Every Man

DEREK LLEWELLYN-JONES

Every Man

PETER BEDRICK BOOKS

NEW YORK

First American edition published in 1983 by
Peter Bedrick Books
125 East 23 Street
New York, N.Y. 10010

© *Derek Llewellyn-Jones 1981*

Published by agreement with Oxford University Press, Oxford

ISBN 0-911745-10-6
LC 83-71476

Manufactured in the United States of America
Distributed in the USA by Harper & Row

CONTENTS

LIST OF FIGURES

1
How you become a male

In the absence of testes, regardless of whether or not the ovaries are present, the genital tract, including the external genitals, will differentiate in a female direction.
Femaleness represents the innate tendency of the foetus.
The development of maleness is complex and precarious, a continuing struggle against the basic trend to femaleness.

Sexuality constitutes the most significant area between biological givens and cultural values in human emotional life.

Laurence Kolberg

TO BEGIN AT THE BEGINNING. DEEP IN THE DARK, MOIST, warm innermost recesses of the vagina, three hundred million spermatozoa (sperms) are ejaculated from the pulsing male penis at orgasm. One of these three hundred million will, with luck, succeed in making the 12-centimetre journey through the uterus of the woman and will penetrate the 'shell' of a single egg which lies waiting in her oviduct. The egg, or ovum, which has been expelled from the woman's ovary at ovulation, has been gently propelled into her oviduct by the finger-like fronds which surround its internal opening.

The journey of the sperms is only possible within a period of two days on each side of ovulation, for it is only during this short time that the sperms can penetrate the mucus which fills the canal which leads into the uterus. Only at this time does the mucus alter from an impenetrable mesh to long strands through which twisting, turning channels form. Through these helical tunnels several million sperms pass, of the three hundred million ejaculated, propelled by the thrashing of their long threadlike tails. But only those sperms

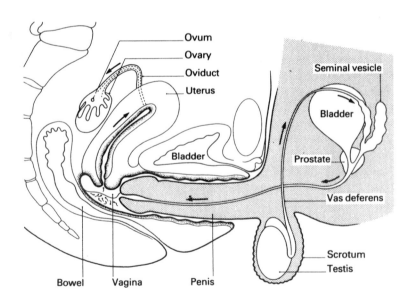

1 The journey of the sperm to reach the ovum

whose heads are of the right size can get through; sperms with abnormally big heads are trapped.

Of the several million which reach the uterus, only a few thousands will survive the journey through its cavity, and even fewer will survive the journey along the oviduct. One, and one alone, will penetrate the shell of the ovum. As its head fixes deeply into the substance of the egg cell, it loses its tail, and the free head fuses with the nucleus in the ovum. A new individual, male or female, has been formed.

Each of the sperms ejaculated into the vagina carries in its head in twisted material, like a bank of computer tapes, all the genetic information needed to make the new individual unique. The twisted material is separated into strands called chromosomes. This genetic inheritance from father and mother, and their father and mother, and their father and mother, combines in an almost infinite variety of ways, suppressing some inherited characteristics, exaggerating others, so that family resemblances appear in the new individual, but not so much that the individual is identical with its parents or ancestors.

The core genetic material in the head of each sperm fuses with the core genetic material in the ovum to make a new mix – a new individual who will be formed as the fertilized egg cell divides repeatedly in complex ways. Once the individual has been created, each cell in his or her body has the genetic material within it capable of forming another new individual, but through aeons of evolution

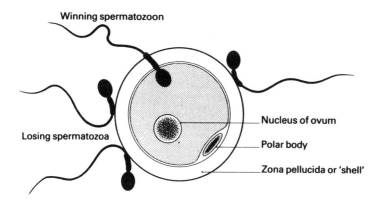

Winning spermatozoon

Losing spermatozoa

Nucleus of ovum

Polar body

Zona pellucida or 'shell'

this facility has been suppressed, and only two specialized cells are capable of this function. These are the female and the male cells, the ova and the spermatozoa. Each human body cell, except the sex cells, carries 46 chromosomes in its nucleus. Forty-four of these determine the individual's appearance, 2 determine its sex. The sex cells contain only 23 chromosomes, half the human number, so that when the sperm head (containing 23 chromosomes) fuses with the ovum (also containing 23 chromosomes), the normal human number of 46 is restored. Each ovum carries one sex chromosome, called an X chromosome because of its shape. Each spermatozoon also carries one sex chromosome, but about half of the spermatozoa carry an X chromosome, and the other half carry a smaller chromosome which resembles a Y.

If an X-carrying spermatozoon fertilizes the ovum, the resulting new individual becomes a female. If a Y-carrying spermatozoon fertilizes the ovum the resulting individual is a male.

Since only spermatozoa carry either an X or a Y chromosome the sex of the unborn child – at this stage only the size of a pinpoint – is

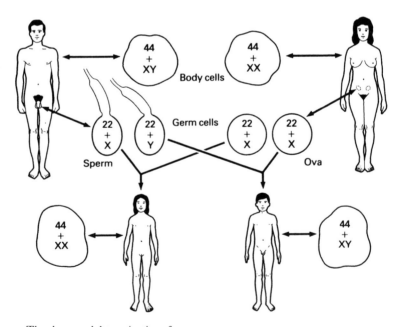

3 The chromosal determination of sex

determined by the child's father. So if a man sires many daughters but no son, he cannot blame his wife. The sex of each of his children is his responsibility!

With the fusion of the nucleus of the sperm head and that of the ovum, a new life has begun. Quite rapidly the single cell accumulates energy and divides, and then divides again, so that 2, then 4, then 8, then 16, then 32, then 64 cells are formed. Each of these cells contains in its nucleus a chromosome count of 46 of which two are sex chromosomes, one X and one Y. In genetic shorthand this is written as 46XY or 46XX.

Occasionally, for incompletely understood reasons, something goes wrong to upset this seemingly simple system and extra X or Y chromosomes are added, or are taken away, or otherwise distorted. Such cell lines may continue and the individual, when born, may be sexually abnormal.

The dividing cells form a sphere, which looks rather like a mulberry within 3 days, and a day later the sphere has entered the cavity of the uterus and has become attached to its lining.

Growth occurs rapidly, and the sphere changes shape. One part of it, where several layers of cells collect, forms the embryo and, later, the foetus, while another part forms the placenta.

Three weeks after fertilization, the embryo, which now looks reptilian, has developed a gut cavity. Along its back surface, two ridges appear, one each side of the midline. These ridges will form the sex glands, or gonads. Into these ridges sex cells migrate from a nearby area, and rapidly divide and divide again.

At this stage of development it is impossible to tell the sex of the embryo by looking at the sex glands, but the cells of the sex glands have been programmed by the sex chromosome they have inherited. If the cells contain a Y sex chromosome, the gonads develop into testes and, provided the embryonic testes function properly, the remainder of the sexual anatomy will develop as a male. This is because the Y chromosomes in each of the cells which make up the embryonic testes induce it to manufacture quantities of the male sex hormone, testosterone, and a much smaller quantity of the female sex hormone, oestrogen. If the sperm which fertilized the egg carried an X chromosome, not a Y chromosome, the gonads will become ovaries, which produce quantities of oestrogen and a much smaller quantity of testosterone. In other words, the testes and the ovaries produce both male and female sex hormones, but in different quantities. The embryonic testes also produce another substance called the female duct-inhibiting substance which is important in determining the sex of the embryo.

There is, of course, more to the sexual apparatus of a male than testes. From each testis, on each side of the body, a twisted, hollow tube runs to join a similar tube from the other testis, at what will eventually become the prostate gland, and opens into a pit at the rear end of the embryo called the cloaca. By now, about 7 weeks after conception, the embryo also has a set of female ducts – oviducts, uterus, and upper vagina. Under the influence of testosterone, the male ducts grow and the female duct-inhibiting substance·causes the female ducts to wither away. If it so happens, as occurs rarely, that the embryo has a testis on one side and an ovary on the other, the side with the testis will produce a male duct and that with the ovary will produce a female duct. The child will be born a hermaphrodite.

Normally, testosterone and the female duct-inhibiting substance secreted by the testes make the male ducts grow and the female ducts wither. The embryo is well on the way to becoming a male.

He has to go through another stage of development before he does. The male ducts, at this period of development, terminate in the cloaca where the gut also ends. Just in front of the cloacal pit (that is on the embryo's front side) a small lump appears, and two swellings grow backwards to make a raised edge to the pit. Looking from the outside, it is impossible to tell if the embryo is a female with a big clitoris, or a male with a small penis and a split behind it.

Quite soon the sex of the embryo becomes clear. If the embryo is a male, the cloacal cells absorb the testosterone which is circulating in the blood and convert it into a new product called dihydrotestosterone. This, in turn, converts the tissues of the cloaca into male genitals. By the 14th week after conception, the lump at the front has become a tiny penis, and the folds at each side of the pit have joined together to form a scrotum. At this stage of development it is empty. Much later in pregnancy the testes are drawn down into the empty scrotum from their previous position in the foetus's abdomen, and at birth the baby is obviously a boy.

After birth only small amounts of the sex hormones are produced by the gonads – testes in males and ovaries in females – until puberty occurs. Then large quantities are made which have quite marked effects, as I will discuss in Chapter 2.

Very occasionally, because of a genetic defect which affects certain families, none of the cells of the body is able to take up the testosterone made by the testes, or to convert it into dihydrotestosterone. These children will not develop either the male ducts or the female ducts (because the inhibiting substance is produced). The

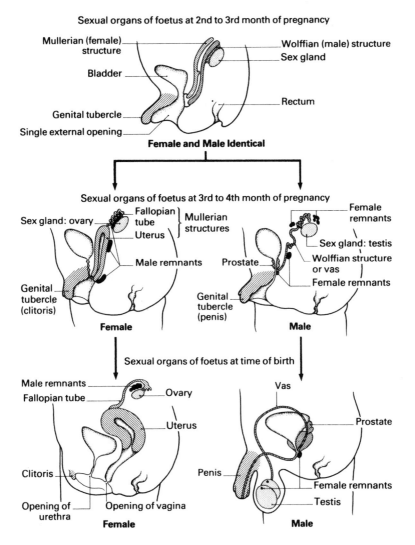

4 Sexual differentiation in the human

cloaca doesn't change into the male form, it remains open, forming a short vagina. The lump at the front becomes a clitoris and the folds fail to fuse. At birth the baby looks like a girl. She is brought up as a girl, and at puberty she develops a feminine shape, because her testes produce some oestrogen. But she cannot menstruate or have children because she has no uterus. She can enjoy satisfactory sexual intercourse because she has a vagina, although it is rather short.

Most children do not have these rare enzyme defects and puberty occurs in the normal way. From this time on the gonads produce sex hormones. The male's testes, and the female's ovaries, start secreting both male and female sex hormones. Males produce more testosterone than oestrogen; in females the reverse happens, but each sex makes both sex hormones. The different effects of the hormones on the body shape of the two sexes is due to the different proportions of the hormones produced. If a greater amount of testosterone is produced then the effects of oestrogen are largely opposed. This means that a boy's penis and scrotum grow at puberty, his chest increases in size, he grows hair on his face, and his voice deepens. The testosterone made by a girl's body during puberty also has a noticeable effect: hair grows on, around, and above her vulva and in her armpits.

Testosterone also has an effect on female embryos. At one time doctors gave women synthetic male-type hormones to prevent them miscarrying. The treatment did not work but was popular in the 1950s. A number of women treated in this way gave birth to babies whose genitals were neither exactly male nor exactly female. Occasionally, the enlarged clitoris was mistaken for a penis and the baby was brought up as a boy. In other cases, the female foetus has an enzyme defect in her adrenal glands. This defect prevents the gland making the cortisone it usually secretes; instead it makes testosterone, which makes the genitals male, and causes other problems which require urgent treatment soon after birth.

*

The development of the foetus as a male happens because the ovum was fertilized by a Y-bearing sperm, because its gonads secreted testosterone and the female duct-inhibiting substance. But this is only part of the story of why a male becomes a male.

The physical changes in the genitals of the unborn male child, which are mediated by testosterone, may have a psychological component.

In small mammals, such as rats, monkeys, and sheep, testosterone made by the testicles of the foetus is known to modify the animal's brain, imprinting on it a 'maleness' in its response to stimuli after it is born. In humans, this pre-natal brain conditioning has only a small effect, which is to modify or blur the child's behaviour towards a male-type behaviour rather than to alter it considerably, as is the case of many other mammals.

The conditioning of the male child's brain may enable the boy to identify more readily with his father (or some other significant male) and to model his behaviour on the way the adult male behaves. At the same time the modified brain response makes the boy treat his mother in a different, complementary way.

This means that, as far as the example of his father is concerned (or his mother's interpretation of how a man behaves), the child responds positively by thinking, 'This is how I am to behave'. In contrast, he responds negatively to the model of his mother by thinking, 'This is how people of the other sex behave, and I must not imitate this behaviour but I must respond in a complementary way'.

*

To sum up, you become a male for several interacting reasons. First, your genes carry a Y chromosome, and this is expressed in every cell of your body. This is your genetic (or chromosomal) sex. Second, because of your genetic sex, your sex glands, or gonads, are invaded by male-directed sex cells. This is your gonadal sex. Third, the male-directed sex cells induce the gonads to secrete the male sex hormone, testosterone, which encourages the development of the male sex ducts, and another substance which causes the withering of the female sex ducts. At the same time testosterone, in its altered form of dihydrotestosterone, induces the tissues at the lower end of the unborn child to differentiate into a penis and a scrotum. These changes make your genital sex. During your life in your mother's uterus, the circulating testosterone may have left a male 'imprint' on your brain cells. This means that after birth, during the vital early years, you are better able to respond positively to and copy male models. First, you copy your father, or another close male figure, and later, other male children of your own age. In humans, in contrast with other mammals, the hormonal conditioning of your brain is only of small significance, adding a flavour of maleness to your more important identification with the male model of your father (or some other male) and the recognition of your mother (or some other female) as a person of the other, complementary sex. These behavioural influences induce you to indicate, by your behaviour to others, that you are a male. This shows your male gender-role. Finally, with the continuing impact of environmental influences, with your interaction with other humans, and with your growing awareness of your male gender-role, you become self-aware of your maleness. This might be called your sexual sex. You have acquired a male gender-identity. You are indeed a man, my son!

*

If we know how a male is made, can we choose the sex of our unborn child? If we could, it could create great happiness for many, and possible problems for the world!

In most cultures, each family desires at least one son to carry on the family name, or to see that the spirit of the father goes to the next cycle of existence after death, or to be able to worship his ancestors, or to prove that the man is really a man who can 'make many sons'.

Because of this desire and because of the patriarchal nature of most societies, many couples would like to be able to choose the sex of their intended child. From time to time reports appear that a doctor, using this or that technique, is able to help couples choose the sex of their child. None of these reports stands up to critical examination. The ancient Greeks thought that men produced boys with sperms from the right testicle and recommended tying off the left testicle to ensure this. The discomfort was great, the results a failure. The method was abandoned.

In more recent times, it has been suggested that the sperms which carry the Y chromosome have a different shape from those which carry the X chromosome. Those sperms which carry the Y chromosome are claimed to have round heads, those which carry the X chromosome are said to have oval heads. As well as this the Y chromosome is smaller and lighter than the X chromosome, and is believed to be more active.

The differences in shape and in weight of the Y chromosome,

suggested to Dr Shettles, who practises in the United States, that because the sperms containing a Y chromosome are different, smaller, and more active, they will reach the egg first, if intercourse takes place at the time of ovulation. He has also stated that because the sperm carrying the X chromosome is larger and slower, but stronger, a female child will be conceived if intercourse takes place 2 or 3 days before ovulation and the couple then abstains from sex. Dr Shettles wrote that the Y-carrying sperm would be helped on its journey if the vagina was alkaline (which meant that the woman had to douche before sex), if she had an orgasm either simultaneously with or before the man, if the man inserted his penis in the woman's vagina from behind so that he could penetrate deeply, and if they had abstained for at least 10 days before having sexual intercourse at the time of ovulation.

In a report of a small series of couples who tried this technique, Dr Shettles claimed that the desired boy was obtained in a high proportion (85 per cent) of cases.

Unfortunately for this theory, no other investigator has been able to reproduce his results. The most accurate investigations have been made when sperm have been put into, and around, the neck of the uterus, using the method of artificial insemination. No preponderance of male children resulted when the insemination was made at the time of ovulation, or of female children when it was done 2 or 3 days before ovulation.

Other researchers have claimed that a preponderance of boys are conceived if intercourse takes place 4 or more days before ovulation, or the opposite, 2 or more days after ovulation. A criticism of the reports of these scientists is that their method of pinpointing ovulation was rather inaccurate. The conclusion is that at present a couple cannot choose the sex of their baby.

There is some interesting work which may let you do this in the future. It has been found that if you add a dye called quinacrine to a specimen of semen, about 45 per cent of the sperms show a glowing spot when they are put under fluorescent light. There is evidence that this glowing spot (sometimes called the 'firefly' test) is associated with a Y chromosome. Unfortunately, to do the test means killing the sperm, but it has enabled scientists to study the glow-spot sperms. One finding, which is contrary to Dr Shettles's beliefs, is that Y sperms do not regularly migrate more rapidly when in an alkaline environment, nor are the glow-spot Y sperms regularly more active in so far as they migrate further and more quickly. But some scientists have found that the male sperms sometimes migrate more quickly in an acid environment. In a series of experiments, Dr Ericsson found that if he put a natural substance called serum albumin in a long tube, added semen, and then centifuged the tube, more Y-carrying sperms were found further up the tube. The sperms which had migrated furthest were more uniform in shape than the rest of the sperms, but most of them were exhausted and, when examined, had very poor motility. Other workers have repeated the experiment but have been unable to reproduce Ericsson's work.

In 1979 a group of doctors in Chicago modified Ericsson's method. They used semen produced by masturbation. This is placed in a test-tube which contains in different layers two concentrations of albumin obtained from human blood serum. The semen is placed on the surface of the top layer. The sperms swim down through the layers towards the bottom of the tube. The doctors have found that more Y-bearing sperms than X-bearing sperms reach the bottom. The bottom layer is separated from the other layers and used to inseminate the woman. Of forty-five women treated in this way, using their husband's semen, fourteen have become pregnant. Seven women have given birth to boys and one woman aborted a male foetus. The numbers of boys born are small and not significantly better than chance, but with further experiments it may eventually be possible to choose the sex of your child – but that is in the future.

At the present time, chance determines whether you have a male or a female baby.

2

What makes a man a man?

An individual becomes the kind of person he is as a result of continuing and continuous interaction between a growing changing biological organism and its physical, psychological, and social environment.

J. J. Conger, *Adolescence and Youth: Psychological Development in a Changing World* (1973)

There seems to be a firmly based principle: physically affectionate human societies are highly unlikely to be physically violent.

J. Prescott (1975)

'WHAT ARE BIG BOYS MADE OF? WHAT ARE BIG BOYS MADE OF?' – INDEPENDENCE, aggression, competitiveness, leadership, task-orientation, outward orientation, assertiveness, innovation, self-discipline, stoicism, activity, objectivity, analytic-mindedness, courage, unsentimentality, rationality, confidence, and emotional control.

'What are big girls made of? What are big girls made of?' – Dependence, passivity, fragility, low pain tolerance, non-aggression, non-competitiveness, inner orientation, interpersonal orientation, empathy, sensitivity, nurturance, subjectivity, intuitiveness, yieldingness, receptivity, inability to risk, emotional liability, supportiveness.

These quotations are from two feminists, Jane Bardwick and Elizabeth Douvan, who investigated the way Americans expected men and women to behave.

How true are these stereotypes? Can the two sexes be fitted into sex-typing so easily and, if they can, are the characteristics of each sex due to inherited psychological sex differences or are they due to learned behaviour?

We all know that little boys and little girls are different. They look different, they behave differently, they belong to 'opposite' sexes. But how exact is our knowledge, how much is it based on myths and on perceptions of what each sex should look like and how it should behave?

If small children were dressed similarly and had similar hairstyles (as they do increasingly), it would be almost impossible to tell if the child was a boy or a girl, without looking at its genitals. The body shape and other physical attributes of all children are very similar until they reach puberty. Up to the time of puberty the average heights, for each year of age, of boys and girls are quite close, as are their weights and the shape of their bodies.

Although boys and girls may have a similar physical appearance (apart from their genitals) most people believe that children of the two sexes have a different inherited psychological make-up, which makes them behave differently. How true is this? 'What makes a man a man?'

A very considerable amount of research has gone into attempts to define sex differences. These have been summarized by Eleanor Maccoby and Carol Jacklin in their excellent book *The Psychology of Sex Differences*.

From their researches it appears that many of our beliefs about sex differences are incorrect, resulting from our prejudices rather than from our observations. It is also evident that the stereotype of masculinity and femininity is a mixture of fact, fiction, and fantasy.

It is claimed that girls are more 'social' than boys, they like to be with people more, they touch people more, and they imitate people more (perhaps by dressing up). It is claimed that boys respond better to things they see than to things they hear, while girls respond better to sounds than to sights. It is claimed that boys understand complicated ideas better than girls while girls are better at rote-learning. This supports the claim that boys are better at mathematics and girls are better at using words. It is claimed that boys undertake tasks for the sake of solving the problem or of completing the task; girls undertake tasks because they want to be complimented or loved for doing them. It is claimed that boys have a greater need to achieve and are more curious than girls. It is claimed that girls are less adventurous, are more timid and more anxious than boys. It is claimed that there is a difference in the temperament of boys and girls, namely that boys are more active, more aggressive, more dominant, less timid, less emotional, and less likely to help others, especially those who are smaller or weaker than themselves. Girls, it is claimed, are more passive, more dependent, and 'naturally' submissive.

How many of these assertions are true?

● There is no truth in the belief that girls are more 'social' than boys. Little girls are no more dependent on those who care for them than are boys. Girls do not spend longer playing with other children, nor are they more sensitive to other children's emotional reactions than are boys. There is one difference which may be of importance to the formation of a child's character and to its behaviour when it grows up: girls tend to form groups of two or three, they have 'best friends' with whom their relationship is intense. Boys, in contrast, tend to congregate in larger groups, or gangs.

● There is no truth that girls are more likely to imitate other people than are boys. In fact, there is a weak trend towards boys being more imitative than girls, namely, that boys are more likely to accept the values of their peer group, rather than their own, when there is a conflict of values.

• There is no truth that girls respond more to sounds and boys to sights. Neither sex is more 'visual' nor more 'auditory' than the other. This is interesting because it is still believed that adult women respond less to erotic visual stimuli than do men, which may be the basis of the publication of a large amount of erotica in newspapers and magazines showing curvaceous, nubile women; while erotica of naked males exposing their genitals are rarely found.

• There is no truth that boys are better at understanding complicated ideas than girls, and that girls are better at rote-learning and doing simple repetitive tasks than boys. Nor is there any truth in the belief that boys can analyse problems better and can reason logically better. This means that the following verse is a libel on women:

> The mind of man is capable of
> Forty different kinds of love.
> The mind of woman, is just an ocean
> Of jealous, immoderate, damp devotion.

It was written by a man, of course!

It does seem that girls do better academically, as judged by school grades, until adolescence is reached, but the difference between boys and girls is not great. And when a boy is aroused to compete, by pressure from his parents or from his age-mates, he becomes a greater 'achiever' than a girl.

• 'Little girls want to please, they work for love and approval, if bright they under-estimate their competence. Little boys show more task involvement, more confidence', Hoffman stated categorically only ten years ago. He based his opinion on the belief that boys had a greater 'need' to achieve, and were more inclined towards achievement for its own sake. Because of this, it was claimed that boys were less cautious and explored more, that they showed a greater involvement in a task and persisted at the task longer. Girls, on the other hand, it was said, only achieved well in matters relating to persons, and they did it to please others rather than for the sake of the task itself. They also had a low self-confidence about achieving. There is no truth in these beliefs. Girls, in childhood, are as self-confident and have as much self-satisfaction as boys.

● There is probably no truth in the belief that there is a difference in the general temperament of the two sexes. There is a suggestion that very small boys (under the age of $2\frac{1}{2}$) are more active than girls, but after this age the difference disappears. Both sexes cry as much, at least up to the age of 3, when parents teach boys not to cry. This means that to conform to what a boy should do, a boy has to bottle up his emotions. This, in turn, may be the reason for the finding that boys react more strongly and loudly to a situation in which they are frustrated and that they lie more easily than girls.

Girls are said to be more timid and anxious, but there is no evidence that this is so, at least until the age of 9. After this, girls do appear to be more fearful. It is doubtful if this is due to an 'innate' character failure. It is more likely to be due to the fact that girls are taught by parents to fear sexual molestation, and that boys have learned to lie to hide any fear, because it is 'unboyish' to be afraid. Some child psychologists are concerned we may be damaging the emotional health of males by our insistence that boys hide their emotions, lie about fear, and react more fiercely to frustration.

Table 1 Behavioural differences between boys and girls

Infancy to age $2\frac{1}{2}$

	Boys	Girls
● Activity level	High	Lower
● Physical impulsiveness	More	Less
● Exploration	More	Less
● Aggression, acted out	More	Less
● Dependency	Less	More

Childhood from age $2\frac{1}{2}$ (when the baby is perceived by an adult to be a child)

● Dependency	Not permitted	Encouraged
● Showing emotions	Not permitted	Encouraged
● Touching	Discouraged	Encouraged
● Verbal skill	Less	More
● Manipulative skills	More	Less

Girls are said to be more nurturant than men, that is they are more likely to give aid or help to others, especially those who are younger, weaker, or damaged in some way. It is true that girls and women do undertake the care of babies and children more often than do boys and men, and more often care for elderly relatives than do men. But the evidence is that this nurturant behaviour occurs because of circumstances, and that in special circumstances men can be as nurturant as women. Biologically, women are better equipped to care for babies, as only a woman can give breast milk to the infant; but in single-parent families, men cope with child care as efficiently as women. Socially, women are taught to believe that the care of elderly relatives is their duty – some sacrificing their happiness for the whims and obsessions of a demanding widowed parent – but when men are forced into a similar position they cope equally well.

A small difference in care-taking roles is found in monkeys and may apply to humans, although there is no definite evidence. This is that female monkeys respond more rapidly to care-taking needs than males. Male monkeys take longer to accept the care of infants, but once they accept the infant, they care for it in exactly the same way as do females. This could be because the pre-natal conditioning by the male animal's brain tracts by testosterone makes it slower to respond. In other words, a male may have a higher 'threshold' to nurturant activities, but we do not know to what extent this applies to humans.

*

With adolescence changes appear in the behaviour and the temperament of boys and girls. These changes are not due to innate sexual differences, or to hormones, but more to the way in which girls have been reared. Girls have been conditioned, by parents, by peers, by society, and through the media, to believe that they should be attractive, co-operative, sympathetic, and loving, while boys are taught to be competitive, ambitious, energetic, practical, and powerful. By adolescence, girls have been taught, and accept, that boys are better achievers (which is not true). They accept that boys will get the more interesting jobs and will rise to higher levels in their jobs (which is true).

In stories and on television most good things happen to the male characters, and they are usually the result of the man's own initiative or action. When a good thing happens to a female character (and this occurs much less frequently) it is usually because of someone else's initiative, or grows out of a situation in which the woman finds herself.

Many adolescent boys fear failure, but many, perhaps most, adolescent girls fear both failure and success. They fear success because it puts them into direct competition with men and may diminish their attractiveness to men. By accepting these views many girls diminish their potential; they believe that they have less ability than boys and will never achieve as much. They accept that women are 'inferior' to men. They accept the inevitability of patriarchy – that men will always dominate society, and that women will always be submissive.

*

Are women more submissive (in all ways, including sexuality), are they more dependent, are they more likely to 'cling', are they more likely to ask for help when facing a problem, than men? Do women require more social approval, do they prefer to work with others, rather than working independently, than do men? Do women withdraw from attacks (rather than counter-attacking) more often than men? In a word, are women more passive than men? Helene Deutsch, whose book *The Psychology of Women* has had a considerable influence on people's attitudes to women, believes that they are. In 1944 she wrote, 'The theory I have long supported – according to which femininity is largely associated with passivity and masochism – has been confirmed in the course of years by clinical experience . . . I venture to say that the fundamental identities "feminine passive" and "masculine active" assert themselves in all known authorities and races.' Many people would still agree with her.

It is of considerable importance to both men and women to know the truth of this assertion. The evidence is that if women are passive it is because of learned behaviour, judged by society as appropriate for females, rather than due to any innate psychological feminine characteristic. In studies of infants, pre-school children, and schoolchildren, no more passivity has been found in girls than in boys, except in one area. This is that small boys engage in more rough-and-tumble play than do small girls.

It is also true that boys are more aggressive then are girls. By aggression I mean the desire of a person to frighten or to hurt another person, either for its own sake or to control and dominate others. Aggression can take several forms, some of which are not generally perceived as being aggression. Direct aggression, by hostile attacks on others, is obvious. Indirect aggression is less obvious and far more insidious and sophisticated. In this type of aggression the person gets what he or she wants by subtle means – by flattery or bribery or by deception.

Scientists who study animal behaviour have established that aggressive behaviour characterizes males rather than females in most species of mammals. In small mammals, such as rats and mice, and in sheep, the aggressive behaviour is dependent upon the effects of the male sex hormone, testosterone, imprinting on the brain cells, in the period before and just after birth, a receptiveness to specific behaviour. If a newborn male mouse or rat is castrated on the day of birth, its aggressive behaviour, when adult, is markedly reduced, but such behaviour can be restored by injections of testosterone. However, extra injections given to an uncastrated adult male rat do not increase its aggression. This implies that, in rats, testosterone given in the critical period before and just after birth imprints on brain cells a responsiveness to a pattern of behaviour and facilitates its expression in later life; but when given later after birth, the hormone does not increase aggressive behaviour.

Similar findings were obtained from studies on rhesus monkeys. Such studies are important, as monkeys and man are much closer in the evolutionary ladder. In one experiment, female rhesus foetuses were given injections of testosterone. After birth, their behaviour was indistinguishable from that of normal male monkeys, who are more active and play more mock threatening, chasing, and rough-and-tumble games than female young monkeys. In another experiment, male monkeys castrated at birth continued to show male patterns of behaviour in childhood, although they produced very little male sex hormone. These experiments suggest that, in monkeys, pre-natal brain hormonal conditioning is crucial to sex-linked behaviour in the animal's childhood.

It would be unethical to conduct such experiments on humans, so that the relative importance of pre-natal brain imprinting is difficult to determine. By chance, an opportunity to unravel to what degree the sexual differences in behaviour in humans are due to pre-natal hormones occurred in a rather unfortunate way.

In the 1950s a number of doctors treated pregnant women, who were threatening to abort, with drugs called 'gestagens' (they are also called progestins). These drugs, which are derived from a synthetic substance resembling testosterone, were given because they were thought to act in a similar way to the natural female sex hormone, progesterone. It was thought, erroneously as it happened, that progesterone and consequently the gestagens would prevent the abortion from occurring. The drug was given by injection, from the 7th or 8th week of pregnancy, often twice weekly for as long as 20 weeks. A number of female children born to these treated mothers were found at birth to have external genitals which resembled those of a boy.

At the same time another group of girls was identified. These children had a genetic defect of their adrenal glands. Because the glands lacked a specific enzyme, the girls were unable to manufacture cortisone in their adrenal glands. Instead, they manufactured the male hormone, testosterone. Testosterone circulated in their body almost from the time they were embryos, and altered the appearance of their external genitals to resemble those of a boy. The girls had a rudimentary penis or, more accurately, an enlarged clitoris, and an apparent scrotum.

Over a period of years, Dr John Money and his colleagues at Johns Hopkins University in Baltimore, U.S.A., have been interested in these two groups of children. After birth, when their correct sex was diagnosed, they required treatment. The girls whose mothers had been given the gestagens in pregnancy usually needed surgery to remove their enlarged clitoris. The girls with the adrenal gland defect needed surgery to remove the big clitoris and cortisone pills to enable them to survive. Both groups of children were reared as girls by their parents, as this was their genetic sex.

When they were between 10 and 14 years old, Dr Money thought that he would try to find out how their behaviour compared with that of matched 'normal' girls (matched, that is, for age, socio-economic background, and I.Q.).

He compared the behaviour of twenty-five affected girls with that of twenty-five normal girls, and found that the affected girls used more energy than normal girls, were judged to be more tomboyish (by adults), preferred what were considered to be boys' toys – guns and toy cars – rather than those usually thought of as girls' toys, and had a higher I.Q. Most were indifferent to dolls.

Dr Money's work suggested that pre-natal testosterone increased a child's intelligence, her energy, and her tomboyishness. These findings have been criticized on several counts. First, the normal girls he used may not have been good 'controls'. The mothers who had been given the gestagens, and who had seen their child's 'abnormal' genitals, may have had different expectations of their child, and may have behaved differently to the child. Alternatively, they may have been more anxious about how the child would develop, and may have over-compensated for this anxiety by being more indulgent.

Second, when the intelligence of the affected girl's parents and that of her brothers or sisters was tested by two of Dr Money's colleagues, they found that the affected girl was no more intelligent than anyone else in the family.

Three subsequent studies of the children of mothers given gestagens have also failed to find any increased intelligence among them when tested at various ages up to the age of 16.

What can be concluded from these important studies? Only that pre-natal hormones may have a small effect on behaviour after birth, at least in choice of toys and in tomboyish activity, and that the hormones may alter the person's threshold to certain activities.

This possible influence can be examined in another way. A small number of male foetuses have a genetic defect which renders the tissues of their body insensitive to the testosterone secreted by their testes, although the other substance which inhibits the growth of the female ducts is secreted and is effective. These children are born with female external genitals and a very short vagina (but no internal genitals). They look exactly like baby girls and are brought up as girls. At puberty, their breasts develop like those of other girls, but they fail to grow body hair and they fail to menstruate. This leads to an investigation when the true situation is disclosed. Although these children are genetically male, all their behaviour in childhood, their sexual hopes, their dreams, and their fantasies are feminine and the children tend to be non-aggressive. While this could be entirely due to childhood conditioning, as the children are considered to be girls by their parents from birth, it is possible that their lack of sensitivity to testosterone has prevented the 'male' imprint on their brain cells occurring. Dr Money suggests that these findings are evidence that in humans, as in other mammals, the sex hormones imprint a pattern on the foetal brain. But it seems, as I mentioned in the last chapter, that the effect of pre-natal testosterone is to 'blur' or 'flavour' the behaviour of the child, rather than modify it markedly.

This theory would be strengthened if it could be shown that male and female foetuses have different levels of testosterone circulating in their tiny bodies. And they have! If the foetus is male, it makes a larger quantity of testosterone than if it is female, particularly between the 10th and 30th weeks of pregnancy. This could presumably give the 'blurring' to the behaviour of the child after birth, although there are two problems.

The first is that, although more testosterone is made by male foetuses, there is an overlap; some female foetuses produce as much testosterone as do males. The second is that from the 30th week of pregnancy there is very little difference in the amount of testosterone produced by either sex. This may be important as the brain cells grow more quickly and make most of their connections with their neighbouring brain cells, to complete circuits, after the 30th week of pregnancy.

The effect of testosterone during the time the boy is in his mother's uterus may also condition or permit boys to learn aggressive behaviour earlier and more easily than girls. In boys, aggressive tendencies begin at about the age of 5. Small boys indulge in more rough-and-tumble play, push other children more, and hit them more than little girls do. Small boys imitate aggressive acts more often than girls after seeing aggression on television or at a film. More small boys *choose* television programmes in which there is more aggression, than do girls. Small boys, who form groups more frequently than girls, are more hostile to a newcomer seeking to break into the group. Small boys are verbally more aggressive and have more aggressive fantasies when day-dreaming, than do girls. But once again there is a problem in accepting that the behaviour is due to testosterone rather than to the ways boys are reared.

In several experiments, males and females aged from 18 to 22 were asked to help teach something to a 'target person'. If the 'target person' gave the wrong response, the 'teacher' gave him or her an electric shock, and could choose how strong a shock he gave and for how long, by turning a dial and holding the shock-button down. The 'teacher' did not know that the 'target person' was a confederate of the experimenter and did not receive a shock in reality! In every experiment, males were more likely than females to give a stronger shock for longer. If the 'target person' was a male and appeared physically disabled or reacted more, the males delivered more intense shocks, the females gave less intense shocks. But if the 'target person' was a female, 'teachers' of both sexes gave less intense, and shorter, shocks.

There seems no doubt that boys and men are more aggressive than girls and women. Women learn about aggression but do not act on their knowledge. This is not due to timidity, or to fear of being punished, because boys receive more punishment for aggression than girls. The aggressive behaviour may be due to the way boys are brought up, or it may be due to the effects of pre-natal testosterone conditioning, or both mechanisms may be involved. Another factor may also be important. Small boys may be aggressive to other small boys for the 'pleasure' they get from hurting others, or it may be for a desire to achieve dominance in the group. In monkeys, dominance seems to be the main reason for aggression, and it is possible that this is the reason for aggressiveness in small boys. When the victim can only escape by becoming a solitary or by seeking the company of girls (which is 'unboyish'), he has to accept the aggression. But among bigger boys, aggression is less useful to obtain dominance, as bigger boys are more easily able to escape or to retaliate, and a leader has to use other methods to maintain his position in the group.

Among male adults, direct aggression is only used as a means of dominance in a few sub-cultures, and leadership is obtained and maintained by indirect methods of aggression or because the leader has a higher status or is more expert on the subject.

We do not know why males are more aggressive. We can speculate that male aggressiveness is probably due to learned behaviour which is more acceptable to the brain cells and circuits that have been flavoured by pre-natal testosterone.

Parents behave differently towards their infant sons and daughters, and this begins almost as soon as the child is born.

*

The different attitudes and different behaviour towards boy-children and girl-children seem to be common to all societies, from those which are classified as primitive to those classified as culturally civilized. In the wide variety of human societies, the behaviour of parents and other adults towards boy-children and girl-children can, and does, vary considerably, but in all societies studied a distinctly different behaviour was shown towards boys and towards girls. The way people behave to a child and the different expectations they demand of the child, depending upon its sex, 'imprints' a distinct pattern of behaviour upon it so that it reacts in a distinctly masculine or feminine way. Once the child's brain is conditioned in this way, it is difficult to reverse it, unless the society in which the child is reared normally expects such a reversal of sexual identity. Some primitive tribes, notably some North American Indian tribes, and some in the South Pacific, do in fact induce a change in sexual identity in children who do not apparently conform to the expected pattern of male behaviour.

A child's masculine or feminine behaviour, depending on its sex, has two components. The first is its sex-typing or its gender-role. This is the way a person behaves to others to demonstrate he or she is a male or a female. The second is even more important. This is the person's own awareness that he or she is a male or a female. This is the person's gender-identity. Until a child has developed a gender-identity it is confused about its sexuality, and about its gender-role.

In Western societies, a complete reversal of gender-identity can be made with relative ease before the age of 4, but after this time the change is only possible in highly motivated individuals who have had doubts about their real sex induced by the doubting attitude of their parents, or who are exceptionally insistent upon the change, such as transsexuals.

John Money reports an illustrative and fascinating case which supports this view. Two identical male twins were circumcised at the age of 7 months. During the operation an accident occurred and one infant's penis was inadvertently amputated, flush with his abdominal wall. Over the next year the parents consulted many authorities and pondered over what was best for their sexually damaged boy. Eventually, they made a decision: the boy would be treated by plastic surgery and reared as a girl. The first reconstructive operation was undertaken when he was 21 months old. This consisted in removing his testicles. The second operation, that of making a functioning vagina, would be delayed until puberty when the child would be given female sex hormones to produce breast development and the female distribution of fat.

Following the first operation the parents changed the boy's name to that of a girl, and began to treat him as a girl. Dr Money has now followed up this family for twelve years and the rest of the story is based on his reports.

Within a year of sex reassignment, the child, now treated as a girl, behaved in a way which was markedly different from her brother's behaviour. She became neater and cleaner. She preferred 'feminine' dresses, and preferred helping her mother in the home to helping her father. As time went on, she copied her mother's behaviour to her father, while her brother copied his father's behaviour to his mother. At Christmas she preferred girls' toys, which emphasized a feminine maternal role, rather than the boys' toys chosen by her identical twin, which emphasized a masculine work role. The only real difference between her and her girlfriends was that she sought to be dominant in the group, had a high level of physical energy activity, and was classified by her teacher as stubborn and tomboyish. These are characteristics Dr Money believes are due to pre-natal conditioning by testosterone.

Dr Money's report, and many others, confirm that parents have different feelings to their children of different sexes and reinforce, both subconsciously and consciously, the sexual role the child is expected to play. A boy would be criticized for being unadventurous or unaggressive, while a girl would be criticized if she were.

The gender-role in children fostered so assiduously by parents induces the child, if a boy, to behave as a boy should behave in our culture, and also to feel that he is a boy. In other words, he develops a gender-identity. He *knows* he is a boy and accepts that he will behave to others in a specific male way. The lack of ability to have a completely male gender-identity, at least in erotic matters, is a problem faced by homosexuals in our critical, disapproving, society.

The contribution of the parental (and later peer-group) behaviour towards the child in the development of his gender-identity is further emphasized by studies of intersex children. These children are genetically of one sex, in other words they are XX-female or XY-male, but because of the abnormal development of their external (and sometimes internal) genitals they are classed, at birth, as being of the other sex. They are 'intersex'. The child can be brought up happily, and confidently complete in its adopted sex, and will behave in a manner conforming to that gender-role once it has developed the gender-identity of its adopted sex.

The evidence shows that the process of change is met with the least disturbance if the parents decide (after advice) which sex they wish the child to have and if, having made the decision, they (and all other people) behave consistently towards the child as if it were of that sex. They will be helped in their behaviour if surgery is used early to correct an obvious genital ambiguity. This is because many parents find it difficult to behave to the child as if it were a girl, if it has an apparent penis; or as if it were a boy if the child has only a tiny phallus, with a urinary opening in the female position.

In most cases, the decision is made to rear intersex children as females, and to perform surgery on the external genitals to make them concordant with the chosen sex. This is a sensible approach, for the 'girl' can have a reasonable psychosexual life after puberty when additional surgery and hormones can make her into a woman, capable of enjoying sexual intercourse although, of course, unable to bear children. Conversely, if the child is made into a male, he will always be defective sexually because of his small abnormal penis, and will fear the mocking of his companions and the distress of any female partner he may find.

In a few cases, the parents continue to be in doubt about the desired sex of the child, and transmit this doubt to the child by their behaviour. These children also have ambiguous genitals, and can observe that they are different from other children – the girls have an apparent penis, the boys have an inadequate penis and pass urine in a non-male way. These psychological and anatomical un-certainties may lead to emotional conflicts in the child and to failure at school and in human relationships. When sex reversal is made early, when the surgery is skilful, and, most importantly, when the parents (and the community) accept and behave to the child as if it really belonged to the chosen sex, the adopted sexual identity of the child is strongly established. It becomes an individual of that sex.

It would seem from the study of these children that gender-identity is not preordained by the genetic or chromosomal sex of the child, nor by pre-natal hormonal effects on its developing brain circuits, although these play a part in modifying some behaviours, but is due to the way others behave to it in its first four years of life.

A criticism of this theory is that the children in these studies had surgery to correct (as far as possible) the ambiguous genitalia and to remove their testes, so that no male hormone was secreted, particularly at puberty when the quantity of testosterone in the blood increases considerably. In the absence of this surge of testosterone, the individual is likely to remain in his assigned sex, and the pre-natal 'imprinting' of maleness does not become apparent.

In a remote area in the Dominican Republic thirty-eight individuals (whose chromosomes are the normal male 46XY) have been found to have a rare enzyme disorder. This disorder prevents testosterone from being converted into dihydrotestosterone, so that in foetal life their genitals are not converted into male genitals and at birth they resemble those of a girl, although they do not look completely like those of a girl. Nineteen of these individuals were reared as girls, and behaved as girls, until they reached the age of between 9 and 12 when strange events occurred which coincided with the surge of testosterone production accompanying puberty. The high quantities of testosterone in the blood permitted the enzyme to convert some of it into dihydrotestosterone. The circulating hormones led to unexpected changes. The 'girls'' breasts failed to develop, their small phallus began to grow into a penis, two lumps appeared in their labia, and their voices deepened. They also began to feel they were not girls, and to have male sexual fantasies. As the years passed, they developed a strong male gender-identity, and began to have orgasms and ejaculations. By the age of 16, the individuals believed themselves to be men, although they were worried about being ridiculed because of the small penis and because they urinated like women. However, they felt that they were men and fifteen are living with women and have sexual intercourse.

The investigations of these individuals suggest that perhaps testosterone has a stronger role in developing a gender-identity than John Money thought. Their 'sex changes' suggest that testosterone in pre-natal life may sensitize the brain circuits concerned with gender-identity, and if this is followed at puberty by the testosterone surge which occurs in genetic males who have testicles, a male gender-identity will be activated, and a male gender-identity will be confirmed.

There are problems about this theory, as the Dominican individuals' genitals were not identical with those of a girl, but only *resembled* a girl's vulva, and the children may have been treated in such a way that the parents expressed doubt about their gender-identity. Moreover, in their society there are considerable advantages in being a man, and when a choice appeared the individuals would have opted to be identified as males, to be able to pursue masculine activities.

Males seem to have greater difficulty in establishing an exact, clearly defined gender-identity than females. This is suggested by the fact that there are more male homosexuals than there are female homosexuals. It is also suggested by the observation that exhibitionists, voyeurs, and narratophiliacs are rarely women. A male exhibitionist is only able to become aroused sexually if he exposes his penis to a shocked female who flees from the sight. A voyeur only gets his sexual 'kicks' by spying on a woman as she undresses. A narratophiliac only gets sexual arousal and can only reach orgasm while talking in a 'dirty' sexual manner over the telephone to a woman who usually does not know his identity. There may also be a sex difference in the way men and women are sexually excited, although this is now disputed. More men appear to be sexually aroused by vision than women; more women appear to be sexually aroused by touch than men. More boys than girls masturbate in adolescence, and more fantasize about visual images during masturbation, or have visual images during wet dreams.

Recent research casts doubts on the sex differences in sexual arousal. It has been found that many women are sexually excited by the sight of an attractive man, and many men are more aroused by body contact with their lover than by the way she looks.

*

How does a small child learn that it is a boy or a girl, and *feel* that it is of a particular sex? In other words, how does it develop its gender-identity? Linked to this is the question of how and when a small child begins to behave to others to demonstrate to them that it is male or female. In other words, how and when does it develop its gender-role?

If you observe small babies, you will find that they show no awareness of belonging to either sex, at least until they are more than 9 months old. During these months most people are unable to tell what the sex of a baby is except by the way it is dressed or, for accuracy, by looking at the baby's genitals and seeing if it has or has not got a penis.

Because parents know their baby's sex from the time of its birth, it is inevitable that they start forming a gender-role in the infant from its very first days, by their behaviour to it.

Child psychologists believe that children develop their attitudes and learn to behave in specific ways only by contact with other humans. They also believe that most of this learning occurs by 'role-taking', that is we learn the attitudes of others by putting ourselves in their shoes, and by imitating what they do so we may obtain their approval.

Obviously, when the baby is very small it can only learn about its gender-identity from the way it is treated by its parents.

From about 9 months of age the baby becomes more mobile and begins to receive a much wider variety of information from its observations. These observations suggest to it its sex, and fix 'memory traces' on its brain. But the exact way in which a boy can say with conviction, 'I am a boy' (in other words establish his gender-identity), is unclear.

There are three main theories, none of which escapes criticism. Freud and his followers believe that the child's gender-identity develops through various stages, all of which are characterized by the child's desire for immediate pleasure and its other desire to avoid pain.

Very small babies obtain pleasure, as well as obtaining food, from sucking. This is the oral stage of sexual development. It is followed by a second stage. Now the small baby gets pleasure from being able to open its bowels or to prevent itself from defecating. This is the anal stage; in it the child has learnt to say Yes or No! It has learnt to give or to withhold.

Freudians believe that these two stages occupy the first two years of a child's life. It then enters the phallic stage. It becomes aware of its genitals and of the pleasure it can obtain from manipulating them. It also becomes curious about objects around it and wants to put its finger in things. Freudians believe that in this phallic stage a child develops an erotic attachment to the parent of the opposite sex and a feeling of rivalry, perhaps of aggression, to the parent of the same sex. But the child has a problem.

For example, if the child is a boy, Freudians believe that he 'instinctively' wants to possess his mother sexually and at the same time feels aggressive to his father, who already possesses her and whom he sees as a rival. This puts the boy in an emotional dilemma. In the first place, he does not have the capacity (or the knowledge) to possess his mother. In the second place, although he is aggressively jealous of his father, he also loves (and fears) him. The two conflicting emotions produce guilt. He believes he deserves to be punished, and this punishment will involve him having his penis hurt, or cut off. If he has noticed that girls have no penises, his fear is confirmed – they are mutilated boys!

To resolve his guilt and escape his fear of genital damage, he gives up his erotic desire for his mother and imitates his father, so that he may obtain his love and, some day, his father's prerogatives. Once the child has resolved his dilemma and identified with his father he has begun to develop a male-identity and has started to establish his gender-identity.

The second theory rejects Freudian psychosexual psychology, and believes that sexual identity is formed by copying, but that a boy child, for example, copies his father initially because of some 'innate' tendency towards being a male, perhaps due to the effects of pre-natal testosterone. Once the child forms the identity-link with his father (or some other male), he models his behaviour on his father's, so that he can obtain his father's love and approval. In this theory a child learns his gender-identity in the way he learns about other concepts. He learns that a furry object with a small face and four legs, which purrs, is called a kitten. He learns more about the kitten as he hears other people talking about it, and as he observes how it drinks milk. He learns even more by playing with it.

By the age of 2, a child has learnt to identify a large and increasing number of objects, but is still learning to identify men and women, boys and girls, by the way they look, by what they wear, by the way their hair is cut, by the absence or presence of hair on their faces, and by watching and listening to them as they discuss each other. In other words, he identifies that men and women, boys and girls, tend to have different appearances and to do different things, or the same things in a different way. He learns that women stay at home, look after children, cook, keep houses tidy, shop, gossip, and are likely to cuddle him. He contrasts this with the observations that men – including his father – do not stay at home, go out more, work, do certain things involving strength and power (like putting out the rubbish, cutting the lawn, or being soldiers and policemen), and are less likely to cuddle him. He is learning that people have gender-roles, but he has not yet learned that *he* has a gender-identity. That comes a little later.

In this theory, the child learns how to behave sexually by observation and imitation in the same way he learns other social behaviours.

Any child observing the behaviour of others ('models') can take one of three actions. It can ignore the behaviour; it can imitate it; or it can behave differently. Children tend to imitate if they see the 'model' as similar to themselves, or as powerful, or as friendly, or as someone who will reward them. If the 'model' is seen to have all these attributes, the child will imitate; the fewer the attributes, the greater the chance that it will behave in an opposite way.

A boy child tends to copy male figures because he perceives them as similar to him and as powerful, and this copying is reinforced by the behaviour to him of his parents, other adults, and other children. Parents encourage him to imitate his father and discourage him from imitating his mother.

A third theory suggests that a child obtains its gender-identity as part of the growth of its observational powers, which adds information to its brain cells. The behaviour of its parents and other visitors to it, when it is very small, starts the process.

As I have said, people treat boy babies differently from girl babies from the earliest days after birth. As the child becomes increasingly mobile, these early memories direct it to look at, and assess, men and women differently. It does not do this for rewards of parental approval, nor to identify with one or other parent, but because it makes a value-judgement of what it wants to be. It sees its father, or some other male, as stronger, more powerful than its mother. A boy child has already had 'memory traces' on its brain that it resembles a male, more than a female, and this is the impetus for it to begin to identify with males. As the child identifies, it models its behaviour on the male behaviour it observes, not for any reward or approval, but because of its 'memory traces'.

During the years between 2 and 7 the boy's gender-identity and his body concepts may be influenced by other information he receives from the outside world and absorbs, but his inclination is to value things which his own sex does and to note, but not act on, things the other sex does. Quite quickly the boy child develops a sex stereotype, which is a shorthand way for him to recognize his own sex.

Later, in early adolescence, many boys and girls develop an emotional attachment to a person of their own sex. A boy, for example, seeks the approval and recognition of the chosen male and does all he can to get that approval, by behaving in a way he expects will be rewarding. As the boy develops physically he replaces this emotional attachment with emotional attachments to girls.

Whatever the mechanism, each child seems to go through several stages. Up to the age of 2 or $2\frac{1}{2}$ the boy does not know his own sex. By the age of 3, a boy child is able to answer correctly, 'I am a boy', and knows what a boy is and in what ways he is different from a girl.

By the age of 4, a boy can identify other children as boys and as girls by clothing, hair, or other physical characteristics. And one or two years later, a boy (and a girl) believes that its sex is firmly unchangeable. A boy will always be a boy. Rather surprisingly perhaps, a knowledge of the differences in its own genital anatomy and that of girls seems to be relatively unimportant. This suggests that gender-identity is not determined by a child's instinctual wishes but by observation of the general behaviour of each sex.

What has been written should not be taken to imply that gender-identity is fixed in *all* instances. The wide variability of human perceptions, thoughts, and behaviours means that some individuals do not obtain a fixed gender-identity.

It is also important to understand that behaviours appropriate to gender-identity are constantly changing. For example, men today do many household chores which forty years ago would have been considered inappropriate, and women do many things which, in the past, were considered to belong to men exclusively. Another example can be found in dress, in the use of jewellery, and in hair-styles. In all these areas there has been a trend to a 'unisex' position, and the firmly held beliefs of what dress, jewellery, or hair-style was appropriate to men and women have been abandoned.

*

The problem in accepting any of the theories of sexual differentiation is that the differences in behaviour are so subtle and so different at different ages that no clear picture can be obtained to answer the question: how does a child become aware of its gender-identity?

There is also the problem that if children model their behaviour on that of the same-sex parent (or some other same-sex individual) why do they do so? In some cultures, it may be because the child (at least after the age of 2) has a greater contact with the same-sex parent and relatives. In Indian villages, girl children stay with the women of the extended family and do 'women's jobs'! Boys, once weaned, stay mainly with male members of the family and do 'men's things'. Both learn how to behave by observation and by copying, and this is encouraged by older people. In our more mobile society these conditions do not apply so exactly. Both boy and girl children are principally cared for by their mother. The father is only seen briefly when he comes home from work and at week-ends. If the child copies the most available person, both boys and girls should have similar behaviour. If the child copies the most powerful parent, then girls would copy the father, as he is perceived in our society as being dominant in a family group. Children would only copy the same-sex parent if changes in power or in caring occurred within the family as time passed, and there is no evidence that this happens.

All this assumes firstly, that parents behave similarly to children of both sexes; and it assumes secondly, that a child's idea of copying is the same as an adult's. We know that when a child is given a complex sentence, it simplifies it. Perhaps a child may simplify the way it copies a model. Equally, it may be that a child sees and absorbs both sex models, but because of its increasing awareness of things about it and its attempts to classify them into things like it and things unlike it, it selects those things it feels appropriate for its own sex.

This implies that the child must have a rudimentary idea that there are two sexes. It could obtain this idea from the way parents (and other significant people) treat it.

In most ways, parents do not treat their children very differently. They show the same warmth to children of each sex, and reward or praise each to the same extent. In some ways they make a distinction: boys receive more punishment than girls, in part because they are less obedient, and in part because our upbringing inhibits us from inflicting physical pain on girls. But there is no difference in non-physical discipline: both boys and girls are threatened with the parent's withdrawal of love if the child is naughty.

In a few ways, parents base their behaviour to a boy or to a girl on their conception of what the child of a particular sex should be. They encourage the child to do what is 'natural' for that sex, and discourage it from doing what is 'unnatural'. They pay particular attention to training children in what they believe are the 'natural' strengths and weaknesses of each sex. Boys are encouraged to be competitive and are known to be more aggressive, so parents direct a boy child to be competitive and to be aggressive (but they control this). They direct a boy away from doing 'sissy' things, encouraging a boy to do 'boyish' things and girls to do 'feminine' things.

There is one important difference in parental behaviour towards boys. Boys are taught, quite early in life, to avoid showing emotions and to refrain from touching and cuddling. To show emotions, to cry, or to want to cuddle and be cuddled is 'sissy' in our culture. How much these learned restraints damage men's ability to relate to other people, to communicate properly with their sexual partner, and to enjoy mutual sexual pleasuring (which is essentially a touching enjoyment) is unclear, but the psychic damage could be considerable.

James Prescott, an American neuropsychologist, believes that male adult aggression and violence are due (at least in part) to a lack of cuddling and of bodily pleasure in the early years of a boy's life. He recalls that studies in the University of Winsconsin Primate Laboratory showed that baby monkeys which were prevented from touching any other monkey in childhood (although they could see, hear, and smell the others) became violent when adults. He also recalls that psychiatrists have found that parents who physically hurt their children invariably had themselves been deprived of physical affection and touching during their childhood. Dr Prescott's strongest support for his theory came from a study of other societies. He found that those societies which gave their children the most physical affection (by cuddling, by touching, and by letting the child show its emotions) during infancy and early childhood had less violence, theft, and assaults than societies which treated their children harshly and disapproved of physical affection.

He says, 'we seem to have a firmly based principle: physically affectionate human societies are highly unlikely to be physically violent', and he argues that we should encourage touching, holding, and body contact with and by our children, especially our boys. Dr Prescott's opinions are supported by Dr Richard Leakey, who for many years has been studying primitive societies and the fossil remains of societies long since disappeared. He says that man is not innately aggressive, but co-operative. Aggression only began when man ceased to be nomadic and settled in areas to grow crops. In other words, human aggression is due to the way in which society evolved; it is not inborn.

*

Between the ages of 4 and 10, boys are disadvantaged compared with girls in several ways. They must be neither too aggressive (or they are disapproved of as 'bad boys') nor too passively dependent (or they are disapproved of as being 'mother's pet' or 'sissies'). And because they are less able to interpret verbal and non-verbal cues of parental disapproval (or that of other adults) as quickly or as accurately as girls, they are more likely to be confused. Boys consequently find it harder to conform and learn to accept their gender-identity later than girls.

As males are more aggressive and more dominant, should not the present patriarchal society be maintained for ever, and women relegated mainly to the dependent 'nurturant' (child-care) activities, otherwise they will be disappointed in their encounter with dominant men when they seek to do 'men's' jobs?

In primitive societies, where gender-role activities are very distinct, and where frequent child-bearing is usual, this view may have value. In societies which have jobs needing great physical exertion it is likely that men, who have a larger muscle mass, will do them better.

In our type of society neither of these conditions applies. Most women limit the number of children they decide to have. In our society, most women conceive their last child before the woman is 28 years old; and a woman's 'nurturant' functions have ceased by the time she is about 35 or 36. Most jobs do not demand great physical strength, machines have replaced muscle. It is true that only a woman can conceive, can carry the foetus in her uterus, and can breast-feed it, but there is no reason why her man cannot help in its nurturance. It is also true that women can do most jobs presently reserved for men as efficiently and as effectively as men if given the opportunity and training.

*

Although there are considerable differences in behaviour believed appropriate for men and women in different cultures, some behaviours seem general. In the following list, decide which of the behaviours you believe are appropriate for a man and which for a woman.

Man

A man should be competitive, striving to do better than other men, and never admitting defeat.

A man should be responsible financially for his family.

Woman

Unless a woman marries and has children she has failed to fulfil her biological destiny.

A woman may work if she wants to – and if her husband allows it – but her *real* place is in the home, where her role is to be a good wife and mother. Her family's well-being is more important to her than her own needs.

A man can do any work outside the home, however menial, but within the home he is only expected to help, which he does with relative reluctance and inefficiency.

A woman should not compete with or surpass her man, or her male colleagues, in any kind of achievement outside home or child-care, because this threatens the man's self-image.

A man may show affection openly for his family, but not for anyone else – certainly not for another man.

A woman may show affection openly for other women, and for some men, but only in a playful way. A woman may flirt but must be careful that it is within the conventional limits and that it enhances her husband's standing with his friends.

If a man wants to show affection for another man, he makes a mock attack on him – slapping him on the back or lunging at him.

A man is permitted to fight with other men, but should never hit a woman. He should never cry.

A woman is not expected to fight or to engage in any other 'unladylike' behaviour, but she is permitted to show emotion and to cry.

Sex is important to a man. In a male group he may brag about his real or imagined 'sexploits'. He may be bawdy in male company but if women are present he uses different words and does not talk openly about sex.

Sex is not very important to a woman, except as a means of making her man 'happy'. Women do not talk about sex, or about their sexual desires and needs, because it is not 'nice' to do so.

He can seek and obtain other female sexual partners, but would be horrified if his wife sought other men for sex.

It is unfeminine if a woman obviously seeks men. Women are taught to respond only if a man shows interest in them. But women may be wily and deceitful in getting the man, and may show cunning in manipulating him by playing on his 'higher', more urgent, sexual needs.

A man may have sex before he marries – in fact he should so that he is 'experienced' – but he expects his bride to be a virgin.

A woman values her hymen, but may permit petting – so long as she knows when to stop.

Sex without love is fun and appropriate for men, so that they can learn to be 'sexperts'.

Sex without love is scandalous for women.

Some of the behaviours are no longer demanded of each sex, but many are. How do they affect the happiness of each sex, how much do they damage the humanity of each sex? Are they still appropriate? Society has to give an answer to these questions.

*

In every known society, the two sexes undertake different tasks and need to co-operate in a division of labour so that the society may best survive. But the tasks undertaken by one or other sex differ widely, depending on the society. In 1949 Margaret Mead wrote in *Male and Female*:

Sometimes one quality is assigned to one sex, sometimes to the other . . . Some people think of women as too weak to work out of doors, others regard women as appropriate bearers of heavy burdens 'because their heads are stronger than men's' . . . In some cultures, women are regarded as sieves through whom the best-guarded secrets will sift, in others it is men who are the gossips. Whether we deal with small matters or with large, with the frivolities of ornament and cosmetics or the sanctities of man's place in the universe, we find this great variety of ways, often flatly contradictory, in which the roles of the two sexes have been patterned.

There are only three absolute, biological, unbridgeable differences between the sexes. These are that only a man can impregnate a woman (although to do this sexual intercourse is not essential, as in the case of artificial insemination of a woman with a donor's semen). Only a woman can carry the growing foetus in her uterus and give birth to it, and provide it with breast milk once it is born.

Beyond these biological imperatives the sex hormones impart no more than a 'flavour' to a person's behaviour. Almost all of the way the two sexes behave is learned by observing 'models' in infancy, childhood, and adolescence. This implies that most (or all) differences in behaviour of the two sexes are learned.

In our society, until recently at least, most people had – and still have – fixed beliefs of how men and women should look, how they should behave, and what roles they should perform. These beliefs are beginning to weaken, but are still present to a greater or lesser degree in different sections of society.

In this time of rapid social change, and of more open discussion about the relations between the sexes and about sexual roles, society has two choices.

Society can choose to maximize or to minimize the differences between the sexes. Should we emphasize the differences by encouraging male aggressiveness and competitiveness, by demanding female subordination and compliance, and by confining women (as much as we can) to their nurturant role? This was the ideal of

Hitlerian Germany. Men did the proper work, a woman's place was defined by *Kinder, Küche, Kirche* – children, kitchen, Church.

Or should we minimize the differences, by discouraging male aggression and encouraging male nurturing activities? For example, now that women have fewer children and the time they need to devote to child-rearing is less, should not women be encouraged to compete equally with men for jobs? It is accepted that men are more competitive than women, but the difference is weak and could be due to the fact that girls are trained to avoid competition with men as they fear they will appear less feminine.

At present, women are disadvantaged in opportunities for jobs. They obtain less interesting jobs, get less pay, and achieve lower levels of promotion. This is not due to lack of ability or of desire, but to the patriarchal structure of society. In a male-dominated society, women have to expend more effort, more time, and more skill to achieve a position a less qualified man achieves more easily. This biases the competition strongly in favour of a man: it ceases to be true competition. The lack of success of women in high-status jobs may also be affected by the way girls are reared. Females take orders from authority more easily and comply with them more readily, they are less likely to protest and are slower to become angry, so they are easier to exploit by men and more ready to take less interesting, lower-status jobs.

The subordinate position of women to men, which is initiated by the way the two sexes are reared, tends to be self-perpetuating. Women, brought up in this way, *believe* that they are inferior to men in both intelligence and ability. Even when the work of men and women is of identical quality, women tend to denigrate that of their own sex and to rate a man's work more highly. In an experiment conducted in America, a group of women university students were given six scientific papers to rate. The name of the author of each paper was manipulated by the investigator so that half of the women thought the author was a man and the other half thought the author was a woman. The women were asked to judge the quality of each paper for style, for professional competence, for conviction, and for over-all impact on the reader. Invariably, whatever the subject of the paper, if the name of the author was male, it was rated higher than if the women thought it had been written by a woman.

Why women perpetuate their sense of subordination is not an easy question to answer. Anthropologists have found that many repressed minority groups tend to adopt the attitudes of the stronger dominant group towards themselves. Women may do the same by accepting the submissive stereotype, and by this device are able to escape some of the anxiety which arises if they feel themselves to be oppressed. It is easier to accept the status quo than to rebel against it, particularly if you rationalize that because of your sex you can never achieve as well as a man, but you are better at nurturant activities, and have an important role to play in caring for children and looking after your husband.

In our society, it is better to be a man if you are a person who wants status or achievement. But in other ways, it is a disadvantage to be a man. A man has a higher risk of dying prematurely. He is more likely to develop heart disease, he is more likely to become a victim of many diseases of civilization, as I describe in later chapters in this book.

While you cannot change your gender-identity, the differences between male and female gender-roles can be diminished.

There are those who fear that any reduction in the differences between how the sexes look and behave and what they do in sexual encounters, in work, or in play, will lead to a destruction of the fabric of society. This is a false fear: equality of opportunity for women in all spheres of activity will not reduce the gender-identity of women, but rather will permit women to develop as freer human beings. The reduction in a man's competitiveness and aggression and the social permission for him to show emotion and affection will not reduce his male gender-identity but will enable him to relate more freely and equally with other human beings, irrespective of their sex.

If the stereotypical sex differences are reduced, it will not mean social chaos. That is more likely to occur if the more conservative elements in society try to prevent the increasing questioning about sexual roles, values, and behaviours which are currently conventional. In this period of rapid and unpredictable social and technological change, only societies which are sufficiently flexible to tolerate experimentation and to allow a variety of different sexual responses will survive.

3 Growing up

Peers have a widespread influence and they often perpetuate misinformation and spread sexual myths. There is a need to provide accurate information to young people and to help parents to take a more positive role. To make peer influences more benign the skills of two significant institutions must be increased – families and schools, which we see always as complementary one to the other.

Royal Commission on Human Relationships (Canberra, 1977), vol. 2

Morris Carstairs asked, in his Reith Lectures of 1962, 'But *is* chastity the supreme moral virtue?' and went on to point out that 'many societies get on quite well without premarital chastity'. That our society does not want to get on better – the unwanted pregnancy rate is still far too high – is not due to sex education, which so far has had little effect. Schofield reports that 'in every ten adults of twenty-five, four feel their knowledge of sex is inadequate . . . It is the lack, not the surfeit, of knowledge that is the cause of distress to young people.'

Anthony Storr (*Sunday Times*, 29 May 1977)

UNTIL RECENTLY, BECAUSE OF THE INFLUENCE OF FREUD, IT was believed that once a child had found its gender-identity it entered a period of sexual latency which lasted until puberty. It was reluctantly accepted that small children were sexual in so far as they enjoyed fondling their genitals and in masturbating, although it was doubted if the child perceived this activity as erotic. But it was believed that by the end of its fifth year a child entered a period of sexual latency, because, by that stage of its development, a boy had repressed his guilt for desiring his mother sexually and had resolved his fear that his father could retaliate by cutting off the boy's penis. Having resolved the so-called Oedipal conflict, the child's sexuality ceased. 'During this lull period,' Freud wrote, 'it is at a standstill and much is unlearnt and there is much recession. After the end of the period of latency, as it is called, sexual life advances once more with puberty.'

It is now known that there is no latent sexual period. With the widening variety of experiences, the child's interest moves away from obtaining pleasure by fondling its genitals, but masturbation continues throughout childhood, and in some cultures sexual intercourse takes place.

In our type of society such activities are condemned and because, for most children, sex is not mentioned, or is mentioned in a condemnatory manner, many children form the opinion that sex is dirty and feel guilty if they enjoy fondling their genitals. As two American sociologists, William Simon and John Gagnon, say: '. . . learning about sex is learning about guilt: conversely, learning how to manage sex constitutes learning how to manage guilt'.

The belief that sex is dirty is encouraged by small actions. Boys are taught it is 'bad' to fondle their penis ('If you don't leave it alone, I'll cut it off'). Small girls are taught to cover their chests long before any breast development has occurred, and to sit with their legs together long before the child's vulva has developed in any way. Both sexes are taught that their genitals are a 'shameful' area, and that it is 'good' to keep them covered at all times.

A child's sexuality increases throughout its childhood, but only becomes intense following the physical and emotional changes which occur at puberty and increase in adolescence.

During the childhood years, the child's sexuality can be damaged by the way its parents behave in sexual matters and by their reaction to its curiosity about sexuality.

If parents let the child know, by their behaviour, that they believe the unclothed human body to be indecent, and that the genital area is scandalous and unmentionable, they may plant the seeds for later sexual disability. Many parents encourage their children to be competitive, even if this requires violence, but when a child seeks to understand why boys and girls have different genitals and to look at the genitals of a child of the other sex, or play with its own genitals, a frozen disapproval appears and the child is often punished. This induces shame in the child's mind about its genitals. It may also induce guilt, because the child has enjoyed what it was doing, but now feels this was wrong because of its parents' disapproval.

Many parents are uncomfortable about their own bodies and disturbed about their own sexuality. Because of this they find it difficult to let their children become acquainted, quite casually, with naked male and female bodies, and they are unable to answer children's questions honestly and objectively. When a child asks why its father has a penis, they are evasive and embarrassed. When a child asks how babies are made, they retreat into euphemisms or silence. When a child asks what its parents do in bed, the question is brushed off, or answered dishonestly.

Because of this reticence, the information many children obtain from their parents is inadequate and inaccurate and is given too late. Those parents who are comfortable about their own sexuality and who enjoy sex are able to understand their child's curiosity and can talk with the child so that the information it so eagerly seeks is obtained in appropriate parcels. These parents take the initiative in helping their children understand the joy of sexuality, and provide the child with a base so that it can cope better with the usual attitudes of society to sex. These parents are exceptions. Most children do not have their curiosity satisfied and get most of their sexual information, or misinformation, from their age-mates. Children are capable of understanding (or misunderstanding) sex long before puberty, and need guidance so that myth and fact, sensuality and sentimentality, eroticism and love can be differentiated.

*

Puberty starts in a complex way and merges complexly into adolescence, which is made even more complex because the terms 'puberty' and 'adolescence' are difficult to define. *The Oxford English Dictionary* defines puberty as 'the state or condition of having become functionally capable of procreating offspring'. This definition has certain defects, as menstruation marks puberty in girls, but in the first year or so after menstruation has started most girls are incapable of becoming pregnant. Puberty in boys is marked by the ability to ejaculate, but in the first months the quality of sperms ejaculated is poor and the quantity small, so that a boy's ability to procreate is limited.

Perhaps a better definition of puberty, for our purposes, is that it is a period of hormonal secretions, particularly of sex hormones, which lead to increasing bodily (including genital) differentiation of males and females, and which culminates in each individual's ability to reproduce. In males, it means that orgasms are associated with ejaculation of good-quality sperms; in females, it means that menstruation (and later ovulation) occurs.

The definition of adolescence also causes problems, because it has no definite beginning or end. *The Oxford English Dictionary* says it is 'the period between childhood and maturity extending from 14 to 25 in males and 12 to 21 in females', which may make a large number of young men rather angry! It is a period of emotional turmoil, during which society begins to recognize the sexual capacity and social independence of the person, who starts mentally scripting his or her sexual drama, through fantasy and actions.

The physical changes

By the end of the first year of life a child's birth weight has tripled and by the end of the second it has quadrupled. After this, both height and weight increases settle down, in both sexes, to a steady annual gain of about 5 to 7 cm (2 to 2¾ in) a year in height and 2.25 to 2.75 kg (5 to 6 lb) increase in weight.

This steady progress is interrupted by a sudden pre-puberty spurt of height and weight. The spurt in height begins at about 10 or 11 years of age in girls and about 12 to 13 years in boys, and it lasts about two years in both sexes. During the spurt girls add about 16 cm (6 in) to their height and boys add about 20 cm (8 in), mostly because of the growth in the length of the trunk. The spurt in weight lags behind that in height in both sexes and starts later in boys.

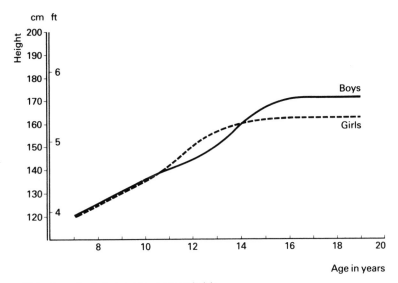

5 Puberty and gain in height in boys and girls

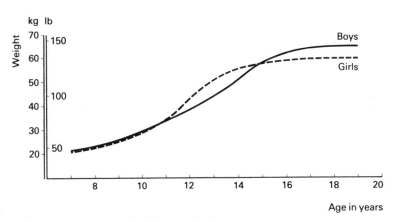

6 Puberty and gain in weight in boys and girls

The two growth spurts change the shape of the bodies of the sexes, so that boys and girls become different physically.

In both sexes, the size of the hands and feet increases first, then the forearms and calf; this is followed by the chest and hips, and then, in boys particularly, by the shoulders. The child is becoming an adolescent! Last of all, the trunk lengthens and the chest deepens. In girls, the chest growth is masked, to some extent, by the development of the breasts. During this period of unequal growth, the child is relatively ungainly and often embarrassed by his or her appearance.

During the early adolescent spurt of growth, sex differences in body shape become apparent. The pelvic region of a girl grows more than her shoulder girdle, becoming wider, roomier, and more shallow than the male pelvis. Fat is deposited over her hips, so that she begins to develop feminine contours. In boys, the reverse occurs. A boy's shoulders become wider and heavier. These changes are due to the secretion of a pituitary hormone – the human growth hormone.

A boy's body growth starts later than a girl's but goes on for longer, until the age of 20 or so, which is why men are usually taller than women.

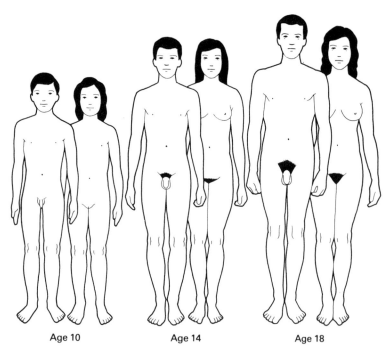

Age 10   Age 14   Age 18

7 The physical and sexual development of males and females between the ages of 10 and 18

The secretion of the sex hormones into the blood circulation produces an even greater difference between the sexes than does the secretion of the growth hormone. In boys the main sex hormone secreted is testosterone, in girls it is oestrogen (but each sex secretes a quantity of the main sex hormone of the other sex). The hormones are secreted by the sex glands, or gonads. These are a boy's testicles and a girl's ovaries. They start producing hormones because they are stimulated by hormones produced in the pituitary gland, called gonadotrophins.

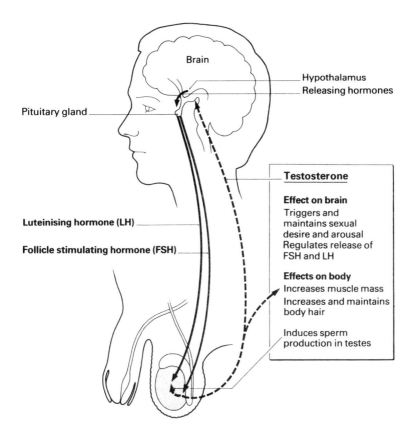

Brain

Hypothalamus
Releasing hormones

Pituitary gland

Testosterone

Effect on brain
Triggers and maintains sexual desire and arousal
Regulates release of FSH and LH

Luteinising hormone (LH)

Effects on body
Increases muscle mass
Increases and maintains body hair

Follicle stimulating hormone (FSH)

Induces sperm production in testes

8 The control of testicular function

Parents often worry either when the boy is a baby, or at puberty, that his testicles are not normal. This anxiety increases if they believe that he will develop abnormally and be unable to father children. Their anxiety may communicate itself to the boy and can cause considerable psychological stress.

In over 99 per cent of boys the testicles can be felt in the scrotum either at birth or within a few weeks, but they may be drawn up out of the scrotum by cold or by crying, so that it may appear empty. If a boy's testicles are 'undescended', it is important that this should be detected before his first birthday. An examination should be made by the doctor at the time of the baby's birth. If testicles are not found in his scrotum, he should be re-examined 6 to 8 weeks later, and if they are still not in his scrotum, again when he is about 9 months old.

Baby boys – about 8 in every 1000 – whose testicles are not found in their scrotum by the first birthday require an operation to bring them down and fix them in the scrotum, so that they grow normally and function properly after puberty. The operation is usually done before the boy is 5 years old.

Until puberty the testicles remain small, when, between the age of 12 and 17, a spurt of growth enlarges them. Many parents (and some boys) are unaware that there is such a wide age range during which the testicles may grow, and become unduly concerned if they think that the testicles are smaller than they should be.

A boy's testicles increase in size because of the effects of the gonadotrophins. These brain hormones induce special cells, called Leydig cells, within the testis, to produce the male sex hormone, testosterone. Testosterone, together with the gonadotrophins, leads to the production of sperms in the 'nests' in the testes. Testosterone enters the boy's bloodstream in increasing quantities and begins the masculinization of his body. The blood carries the testosterone to his brain where it 'stimulates' his sexual interest, so that it becomes more intense. Once so stimulated, testosterone has no further effect on his sexual desire or activity, provided the amount secreted by his testicles remains within a wide 'normal' range. It is for this reason that injections of testosterone are of no value in improving a man's sexual performance or in treating most cases of impotence.

The first obvious sign that a boy has reached puberty is that his penis grows in length and in circumference, so that it is bigger in both dimensions. At first the growth is slow, but by the age of 13 or 14, a boy's penis grows more rapidly and pubic hair begins to appear.

A year or so later, about the age of 15, hair appears in his armpits and some frizzy hair starts tentatively on his upper lip. By now, too, his larynx, or voice-box, has increased in size owing to the circulating testosterone, and his vocal cords have lengthened. These changes deepen the boy's voice, but for a year or so he may have difficulty in controlling the lower register, so his voice may suddenly jump from deep tones to a high squeak.

Testosterone also has the effect (probably in association with growth hormone) of increasing the muscle mass of boys. This affects the boy's shoulders, upper arms, and legs, particularly, so that boys become stronger than girls, and their shoulders broader.

Not all the effects of testosterone are so beneficial. The hormone acts on the sebaceous glands in the skin, leading to acne which disfigures the face and neck of many adolescent boys, causing embarrassment and dismay, and making many concerned about their attractiveness to girls.

*

Does early as opposed to late maturity have any lasting effects on the boy's personality?

A boy who is physically mature at 15 is likely to be regarded with greater respect by his parents, by his peers, and by girls than a boy who is still small and has little or no facial hair. The physically mature boy is able to compete better in athletic contests, which in our society gives him status. Because girls mature about one or two years earlier than boys, the physically mature boy is more confident with girls of his own age in heterosexual encounters.

These observations were confirmed by the scientists in California, who found that late maturers were less well poised, less physically attractive to others, less popular with their peers, more likely to seek attention, and more tense than early maturers. The late maturers needed more sympathy and encouragement to combat their anxiety and distress.

Many of these problems would be avoided if the wide variation in age of physical maturity in adolescence were known by parents, and if they stressed to their anxious son that by 16 or 17 he will be as physically mature as a boy who matures early. Parents and children should know that the physical changes of adolescence can occur at widely different ages in normal young people. The height spurt may occur as early as 11 or as late as 16. The size of the boy's chest may increase at 12 or not until he is 17. He may put on weight, increasing his muscle mass and his strength, any time between 12 and 16. There is no basis for the folk myth that a boy can outgrow his strength.

Similarly, the age at which a boy's genitals increase in size is very variable, and neither the boy nor his parents need be over-concerned if his penis has not grown as much as those of his age-mates, at least until he is 16.

The physical changes associated with adolescence may provoke psychological anxiety as the youth becomes confused about his body's changes, and may become over-sensitive to his appearance, particularly in a society which stresses a stereotype of a young male in advertising. If the adolescent sees himself as different from the cultural stereotype, he may lose his self-respect and feel unattractive and unwanted. Similarly, a boy who matches (or exceeds) the cultural stereotype may receive such a measure of recognition from others that his self-image becomes magnified, and he becomes vain and over-bearing.

The psychological changes

The considerable physical changes which occur during adolescence are paralleled by marked psychological changes as the child matures to become an adult. Psychologists have determined that the adolescent years are a time when learning capacity and efficiency are at their peak and reasoning is easier. At some point during this period the child, for the first time, begins to be able to make decisions, to choose with discrimination, and to become aware of what is possible and what is fantasy.

Above all, as far as the psychological development of the child is concerned, adolescence is a period of adjustment, during which he is searching for an independent identity, so that he can answer the question 'Who am I?' He knows the direction in which he wants to go, but he is unsure where he wants to go and how he is going to get there. Because of this need to see himself as a distinct individual – not as an extension of his parents – he questions authority, and may rebel against parental decisions.

It is not entirely clear how an adolescent finds an identity in which he is comfortable, but the evidence is that it is a slow, continuous process, not a sudden, spectacular vision. A person's unique identity begins to be formed from childhood identifications with his parents or other 'significant' individuals. These identifications leave memory traces, and, as the child grows older, they are added to, modified, changed selectively, perhaps several times, in the light of new experiences, until at last an identity is formed which the adolescent finds comfortable for himself.

To some extent the ease with which he adjusts depends on the security and confidence he has obtained during his childhood years, from his parents and other people. To some extent it depends on the attitude of his parents to his quest for his unique identity. If his parents are autocratic or authoritarian, they will oppose any attempt the youth makes to express his own views and to make his own decisions. This reaction may be because one parent (usually the father) had a difficult adolescence and has suppressed his own awareness of his turbulence at that time. He has retreated into a belief that he always knows best, and that his values are the only ones which his child must adopt. In a rigid society, this approach is possible, but in our pluralistic, mobile society it can create grave problems, particularly when the adolescent compares his lot with that of his friends, whose parents treat their children more as equals. The comparison may lead to deep anxieties and stresses.

The reverse is also true. If the parents either ignore the adolescent's behaviour, or offer only minimal guidance, anxiety and guilt can result, as the adolescent is unsure whether or not he is behaving in a way of which his parents would approve. The most satisfactory way in which parents can behave to enable the adolescent to find his identity is for them to be able to discuss issues about the youth's behaviour, openly and easily. In this way the adolescent can find if his decisions meet with the approval of his parents and if they do not, why not.

If the parents act in an authoritarian way, the adolescent may cease to seek his own identity, modelling himself completely on his father. In this event he may find, later, that he has a confused identity, and is less well able to relate to others. The alternative is for the adolescent to rebel, and to reject all that his parents hold as conventionally proper. If he chooses this course, he may also be hindered in forming his identity, or he may be so confused that his identity goes through multiple changes until he finally finds the one with which he is comfortable.

It is obvious, from what I have written, that parental authority is weakened and parental decisions are questioned during adolescence. But in spite of much publicity, adolescence is not a period of turmoil and chaos, rather it is a period of minor rebellion, bickering, and questioning.

In today's rapidly changing society, parents have to accept that they have to learn from their children, and can hope that their children will continue to learn from them, to trust, and to love them.

It is perhaps unfortunate, too, that the child's adjustment to adolescence may coincide with the parents' adjustment to middle age. The youth wants to expend energy, his parents feel a need to conserve energy. The adolescent looks forward to an exciting future, the parents may be looking back to a romanticized past. The youth is enthusiastic, impulsive, and impatient, his parents have become cautious and compromising. The adolescent is uncertain about his awakening sexuality, the parents may be concerned about their (as they believe) waning sexuality. The youth is anxious that his decisions will make his parents unhappy, the parents are anxious because they know that the youth must learn to manage his own affairs, but they want to protect him from harming himself and from the unpleasant realities of life.

Increasingly in adolescence, the youth is influenced by others of his own age group. Peer group influence starts in childhood but becomes much stronger in adolescence. In the period of adolescent adjustment, his group of friends is important in helping the adolescent to interact with his age-mates, to share feelings, and to solve problems with his contemporaries. The friendships of adolescence, which are often intense, though short lived, may compensate for the weakening of family relationships, particularly if these are emotionally charged, as the adolescent strives to become independent while yearning for the security of dependence. In relationships between parents and adolescents, in which warmth and understanding may be minimal, a deep friendship with one of his friends may provide much needed support and enable the youth to develop his personality.

It is also true that peer group influence can be harmful, as the group influence may induce the adolescent to suspend his own judgement and to behave in a way which he may later regret.

For most adolescents, however, the influence of parents and of peers overlaps. In most cases the values of parents and peers are not very different, and the differences tend to be superficial. The adolescent may dress and behave in a bizarre, unconventional way, but he continues to hold many of his parents' values, rejecting only a few. But if the parents are authoritarian, or ignore him, he may reject their beliefs and adopt those of his peers.

The psychological adjustment to adolescence is complex, and often difficult, both for the adolescent himself and for his family. The adolescent has to adjust to the physical changes in himself and to the demands of his culture and the society in which he lives. As well as this he has to make decisions about whether he will conform to his parents' expectations or reject them.

He has to decide who he is, what he wants to be, where he is going, and how he can get there. In this age of uncertainty, of corporate and governmental dishonesty, of instant television images and influences, of unresolved problems and conflicts, it is not surprising that the adolescent appears to be more ready to reject than to accept many conventional values. Most adolescents, in fact, accept many of their parents' beliefs and behaviours, but this generation is more concerned than their parents' generation with such qualities as tolerance, honesty, friendship, and love, and less with status-seeking, acquisition of money, and competition. Many of them believe that only through a critical reassessment of conventional wisdom, rather than its uncritical acceptance, will mankind survive in the unstable world of today.

Sexuality in adolescence

One of the matters which concerns many people, who are now parents and nudging into middle age, is the more open sexual behaviour of contemporary adolescents. It is likely that the change is less, in reality, than in most people's fantasies; but it is true that today sexuality is more open and more discussed and that attitudes to it are more honest.

Sexuality includes sexual arousal, sexual behaviour, and sexual relationships, and each of these needs consideration.

Sexual attraction and arousal

The precise reasons why one person is sexually attracted to another are unclear. Perhaps the most useful theory is that from early childhood each person develops his or her own sexual arousal pattern or 'scenario'. The scenario – the sexual arousal script – is 'written' by the person. It is based on childhood experiences, memories, and fantasies and added to by experiences, information, and fantasies occurring in childhood and adolescence. As the person grows up he modifies the script, adds to it, rejects parts of it, expands other parts of it, 're-writing' it again and again in his mind until he creates a unique pattern of sexual arousal.

In the scenario the writer creates and identifies the type of person by whom he is sexually excited. In his script he is the hero.

When he meets the type of person he has created, he becomes sexually excited, and if this is reciprocated by the other person (who has developed his or her own unique scenario) the couple make closer contact. During this contact, the couple explore each other's personality and either become closer, wanting to learn more about each other, or the initial excitement fails to be sustained and they separate.

In the arousal scenario all the senses are involved to a greater or lesser extent. In our culture, sight seems to be a most potent sexual arousal stimulus, a fact not unnoticed by advertisers who use women's faces and bodies to induce people, particularly men, to buy their products.

Their opinion is supported by several researchers, notably Dr Ellen Bersheid and Dr Timothy Brock. They have confirmed that in an initial encounter the looks of the person are not just very important, but in many instances are all important. In other words, the physical attractiveness of the person is a stronger stimulus to sexual arousal than his or her intellectual ability or status in society. Although appearance is most important, sexual arousal is increased by the other senses. The sound of a woman's voice can turn a man on; so can her smell, whether natural or due to perfume. It is interesting that in other animals, smell seems to be the most sexually exciting stimulus. When a female animal is in heat she secretes substances called pheromones in her vagina. Human females also produce these substances, but our sense of smell is not as acute as that of other animals. Animals, particularly birds, also use sight to attract a sexual partner. In most species, the male displays to attract the female. Among humans, women are said to dress (or undress) to attract men; but a visitor to any Western country can see that men also dress to attract women, although many men may deny this.

For many people, the touch of body contact is the most sexually exciting of all the senses. Most people experience increased sexual excitement if they have the opportunity to kiss or hug a person by whom they have been sexually aroused. This excitement is increased if the erotic parts of the body are touched. In our culture, the breasts, the genitals, and the buttocks are strongly erotic for most people. Some people are sexually excited from having their feet massaged, their backs rubbed, or their hair stroked. It depends on the scenario each person has created.

By late adolescence the person's sexual arousal scenario is largely complete, and it is less likely to be re-written as the person grows older. For most people the culmination of sexual arousal is orgasm, by either masturbation, or erotic stimulation by a partner, or sexual intercourse.

Sexual behaviour

Studies of adolescent sexual behaviour are limited. The best organized studies have been made in the U.S.A., in Britain, and in Scandinavian nations. As might be expected, there are considerable variations between nations, between the two sexes, between individuals in each sex, and between boys and girls in different socio-economic groups.

'Sex' or 'wet dreams'

One of the early sexual manifestations of male sexual puberty occurs in dreaming. The teenager dreams of some erotic fantasy, and ejaculates in his sleep. Sex dreams are independent of sexual experience, but may be related to the surge of testosterone which accompanies puberty. (Girls are less likely to experience sex dreams, and orgasm, until they have had an actual sexual experience.) 'Wet dreams' may be related to the supposed greater way in which erotic visual stimuli affect men. When a man fantasizes about a sexual experience, after seeing an erotic picture or a film, he is more likely to take the erotic woman in his imagination and to fantasize sexual intercourse. A woman in her sexual fantasy is more likely to want to *belong* to the sexually attractive man in the picture or film.

Wet dreams are normal; they occur most frequently in adolescence and less frequently as alternative sexual outlets become socially acceptable and possible. Masturbation is the earliest, the most normal, and the most universal outlet.

Masturbation

By the age of 15, nearly 100 per cent of boys have masturbated (and, as one commentator has said, those who haven't are liars!). The proportion of girls who masturbate is lower in each age group, but in recent years the proportion is increasing.

It is now accepted by all but a few fearful people that masturbation is a normal sexual outlet and an important sexual learning process, and the anxiety that masturbation will lead to moral or physical decay has declined. Despite this, many adolescents who masturbate feel guilty because they fear that their parents will punish them, and because of inaccurate memories of the dangers of masturbation as discussed by their peers in whispered conversations. The myths which surrounded masturbation have been largely discredited, but they still cause anxiety and guilt.

What are the myths and what are the facts?

The myths	The facts
Masturbation is a sign of moral turpitude and shows that the person is weak and unstable.	Masturbation is usual in all societies and all classes. Nearly 100 per cent of boys masturbate and 70 to 80 per cent of girls masturbate.
Masturbation is an abnormal way of behaving.	Masturbation is a normal sexual outlet, which is most common in adolescence, but which is practised at all ages, by people with and without sexual partners.
Masturbation is unhealthy and evidence of sexual immaturity.	Masturbation is a healthy way of learning to explore your body, of developing your sexuality and your sexual fantasies. All of these are important for a fulfilling sexual life.
People who masturbate subsequently develop sexual problems and are sexually frustrated.	This is obviously untrue, as nearly all people masturbate.
Masturbation cannot give a person full emotional pleasure.	No less pleasure is obtained from masturbation than during sexual intercourse: the pleasure may be different but it is not diminished.

Excessive masturbation leads to bodily weakness, lack of concentration, and eventual mental decay.	There is no truth whatsoever in any of these assertions. What is excessive for one person is normal for another. Masturbation does no physical harm to anyone. The only harmful effect of masturbation is the guilt which it may cause, and there is no need for anyone to feel guilty about masturbation.
Excessive masturbation causes inflammation of the prostate gland, prostatis, because 'a man does not get as thorough an emptying of his prostate when he masturbates as he does in sexual intercourse'.	The evidence for this is dubious, although some doctors believe it.

Despite our knowledge that masturbation is healthy, and that nearly all people masturbate, most people are still ashamed to let it be known that they masturbate. When asked they become reticent and defensive. They are reluctant to tell their friends, lovers, or mates. This is an example of the way in which a normal pleasurable activity has been debased by societal condemnation.

'Petting'

Petting is an American word which is accepted in most English-speaking countries. It implies that the couple extend their sexual arousal to an increased excitement through extensive touching, particularly of the perceived erotic areas of the body. Depending on the degree of sexual inhibitions of each partner, the areas touched may be limited, but in 'heavy' petting all parts of the body are touched, and one or both partners is helped to orgasm by the other, but sexual intercourse does not take place. In recent years, the extent of petting has been reduced, as more young people accept sexual intercourse as a normal expression of enjoyment between two aroused people.

In spite of this change, petting continues to have a useful place in the sexual development of young people. It gives them the opportunity to explore each other's bodies, including the genitals, and it helps them to interact emotionally with each other. It teaches them to learn more about their own and their partner's erotic body areas; and if they are able to talk to each other, to learn about each other's response to touch. It helps them to communicate with each other sexually. It makes each more sensuous, sensitive, and receptive to the other's sexual needs.

As sexual intercourse is prohibited in petting, petting helps men, particularly, to learn the enjoyment of 'mutual' pleasuring of body and mind, and to avoid the conventional male myth that the objective of sex is to 'get it in, get it off, and get it out'.

Sexual intercourse

Although masturbation is now accepted as normal and petting is permitted, sexual intercourse between adolescents remains a matter of considerable concern both to parents and to the adolescents themselves. While some parents accept that their children will have sexual intercourse and only seek to suggest that it is sexually damaging and irresponsible to put the girl in danger of becoming pregnant, or of either partner becoming infected with a sexually transmitted disease, most parents disapprove of pre-marital sexual intercourse, especially for girls.

This creates a dilemma for many adolescents. Their parents' values about sex may differ considerably from those of their peers, and when the parent is perceived as being non-permissive, the adolescent is increasingly influenced by the values of his peers which are likely to be more permissive. This can cause guilt about deceiving parents, and fear should the parents find out. Many parents promote and instil values which reduce sexual permissiveness; many peer values, and the emotional experiences of dating, promote sexual permissiveness.

Sexual relationships

Investigations into adolescent sexuality are difficult to organize and few, if any, of those made can escape criticism. However, the information obtained from Scandinavia, the U.S.A., and Britain is sufficiently important to be recorded so that the reality of current adolescent sexuality can be contrasted with the conventional illusions.

In all three countries, boys are more likely to have had sexual intercourse, with more partners, than are girls; and both boys and girls of lower socio-economic groups are more likely to have had sexual intercourse at an earlier age than those in higher socio-economic groups.

Ira Reiss studied adolescent sexual behaviour in America in 1967. He found that he could divide sexual behaviour into four groups. These are (1) *Abstinence:* pre-marital intercourse is wrong for both sexes, although some kissing and petting is permitted. (2) *The double standard:* this states that as men have a stronger sexual drive than women, and a need to satisfy it, men can 'indulge' in sexual intercourse when they want. A woman either should await marriage or, occasionally, may permit sexual intercourse with her fiancé. (3) *Permissiveness with affection:* if the couple have an affectionate, relatively stable relationship, sexual intercourse is permitted. (4) *Permissiveness without affection:* sex is a universal pleasurable activity for both men and women, and each can enjoy sexual intercourse regardless of the amount of affection which exists between them.

Table 2 Standards of sexuality in the U.S.A. in 1967

	Men	Women
	(percentage of sample)	
Abstinence	28	55
Double Standard Accepted	27	23
Permissiveness with Affection	30	20
Permissiveness without Affection	15	2
	100	100

Source: Ira Reiss, *The Family System in America* (Holt, Rinehart & Winston Ltd., New York, 1971).

Ira Reiss found there was a difference between the sexes and between social classes. You can see in Table 2 that men were more sexually permissive than women. Women were more likely to have sexual intercourse if they were 'going steady', which suggested that most women associated sex with affection. Men were more likely to have sexual intercourse whether they were in love or not, and to 'sample' multiple partners.

In 1971 Robert Sorensen investigated the sexual behaviour of American adolescents. His investigation can be criticized as only 60 per cent of those randomly selected agreed to be interviewed. The parents of most of the others refused to permit the interview, but some of the adolescents who had agreed backed out when the questions were asked. Those who answered were self-selected and were likely to have more permissive attitudes to sex than those who refused or backed out of the survey. Nevertheless, Sorensen's investigation gives some indication of adolescent sexuality in contemporary America. Of the 411 adolescents finally investigated, 52 per cent (59 per cent of men and 45 per cent of women) had had sexual intercourse by the age of 19.

Sorensen also divided those who had had sexual intercourse into 'serial monogamists' and 'sexual adventurers'. Serial monogamists had relationships which lasted for some time, during which both partners had no other sexual attachment. Sexual adventurers were not interested in a relationship, but hoped to have several partners, either simultaneously or serially. Twenty-five per cent of the boys, but only 6 per cent of the girls, were classed as sexual adventurers.

Sorensen's findings were not very different from those of the investigation made by Ira Reiss in 1967, or that of Kantner and Zelnick who found, in 1971, that 46 per cent of unmarried women aged 15 to 19 were sexually active by the age of 19.

These three American surveys of adolescent sexuality, and others, showed that by the early 1970s more young men were sexually active than were virgins by the time they were 19 years of age, and that nearly as many young women were having sexual intercourse as were still virgins.

The American surveys also revealed that adolescents in different social classes had different attitudes towards sexuality. Among young men in lower socio-economic groups there was greater sex segregation in peer groups. Masturbation occurred less often and started later, as it was considered 'unmanly'. Sexual intercourse started earlier than in the higher socio-economic groups. It was often casual and exploited the women, the men being sexual adventurers who avoided any romantic attachment. Within the peer group each member tried to impress the others by his aggression, by physical display, and by his sexual successes. In modern terms, the young man was developing into a male chauvinist pig, who had a strong double standard of sexuality and who perceived women as objects for sexual pleasure.

In the higher socio-economic groups there was far less sex segregation and much earlier masturbation, which was accompanied by sexual fantasy. The young men had sexual intercourse later, often made romantic attachments, and found it less necessary to impress the peer group by physical display, aggression, or sexual prowess.

The differences in sexual behaviour between young women of

different social classes were less marked. Women in lower socio-economic groups masturbated less, but had sexual intercourse earlier and more often, although they apparently had less enjoyment from sex, reaching or being helped to orgasm less often.

It is interesting too that adult concepts of 'bad' when related to young adolescents of each sex were different. Adults accepted that a 'bad boy' could be bad in several ways. He could fight excessively, lie, steal, take drugs, or play truant from school. But to say a girl was a 'bad girl' meant that she was sexually permissive.

In Britain, Michael Schofield investigated the sexual behaviour of adolescents. They were chosen, at random, from lists of school attenders in seven different areas of the country. This selection made the sample as representative as possible of the young people of Britain. They were aged about 17 in 1966, and 66 per cent of them were re-interviewed 7 years later.

The study showed that 72 per cent of the young people had had sexual intercourse before marriage, usually starting between 18 and 21. More men (80 per cent) had had pre-marital sexual intercourse than women (61 per cent), and there was another difference in sexual behaviour. The young men began sexual intercourse at an earlier age than the women, and were more likely to have several partners, but once a woman became sexually active she had sex more often, usually with the same partner, or one other.

Most of those who were sexually active had only one partner at a time, that is they were going steady or were serial monogamists. In the year before the second survey (when the people were aged about 23) 65 per cent of the men and 85 per cent of the women had had sex with one partner only; 11 per cent of the men and 6 per cent of the women had had two partners, but only 17 per cent of the men and 3 per cent of the women were sexual adventurers, having had intercourse with three partners or more.

The first time the adolescents had sexual intercourse was usually unpremeditated. The young women most often had sex with an older man, either at his house or at hers; but in one-third it took place in a car, a lane, a park, at a party, or in a hotel. The man was someone she knew fairly well, and often he was the person she later married.

Forty-six per cent of the men said that they remembered enjoying the first sexual experience, but only 35 per cent of the women remembered enjoying it. There was no difference in the proportion enjoying their first sexual intercourse experience if it took place before, or in, marriage.

More than half of the men and nearly two-thirds of the women found their expectations were not met. They were either disappointed (18 per cent), ashamed (13 per cent), had no feelings either way (16 per cent), or disliked the experience (8 per cent, mostly young women). Very similar percentages were found in the U.S.A. in Sorensen's survey. This negative reaction to their first sexual experience suggests that the young people had either been misinformed, had acquired false attitudes, were worried about the morality of pre-marital sex, or anxious about venereal disease or pregnancy. A few were worried about their ability to perform well sexually.

Neither of the British surveys showed that sexual intercourse 'indulged in by young, immature people leads to irresistible sexual impulses to which the person rapidly becomes addicted', as some concerned older people believe.

Forty-one per cent of those who had sexual intercourse repeated the experience within a week, 50 per cent within 2 weeks, and 60 per cent within a month; but 20 per cent did not have sex again for at least 3 months. Fortunately, with repeated sexual intercourse the percentage enjoying the experience increased to over 90 per cent.

When pre-marital sex was related to the social class of the young people there was a slight difference. The children of middle-class parents and manual-worker parents had pre-marital sex equally frequently, but the children of non-manual workers had pre-marital sex less frequently than the other classes.

Schofield's survey showed that in Britain, by 1973, sexual intercourse was fairly common before marriage, and was widely accepted by young people, but it started later than many older people claimed. Nor was there any evidence that more young people were sexual adventurers than in earlier surveys.

What was disturbing were the findings that over 57 per cent of the young people who were sexually active had a sex problem of one sort or another.

The main problem was anxiety about sexual performance. This concerned 21 per cent of the men and 13 per cent of the women. Fewer married people (16 per cent) expressed this anxiety, compared with those 'going steady' (23 per cent) and those who were single (21 per cent). The second main problem was boredom in sex, which affected 7 per cent of the men and 16 per cent of the women. More married than unmarried couples complained of this problem. The third problem, that of guilt feelings, or of moral concern about sex, was complained of by 18 per cent (21 per cent of the men and 15 per cent of the women). The unmarried, sexually active young people were more likely to be concerned about this problem. The fourth problem was anxiety about masturbation, which concerned 12 per cent of the men and 2 per cent of the women.

These findings relate to surveys of sexual behaviour made in the late 1960s and early 1970s. The question has to be asked: Is sexual activity among teenagers increasing or not?

This has been answered, at least partially, by Michael Schofield's 1973 investigation, by a survey, also in Britain, by Christine Farrell in late 1974, and by a survey in the U.S.A. in 1976 by Melvin Zelnik and John Kantner.

Michael Schofield's second survey demonstrated that changes in sexual attitudes and behaviour had occurred between 1966 and 1973. These changes were more in attitudes than in behaviour. In 1966 the teenagers had rather more sex than they admitted having. In 1973, although some increase in sexual activity had occurred, the men and women, now aged 25, had rather less sexual activity than they said they had.

In 1974 Christine Farrell, on behalf of the Institute for Social Studies in Medical Care, organized a carefully designed study into sexual attitudes and behaviour. Over 1500 teenagers were interviewed and the study represents, as far as is possible, the sexual behaviour and attitudes of British teenagers aged 16 to 19.

The survey showed that 32 per cent of the boys and 13 per cent of the girls had had sexual intercourse before they were aged 16. With each year of age, the percentage who said they had had sexual intercourse rose, and by the age of 19, 75 per cent of the men and 70 per cent of the women were sexually experienced.

The difference in sexual experience between social classes, noted by Schofield eight years earlier, had diminished to some extent by 1974. Similar proportions of middle-class teenage men and women and of working-class teenage women had sexual experience (49 per cent middle-class teenage men; 47 per cent middle-class and working-class teenage women) whereas 60 per cent of working-class teenage men were sexually experienced. These findings are closer to those reported from the U.S.A. than to Schofield's study, and suggest that patterns in sexual behaviour in English-speaking countries are tending to converge.

In spite of the high percentage of sexually active teenagers there was little evidence of promiscuity. Few of the teenagers were sexual adventurers. Christine Farrell comments, 'The majority of young people currently involved in a sexual relationship were having sex with someone they had been going out with for more than six months, and there was no evidence that the pill was encouraging casual relationships.' Most of the sexually active teenagers used some form of contraception, and only one in twelve did not. The form of birth control most commonly used was the condom, followed by withdrawal, and, increasingly, the pill.

In the U.S.A. Zelnik and Kantner's 1976 survey followed the same pattern as their earlier study. They concentrated their efforts on seeing if changes had occurred in the sexual behaviour and contraceptive experience of teenage women. Their findings confirmed an increase in sexual activity by teenage unmarried women. They found that by the age of 19, 55 per cent of unmarried teenage women had had sexual intercourse compared with 47 per cent in the survey of 1971, an increase of 18 per cent. As well as this, they found that teenage women were having sex earlier, and there was a 30 per cent increase in the number of women aged 15 to 19

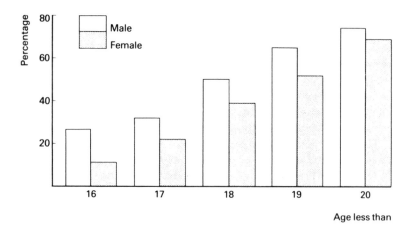

9 Sexual intercourse among British teenagers, 1974

who had sexual intercourse. There had been a tendency, in the five-year interval, for a woman to have more sexual partners, although 51 per cent of the women had sexual intercourse with only one partner by the age of 19. Thirty per cent of women had had sex with two or three men, and 23 per cent were sexual adventurers, compared with 16 per cent in 1971.

Zelnik and Kantner inquired where sexual intercourse usually took place. They found that four out of five teenage women usually had sexual intercourse 'at his place or at mine', with his place being used nearly twice as often. Only 6 per cent of the women said that the first time they had had sex, or the most recent time, had been in a car or at a hotel. This is a change from earlier sexual behaviour patterns, and suggests that parents go out more often – either to work or for pleasure – leaving the house 'reliably vacant at an opportune time', as Zelnik says.

The surveys confirm that most teenagers see nothing morally wrong in pre-marital sexual intercourse, and an increasing proportion of teenage men and, especially, of women are sexually active. This presumes that there has been a reduction in the 'double standard' of sexuality and that women increasingly feel that they have equal sexual desires, needs, and enjoyment as men.

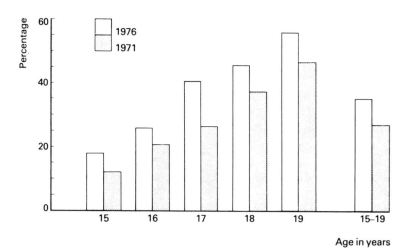

10 Sexual intercourse among never-married American teenage women, 1971 and 1976

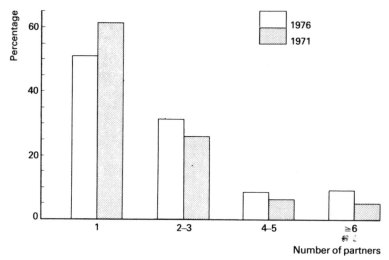

11 Number of partners of sexually active never-married American teenage women, 1971 and 1976

The American survey disclosed that fewer than 40 per cent of the unmarried teenage women had any reliable knowledge of the time during the menstrual cycle when the risk of becoming pregnant was greatest. It also showed that only about 60 per cent had used contraceptives (or their partner had) the last time they had had sexual intercourse. This finding is disturbing, but is none the less an improvement over the finding in the 1971 survey, when only 45 per cent had used contraceptives. It is also encouraging that reliable methods of contraception (the pill and the condom) were replacing the unreliable methods (withdrawal and douching).

Table 3 Sexual freedoms, rights, and responsibilities

Every person has the freedom

- to express affection and love
- to control his own body
- to make his own sexual choices
- to reject sexual exploitation
- to refuse sexual stereotyping
- to know about sexual myths

No person has the right

- to exploit another person's body sexually or commercially
- to conceive or give birth to an unwanted child
- to deny another person his sexual preferences
- to impose his sexual preferences on others
- to spread a sexually transmissible disease

The British surveys noted far smaller class differences in sexual attitudes and behaviour than the American surveys, but there were differences nevertheless. Those more highly educated and earning higher wages were more likely to have had sex before marriage, perhaps because they married later. They were also more likely than those with less education to have an abortion or to continue with the pregnancy and have an out-of-wedlock baby, because they were less likely to be forced into marriage; but as those with more education were more likely to use contraceptives, pregnancy was less likely to occur.

*

It is clear that today young people accept pre-marital sexual intercourse as normal social behaviour. If chastity is no longer believed to be a virtue, society has an obligation to reduce the consequences of the sexual behaviour of young people. These are unwanted, unwelcome pregnancy and sexually transmitted disease, especially gonorrhoea and non-specific urethritis.

Investigations in most areas of the world have shown that in many developed nations adolescent pregnancy and childbirth is causing a considerable problem. Among Western nations the experience of the U.S.A. can be taken as an example. Dr Frederick Jaffe, President of the Alan Guttmacher Institute, pointed out at a conference held in 1976 that 'the nation is experiencing an epidemic of adolescent pregnancy and childbearing'. Adolescent pregnancy rates are higher in the U.S.A. than in many less-developed countries. One million American teenagers (about 10 per cent of all adolescent girls) 'become pregnant each year, sixty per cent give birth and go on to face the adverse health, social and economic consequences associated with early childbearing'. Over half of those who gave birth became pregnant out of wedlock. Investigations showed that two-thirds of the pregnancies and one-half of the births were not intended. Half of the sexually active adolescents surveyed reported that they had not used contraception the last time they had sexual intercourse. Over 300,000 teenagers obtain abortions for unintended pregnancies each year in the U.S.A. Dr Jaffe believes that the situation will only be changed with better education and with more adequate service programmes to provide contraceptives to sexually active teenagers.

If a young woman finds that she has become pregnant she has three choices. She can seek to obtain an abortion, she can marry and have the baby, or she can remain single and become an unmarried mother. In contrast to the U.S.A., in Britain since 1970 the number of extra-marital conceptions has declined, and of those which have occurred, nearly 38 per cent are terminated by abortion, nearly 28 per cent are followed by childbirth after marrying, and in the remaining 34 per cent the mother remains single. The important factor in the decline is the increased use of contraceptives.

The situation regarding sexually transmitted diseases is also of concern. Unfortunately, as the surveys of sexual behaviour in Britain show, many young people have little idea of the symptoms of sexually transmitted diseases.

In addition, many young people are concerned about their sexuality, their sexual performance, and their relationships.

One way in which society could reduce the effects of this lack of knowledge would be to provide properly thought-out sexual education.

At present the quality and quantity of sexual education in all English-speaking countries vary very considerably. Surveys in the U.S.A., Britain, and Australia suggest that although most adolescents would prefer to obtain sexual education from their parents, few do so. Most obtain it from their friends, and it is often inaccurate. One Australian respondent wrote: 'I got my information mainly from my friends, but I didn't learn much.' Another wrote: 'I had some information from other boys, but it was mostly misleading.' Although most adolescents would have preferred to learn about sex from their parents, a complaint of those who did was that much of the information given them was later found to be inaccurate or they had not understood it.

It is clear that if sensible and accurate information about human relationships and human sexuality is to be given to adolescents, and if the misinformation provided by peers is to be reduced, both parents and teachers will have to make a more positive contribution.

Unfortunately, many parents seem unable to provide accurate information, and teachers will have to fulfil this role, so that tomorrow's parents may be educated sufficiently to educate *their* children.

This statement is supported by the surveys reported in this chapter, which suggest that adolescents would prefer to learn about sex from their parents, but believe that teachers are more suitable educators.

They want to learn about sexuality at school and, in most circumstances, in coeducational groups led by well-trained, empathetic teachers. They believe that it is less embarrassing all round to discuss sexuality in the classroom with an impartial, informed adult than at home with uncomfortable parents. They want to know about human relationships in sexuality, as much as about the biological and technical aspects of sex.

I accept that very young children are probably best taught about sex initially by their parents, but this needs to be reinforced by trained teachers in primary school. Because of the inability of many parents to discuss the more complex aspects of sex education, the information should be given to children in the early years of secondary school. This is crucial if tomorrow's parents are to be better informed on sexual matters, and better able to tell their children. The purpose of sex education is not just to provide sufficient factual knowledge, but to become the basis of subsequent sexual development.

What should sex education provide for children of both sexes?

● It should detail the physical, mental, and emotional changes which occur during puberty to girls and boys. This information must include descriptive knowledge of genital anatomy and its variations, and discussions to reduce anxiety about menstruation, masturbation, petting, wet dreams, and sexual arousal.

● It should explain about conception, pregnancy, childbirth, and parenthood. It should also stress the obligations and responsibilities of the couple to each other and to their child.

● It should provide accurate information about contraception and birth control. This should be provided initially before the child reaches puberty and should be reinforced and expanded during later school years, when many students are exploring their sexuality and experimenting.

● It should provide clear information about sexually transmitted diseases.

● It should encourage students to accept people whose sexual practices are discordant with their own.

• Most important, it should provide the basis for sexual responsibility in which the obligations of one human to another are emphasized, the conditions which encourage sexual exploitation are discussed, and sexual mythology is replaced by sexual knowledge.

Some people will argue that sex education will have a damaging effect on the adolescent's sexual morality and will lead to an increase in sexual permissiveness and its consequences. There is no evidence that sex education does this. But there is some evidence that commercial 'sexploitation' by publishers, film makers, and others may have possible damaging consequences, unless counterbalanced by properly presented, factual sex education.

Some people fear that sexual experimentation is psychologically dangerous, even though the hazards of unwanted pregnancy and sexually transmitted diseases are avoided, as it prevents a subsequent stable relationship and a proper 'family life'. The evidence is against this view: sexual experience with a number of sexual partners probably leads to a better permanent relationship (inside or outside marriage), a more stable family life, and perhaps a reduction in the number of those men and women who make fools of themselves in middle age.

There is a fear that sex education will encourage sexual 'perversions' and the spread of pornography. The evidence again denies this. In periods of apparent sexual repression, such as the second half of the nineteenth century in England, commercial sex and pornography were available, although mainly to the wealthy. Child prostitution was common, brothels provided for a wide variety of perversions, unwanted children were sent, soon after birth, to poorly paid wet-nurses in the country and to a near-certain death during infancy. But propriety was maintained by keeping the sexual activities hidden and apart. It is likely that pornography will only have an adverse effect on those who have had to suppress their sexuality in childhood and who have had no education in human sexuality. Sex education is needed to counteract meretricious commercial exploitation. It is needed to encourage sexual responsibility and to improve sexual relationships.

What is presently provided is inadequate and insufficient. Better and more explicit sex education is needed to help young people to share and to enjoy their sexuality.

4
The human sexual response

Van de Velde and Dickinson first dared to investigate and to write of sexual physiology. Yet they were forced to wait until the twilight of their professional careers before challenging public and professional opinion. Obviously, they were shocked when, aside from the expected opprobrium and implication of prurience, the biological and behavioural sciences emphatically shut the door of investigative objectivity. Possibly history will record as Kinsey's greatest contribution, the fact that his incredible effort actually enabled him to put his foot firmly in this door despite counter-pressures that would have destroyed a lesser man.

This text represents the first step, a faltering step at best, but at least a first step toward an open door policy. The door of investigative objectivity must not be closed again.

> W. H. Masters and V. E. Johnson,
> *Human Sexual Response* (1966)

Sexuality is the drive to escape from aloneness, from solitude, to an encounter with another person. The encounter may be in fantasy (masturbation, etc.) or in reality. If it is in reality it may be mainly physical (one night stands, etc.) or a mutual pleasuring of body and mind, in other words, it becomes love. This has been expressed with poetic clarity by Rainer Maria Rilke:

> 'Love consists of this: that two solitudes protect and touch and greet each other.'

DESPITE A GOOD DEAL OF FOLKLORE AND MYTHOLOGY OUR real understanding of a person's response to sexual arousal is new. As sex is 'such a delicate matter' in the minds of many people, including scientists, the investigation of the reactions of men and women to sexual arousal and to sexual intercourse has only been made recently. Dr William H. Masters and Dr Virginia Johnson were pioneers in this research. They were able to recruit volunteers to find out what happens when a person is stimulated sexually. In the course of this research they discovered that many beliefs about human sexuality had no substance – they were myths.

The first of these myths relates to the male sex drive – that is, the urge of a man to initiate a sexual relationship. It has been believed that the average man had a stronger, more urgent sex drive than the average woman. In sexual matters he was the initiator, the aggressor, while the woman was the relatively passive recipient. This is nonsense. It is now known that the sex drive of men and women is essentially similar.

Part of the error lay in a lack of understanding of the sex drive in humans, as no concise definition exists. A reasonable definition of a 'drive' is what occurs when a perceived need or emotion impels the body to activity. The sex drive needs further definition. It has been defined by Brian Heard as 'a fundamental impulse away from the solitary state'. This is true as far as it goes, but even this definition needs further qualification. I define the sex drive as a perceived need to make close contact with another person which impels the body into activity. The activity may be symbolic, as the relationship between Bernard Shaw and Ellen Terry, in which the contact was largely in the meeting of their minds. Usually, though, it is physical. If it is physical it need not be genital, although it is usually. Touch (body to body, mouth to breast, mouth to mouth, genital to genital, or mouth to genital) is an evolutionary imperative, and if one component at least is genital it is usually rewarded by one of the oldest pleasures – orgasm.

The sex drive is very similar to all the other drives which control human behaviour. These drives have evolved over thousands of years and enable a person to seek, or to be attracted to, pleasure and to avoid or escape from pain. For example, if you are frightened, or injured, or hungry, your 'pain centres' are stimulated and messages are sent (through chemical transmitters) which make you ready to fight or to flee, to avoid further injury or to find food, so that the possible dangers you encounter are avoided.

If you do something well (as you perceive it, or as others tell you), or if you have a good meal, or if you achieve something you have long desired, your 'pleasure centre' is stimulated, and messages which make you feel happy, or satiated, or triumphant pass to other parts of your body. You feel good!

Our sexual behaviour is no exception to the 'pleasure–pain principle', but it is unique among the drives, as it is dominated by pleasure, almost to the total exclusion of the 'pain principle'. So when you are sexually aroused, and this leads to a warm sexual contact, and perhaps to sexual intercourse, you feel warm, relaxed, pleasured, and 'great'.

Scientists who study brain structure and function have found that the areas of the brain which appear to control sexual arousal are closely related anatomically to areas of the brain which relay sensations of pleasure. For convenience the areas controlling sexual arousal are called the 'sex centre', although in reality they are systems of interconnected areas in the brain. The 'sex centre' and the 'pleasure centre' lie close to each other in the oldest part of the brain and probably have nerve fibres connecting them. In an experiment which supports this concept, Dr Heath, a scientist, has discovered that in animals orgasm is associated with strong electrical impulses in the pleasure area of the brain. Many men and women, after a particularly arousing sexual experience, feel warm and loving to their partner; they lose hostility and aggression to others, and the pleasurable mood can last for hours.

Although human sexuality and pleasure are so intimately related, it is interesting that, almost alone of the behavioural drives, the sexual drive can be suppressed, modified, or diverted; and a person, if sufficiently motivated, can live for years without needing any sexual release. Equally, if a person who is sexually stimulated is unable to obtain sexual release, it can cause great frustration, unhappiness, and hostility, so the 'pain principle' is not entirely divorced from sexuality.

The reason for these variations is that the sex and pleasure centres receive messages from the genital area and also from the other parts of the brain. In the sex centre, the messages are interpreted and conveyed, as the sex drive, back to the other parts of the brain and to the genitals. In this way all kinds of memories, emotions, experiences, and thoughts can affect the sexual response. Anxiety, depression, or fear can dampen it, fantasy and love can enhance it. This is the basis for full sexual enjoyment and also for the sexual problems which may also arise.

The sex drive is only one of the components of sexual responsiveness. It is the emotional power-house which needs to be translated into the capacity to perform and then into the actual performance. It is both innate, that is biologically determined, and learned, that is determined by experiences.

Sexual drive is not the same as sexual capacity, that is the ability to enjoy sex. The sex drive tells you what you want to do; sexual capacity is what you are able to do. Because of this distinction, psychological problems may arise when the drive powers an inadequate capacity (as in impotence) or results in an inadequate performance, as assessed by oneself or by others (as in premature or delayed ejaculation in men and in lack of orgasm in women). The strength of a person's sex drive may also lead to psychological problems if one partner's drive does not relate closely to that of the other, and the couple are unable to talk about their problem frankly. Usually a compromise is reached, and the urgency of the drive is sublimated, but this may not occur and the individual becomes tense and hung-up.

How a man's sex drive starts and how it is maintained is not completely understood, but the male sex hormone, testosterone, is strongly implicated. At puberty, testosterone is secreted into the blood in increasing amounts, and all mammals (including humans) become sexually arousable.

Evidence that testosterone is essential for triggering a man's sex drive comes from the study of the Dominican villages mentioned in Chapter 2. Once these 'girls' reached puberty, their testes began to secrete testosterone and they began to have male sex fantasies, to masturbate, to ejaculate, and finally to have sexual intercourse, although they were fearful of being ridiculed because of their small penis and split scrotum.

The 'intersex' men not only became male in shape but they developed a male sexual drive. They perceived girls as sexually exciting, they had male sexual daydreams, and when sexually stimulated they ejaculated. In other words, each of them responded as a male would respond to erotic stimulation, although up to this time he had thought himself to be, and others had thought him to be, a girl. The testosterone had triggered his male sex drive.

As the sex centre controlling the sex drive is in the brain, it is here that testosterone operates. Probably it only operates when the brain cells have been sensitized to pre-natal testosterone. This explains why testosterone injections (or tablets) rarely help to raise a woman's sex drive. Before she was born, her brain cells were sensitized, or 'imprinted', by circulating female sex hormones, and remain relatively unresponsive to male sex hormones.

The brain can be divided into three zones. The innermost, and the oldest, is the reptilian brain. With the evolution of mammals, a second zone developed which covered the reptilian brain. This is the old mammalian brain, or the limbic system. With further evolution, more advanced mammals appeared, culminating with man. The more advanced mammals, the monkeys and especially man, have developed a third outer zone, the new mammalian brain, or the neocortex. The neocortex is the area where the erotic part of the sex drive is interpreted. It is the area where man's ability to think, to talk, to write, and to appreciate aesthetics is situated. It may be the area where his capacity to love is situated. But below this, deeper and older in evolution, is the centre for the sex drive. It lies in the limbic area of the old mammalian brain and, in animals, controls mating and copulation behaviour. It is likely that certain smells and some tactile sensations are interpreted as sexual stimuli by this area. Most female animals produce distinctive sexually stimulating secretions in their vagina when in heat, which attract males and lead to copulation. These substances, in monkeys at least, have been isolated and are aliphatic acids. Humans, by contrast, are most attracted sexually by the sight or sound of a potential partner, and such stimuli are interpreted in the cerebral cortex. However, recently scientists have found that women produce exactly the same aliphatic acids, in exactly the same proportions, in their vagina as do monkeys. It is merely that man, like the quoodle, has lost his sense of smell!

The limbic area is closely connected with the hypothalamus where the gonadotrophin hormones originate. These induce the testes to produce spermatozoa and the sex hormones found in men, and the ovaries to secrete the sex hormones which control the menstrual cycle in women.

It also seems, from experiments on male squirrel monkeys, that the messages from the sex centre in the limbic area of the brain which help the animal get an erection and have an orgasm are funnelled through the hypothalamus to the brain stem. It is probable that this also happens in man. A treatment of male sex offenders, practised at one time in Germany, was to implant an electrode in the region of the front part of the hypothalamus and to destroy the nerve pathways by passing an electric current through the electrode. The eleven men treated in this way by Dr Roder lost all their sexual drive after the operation, although they were unchanged in every other way and continued to secrete the male sex hormone, testosterone.

A man's sex drive will only become active if it is 'primed' by testosterone, secreted by his testes at puberty. The continuation of the drive is from stimuli, which are interpreted as erotic by the 'old brain', triggering the physical aspects of the sexual response, particularly erection, ejaculation, and orgasm.

Unless male sex hormone continues to be secreted, the ability to ejaculate diminishes, and in some cases all the sexual urge is also lost. In reported cases of men castrated after puberty there is a very great variation in the time taken for the sexual urge and penile erections to go, if they cease at all. In some men they go quickly, only weeks after castration. Other men retain their sexual potency for years, or for life. What one needs to know is whether men who retain their potency continue to secrete male sex hormones, presumably from their adrenal gland. Until this is known the place of testosterone in the continuation of the sex drive will remain obscure. At present the evidence is that it plays a very small part, once the drive has been primed at puberty. After this a man's sex drive is maintained by emotional impulses which stimulate the sex centre in the brain, and initiate the sexual response.

*

It is rather astonishing that, despite the universality of sexual activity, the details of the human sexual response were not investigated properly until the 1960s. Even today, in spite of the research, the sexual response of a man (and perhaps even more, that of a woman) remains the subject in the minds of many people for surreptitious sniggering, anecdotal myths, and perpetuated misconceptions.

Up to 1940 the few medical scientists who had attempted to find out what really happened during sexual arousal and in sexual intercourse were vilified and rejected by their fellow scientists as eccentrics, or even as sex-mad. In the 1930s and 1940s Dr Robert Dickinson had studied a limited number of couples during sexual intercourse and had produced a carefully drawn atlas of the anatomical changes which occurred. However, his work, of necessity, was relatively superficial.

It was perhaps Dr Kinsey who broke the timidity of the medical scientists to study the physiology and psychology of sex with his 'deafening report', as Noel Coward called it, published in 1948. The medical profession, and the public, found for the first time that behind the silence, the reticence, and the conventional 'delicacy' in human sexuality an astonishing amount of sexual activity took place – masturbatory, extra-maritally, and homosexually as well as within apparently 'normal' marriages. For the first time the American people began to see sexual life in the U.S.A. as it really was. The shock was considerable, and although opponents of Kinsey and his co-workers have tried to slur his admittedly limited findings, the facts he exposed have stood the test of time. Dr Kinsey's persistence, his integrity, and his enormous effort opened the door, only slightly, but nevertheless permanently, to a rational, scientific, unemotional study of this myth-ridden, emotionally charged subject. His work has permitted light to be cast on a previously obscure area and has allowed the current widespread discussions and investigations into human sexuality. Without scientific study of what normally happens during sexual encounters, it is impossible to identify, analyse, and treat the sexual dysfunctions which cause discomfort to so many people and damage large areas of their relationships with other humans.

Human sexuality has been studied in the greatest detail, to date, in the years following 1959. This work, particularly that of Dr William Masters and Dr Virginia Johnson, led in 1966 to the publication of their book *Human Sexual Response*. This book, with its detailed analysis of the sexual response in male and female partners, has given us our knowledge of the human sexual response, and acknowledgement must be given to the careful, contemplative scientific study made over the years at the Reproductive Biology Research Foundation at St. Louis, Missouri.

Until the investigation in St. Louis showed the truth, massive ignorance and accumulated myths surrounded male sexuality.

These 'phallic fallacies' have persisted through the years and still form the basis of 'dirty' jokes. Here are a few:

• *The bigger the man, the bigger his penis* This is untrue, as was demonstrated as long ago as 1907 by the anatomist, George Piersol. The size of the man bears no relation to the size of his penis in the unstimulated state. A coalminer 180 cm (5 ft 11 in) tall, weighing 92 kg (200 lb) may have a smaller penis than a clerk 150 cm (4 ft 8 in) tall, weighing 55 kg (120 lb).

• *The larger the size of the man's penis the better he is as a lover* This is untrue. Dr Dickinson showed in his *Atlas of Human Sex Anatomy* that penises, when unstimulated, have various sizes and usually measure between 7.5 cm (3 in) and 10.5 cm (4 in). But when stimulated to become erect the difference in length is much less. A small penis of 7.5 cm when flaccid doubled to reach 15 cm (6 in) when fully erect; while the man whose flaccid penis measured 11 cm ($4\frac{1}{4}$ in) increased by 5 cm (2 in), to a total length of 16 cm ($6\frac{1}{4}$ in), when fully erect. In other words, the length of the erect penis of different men is not so different. It is true that the diameter, and so the size, of the erect penis does differ. Some men have bigger penises than others. But as the vaginal walls are normally in contact and only separate to accept the penis, penile size has nothing to do with a man's quality as a lover.

• *A circumcised man can last longer during sexual intercourse before ejaculating because his glans is relatively insensitive. An alternative myth states that an uncircumcised man lasts longer before ejaculation* Masters and Johnson have dissipated this myth. There is no difference between the two. The degree of ejaculatory control is not affected by the presence or absence of a foreskin.

• *Sexual intercourse, especially ejaculation, weakens a man, particularly if repeated frequently* This has led to the advice given by sports coaches of 'no sex before football' and to the myth that 'athletics and sex don't mix'. There is no truth in these assertions. In fact, a sexually tense and unrelieved sportsman, or woman, may perform less well than a sexually fulfilled person.

This false belief may also affect the sexual performance of middle-aged business men and other executives, who feel they have to concentrate on their work to achieve the next promotion and become eligible for a larger pension on retirement. Because they believe that sex is weakening they avoid sex, which can be destructive to their relationship with their partner.

● *If a man does not have regular sexual intercourse, especially if he is impotent, his penis shrinks in size* This is not true; the sizes of men's penises are not altered by the number of times that the man has intercourse. This is because the penis is not a muscular organ, but is made up of spaces which fill with blood when the man is aroused sexually.

● *If a man does not have sex frequently, in which he has orgasms and ejaculates regularly, his testicles will become swollen with unreleased sperms and will ache intolerably* (in America this condition is called 'blue balls') This male-oriented myth is untrue on two counts. First, the sperms only form a small proportion of the semen, most of which is composed of secretions from the prostate gland. When sperms are formed and not ejaculated, sperm production slows down and no increased tension occurs in the testicles. Moreover, men who have had a vasectomy do not get painful testicles. Any pain a man feels in his testicles, if he does not ejaculate often, is due to psychological, not to physical, factors.

It is true that if a man is stimulated and stays in the plateau phase of sexual arousal for a long period of time vasocongestion of his testicles will occur, and their size can increase by as much as 75 per cent. In this situation the man may get testicular pain, which is relieved by orgasm. This is a normal sexual response and is not to be confused with the mythical 'blue balls' which is said to occur if a man does not have sex often.

The second count on which the myth is untrue is that if a man feels the psychosomatic testicular pain from insufficient sex, he can masturbate to orgasm. He does not need to have sexual intercourse.

● *Men are sexually aroused more readily and need sex more often than women* The response, both mental and physical, to sexual stimulation follows a similar pattern in both men and women. There are variations, of course, and an uninhibited response is rare, for we are conditioned, all of us, by our childhood upbringing, and by our hang-ups. These can, and do, modify our response to the stimuli. Lord Curzon is rumoured to have said that during sexual intercourse 'a lady does not move'. If a woman has been taught that this dictum is correct she will undoubtedly modify her physiological response to sexual stimulation. Luckily, Lord Curzon's remark is today recognized as the ignorant, obscurantist remark of a Victorian who approved of a double standard in sexual conduct. It is now recognized that men and women respond to sexual stimuli in similar ways, and it is the similarities rather than the differences in the anatomical, physiological, and psychological responses which need to be stressed.

*

What is it that attracts one person to another while both ignore a third? Female animals when in heat produce scents from their vaginal secretions called pheromones, which attract the males. Although women produce the same scents, mankind's sense of smell is too rudimentary to detect them, so this cannot be the explanation. There is another difference between female animals and women. Female animals are only sexually aroused when in heat, while a human female is capable of being sexually aroused and is sexually responsive at most times, if the stimulus is right. It is true that a woman's physiology has not entirely escaped from her evolutionary ancestry. Her sexual excitement varies during her menstrual cycle, and, like that of other mammals, is often greatest at ovulation time – that is, half-way between her periods. This is only a minor factor, as most women's sexual arousal depends more on sexual attraction and sexual stimulation than on the levels of her sex hormones.

Sexual attraction and sexual arousal are not understood fully, but a probable reason is that each person develops his or her sexual arousal script as I have described in the last chapter. In the script, the person is the hero, to whom sexually exciting adventures occur. When a man meets a woman who resembles his fantasy partner, his sexual drive is started. He becomes sexually aroused. What happens to his body during sexual arousal has become clear from the research of Dr Masters and Dr Johnson. To help them analyse the physical components of sexual arousal they found it convenient to divide the rising sexual tension into four phases. They realized that the phases merged one into the other, and that the duration of each phase varied between individuals and with the strength of sexual arousal. The phases are, first, the excitement phase; second, the plateau phase; third, the orgasmic phase; and fourth, the resolution phase.

The excitement phase is explained by its name. The individual responds, sexually, to any stimulation which his (or her) brain interprets as a sexual invitation. The stimulus, in our culture, is usually visual or tactile, but may be, and often is, enhanced by smell or by sound. The stimulus must be of sufficient strength, or be reinforced by additional stimuli, to permit a sufficient increase in sexual desire to extend the phase into the second, or plateau, phase. The opposite can also happen. An advance by a man (or by a woman) may be rejected by the other, and unless the individual's sexual desire is so heightened that he (or she) persists, the excitement phase will be terminated. On the other hand, an obvious response by the person approached, particularly if welcoming, will increase the intensity of the response and bring the individual more quickly into the plateau phase. In our culture, men, especially, are

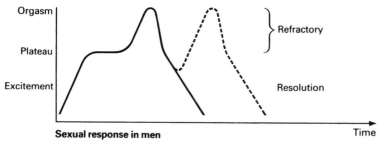

Sexual response in men
Only men have a refractory stage, which may last minutes (as in this diagram) or hours

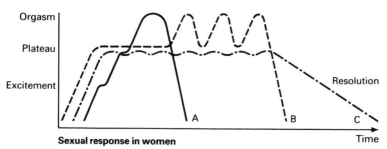

Sexual response in women
A   Short plateau single orgasm
B   Longer plateau multiple orgasms
C   Plateau but no orgasm, slow resolution (this may also occur in men from time to time)

12 The sexual response in men and women shown graphically

said to be stimulated erotically more by vision and women by touch; but this may not be true, as I have mentioned.

It is also believed, in our culture, that a woman is normally only responsive to one man, while a man is able to respond to a wide range of sexually attractive partners. This is an example of the double standard and, with increasing women's sexual liberation, has been shown to be a myth. Both sexes probably respond equally to visual and to tactile erotic sensations and both can respond to multiple partners – if they want to.

In the excitement phase of sexual arousal many changes occur in the bodies of both sexes. The principal, most obvious sign in a man is that his penis becomes erect. In a woman, the main sign of sexual arousal is less obvious, but no less important. Her vagina becomes softer and moister and its entrance rather swollen.

Many men believe erroneously that the vagina is a hollow tube waiting, open, ready to accept a penis. In fact, the walls of the vagina are normally pressed together, and when a woman is not sexually aroused, her vagina is a slightly moist potential space. The sexual arousal of the excitement phase converts this potential space into a well-lubricated, wet, soft, cushioned, warm space to encompass an erect penis. In sexual intercourse, the vagina expands only just enough to stay closely touching the man's penis, whatever its size.

The exact way in which a man gets an erection is now known. It is complex and fascinating. It is essentially due to a reflex over which a man has little or no voluntary control. You cannot will yourself into having an erection, although by using fantasy you may create one; and you can get an erection by stimulating your penis with your hand.

The first kind of stimulus is due to sound, sight, taste, smell, or imagination arousing the sex centre in your brain. The sex centre then sends messages down the spinal cord to its lowest, or sacral, part. In this area the messages are relayed to branches of nerves belonging to a specialized (autonomic) nervous system which reach out to the penis, bladder, and other organs in the pelvis.

The autonomic nervous system is so called because you have little or no conscious control over its activities. It functions in spite of your wishes, to keep you alive and well. It is made up of two different kinds of nerve fibres. The first are the sympathetic nerves, which release adrenalin and, by toning up your muscles, make you ready for fight or for flight. The second kind of nerves are the

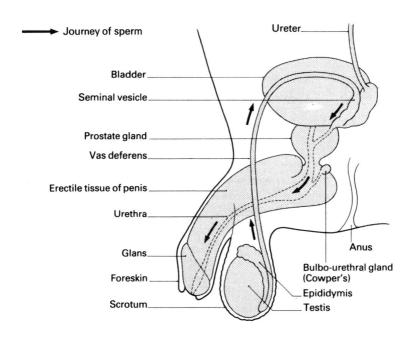

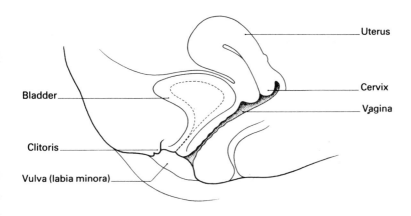

13 The external and internal male and female genital organs

parasympathetic nerves which control (among other things) the blood flow into various organs.

Both types of nerve fibres reach most organs of the body. They control the rate at which your heart beats and the strength of each beat; they control your digestive processes; they control your breathing; and they control your ability to have an erection. Stimulation of the parasympathetic nerves which reach your penis leads to an inflow of blood into your penis and it becomes erect, which is why these parasympathetic nerves are called the 'erection nerves'. But stimulation of the sympathetic nerves supplying your penis, for example by anxiety, or a sudden frightening noise, or fear, can inhibit an erection, or reduce one.

Because erections are necessary to permit sexual intercourse and perpetuate the race, man has evolved, through evolutionary processes, a second system, should the first fail or be damaged, perhaps following a spinal injury.

In this second system, nerve fibres which travel outside the spinal cord in the thoracolumbar trunk connect the higher centres of the brain with the penis, missing out the spinal parasympathetic nerves. Erotic stimuli perceived by the brain excite the thoracolumbar trunk and an erection follows.

This enables some men who have had a spinal cord injury and are paraplegic to get erections, from psychological stimuli, although their spinal parasympathetic nerves are cut off from the erotic messages sent by the brain.

The second way in which a man can get an erection is well known to almost every man. This is by directly stimulating the penis with his own hand, by having it stimulated by his partner's hand or mouth, or by the touch of his partner's body. When a man's penis is stimulated in one of these ways, messages pass along the pelvic nerves to the spinal cord. There they are relayed and the message is transferred to the erection nerves, which send messages back to the blood-vessels supplying the penis. These messages pass directly back to the penis without going to the sex centre in the brain. The mechanism is called a reflex, and the brain is not involved.

Most paraplegic men can get an erection in this way. If the man's penis is stimulated, an erection will occur, although he can feel nothing, and has no nerve connection between his brain and the lower part of his body. The erection occurs because of the erection reflex which does not involve his brain.

The erection nerves end in the walls of the arteries which supply blood to the penis, and the impulses cause the arteries to become wider, so that an increased amount of blood flows into the penis. Normally, blood flows in and out of the penis at a steady rate, but if the penis is sexually stimulated, the blood flows in faster than it flows out, and an erection results. You can appreciate this better if you can imagine a hollow plastic cylinder shaped like a penis, closed at one end and filled with sponge. If you dip the open end of the model in water it will rapidly become heavier and stiffer. This state will continue as long as the liquid remains in the cylinder.

This is what happens when the arteries supplying blood to the penis dilate. Blood flows in, and the sponge-like cylinders of the penis become engorged with blood so that it becomes firm, stiff, and erect.

In some diseases, such as diabetes, the blood-vessels which supply the penile cylinders may become narrowed (or atherosclerotic). These damaged blood-vessels are unable to dilate in spite of parasympathetic nerve stimulation and the man is unable to achieve an erection – in other words he has erectile impotence.

When the spinal cord is intact, the sex centre in the brain controls the spinal erection reflex. If the messages coming into the brain sex centre are erotic, from memories or fantasy or thoughts, the erection reflex works more easily and rapidly, in other words, it is facilitated. But if the messages received by the sex centre from other parts of the brain are disturbing, because of old unhappy memories, depression, anxieties, or hang-ups about sex, or because of anxieties about other matters, or because of hostility to one's partner, the erection reflex is damped down, or inhibited. This inhibition may be so strong that the erection fails to occur, or if it occurs it may be only transitory.

With increasing age, the facilitating messages from the brain become reduced, and perhaps the reflex from the stroked penis is less easily started, so that older men often take longer to get an erection. But even very old men can get an erection if the penis is stimulated for long enough.

Erection is the most obvious sign of sexual excitement in men, but it is not the only change. Other genital organs also become congested. The man's scrotum becomes swollen and his testicles increase in size and rise up towards his crutch. In women, as well as vaginal lubrication and congestion-swelling of the tissues which

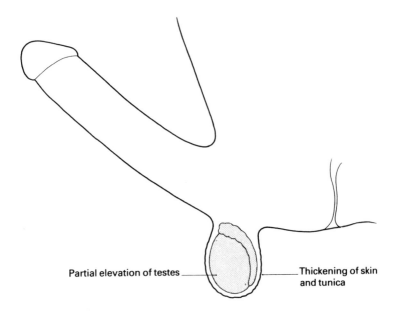

Partial elevation of testes _____ Thickening of skin and tunica

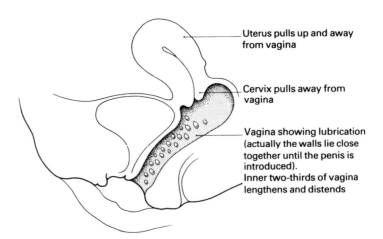

Uterus pulls up and away from vagina

Cervix pulls away from vagina

Vagina showing lubrication (actually the walls lie close together until the penis is introduced). Inner two-thirds of vagina lengthens and distends

14 The stages of sexual response in men and women: the excitement stage

surround the vaginal entrance (the lips or labia), the lips open out to expose the vaginal entrance, and the vagina becomes congested, its colour deepening to a purplish-red. A woman's clitoris (which is the equivalent of a penis) increases in size and length – the same reaction as occurs to the man's penis, when sexually stimulated. In women (but less often in men), a sex flush appears on the breasts and upper abdomen. In both sexes the heart beats faster and the blood pressure edges upwards.

The second, or plateau, phase of the sexual response is a time during which sexual arousal and desire is intensified, and may ultimately reach the stage when orgasm is inevitable. In this phase all forms of stimuli can intensify sexual desire, but the strength of the desire may be diminished by extraneous factors. A knock at the door, an insistent telephone ringing, or a sudden noise can so reduce sexual tension that the man moves away from orgasm and his sexual tension may even dissipate.

The principal stimuli in this phase are those of touch and smell. Stimulated, initially, by the looks of the sexual partner, by his or her voice, in the plateau phase touch becomes as important. Stimulation occurs from the touch of the partner's lips, the exploring tongue, the feel of a man's penis and scrotum, or a woman's breasts, body, and soft vulva. These stimuli enhance sexual desire, lifting each partner into the later plateau phase when the desire to reach orgasm becomes intense. The term 'plateau' is perhaps a misnomer, for sexual tension increases during this time; but a man who is a considerate lover and finds that his partner is not so aroused as he is will want to help her to reach his degree of sexual tension, and will consciously 'hold back', so that he remains highly sexually stimulated in the plateau phase, but does not enter the orgasmic phase too quickly.

The duration of the plateau phase depends on the urgency and strength of the sexual desire, on the effectiveness of the sexual stimuli given by the partner, and on the quality of the communication between the partners. If a woman is slow to reach the orgasmic phase, but does not tell her partner that she needs additional stimuli to bring her to orgasm, she can only blame herself, or her inhibitions, should her man reach orgasm and fall sleepily into the phase of resolution, without having helped her to reach orgasm to relieve her sexual arousal.

During the plateau phase, a man's penis increases in size,

particularly the size of the lower part of his glans; his testicles increase to one and a half times their non-stimulated size, and they rise up even closer to his crutch. Late in this phase, two or three drops of fluid may seep out of the 'eye' of his penis, and occasionally active spermatozoa are found in this fluid, which is one reason why the method of 'withdrawal' is a relatively inefficient method of contraception. The man's breathing increases in rate, his heart beats faster, and his blood pressure rises further. If he has developed a sex flush, this increases in colour and spreads. Sometimes the muscles of his face and abdomen contract spasmodically.

In a woman, the swellings of the tissues around the lowest third of her vagina increase, so that 'cushions' of soft tissue are formed and the vaginal lubrication increases still more. Her upper vagina expands in size, and her uterus is pulled upwards giving a 'tenting effect'. Her labia becomes increasingly congested with blood and dusky in colour. Her clitoris, now swollen, pulls in towards her pubic bones.

The other changes – the increased heart rate and the sex flush – are similar to those which occur in a man, but, in addition, the woman's nipples increase in size, as do her breasts.

The orgasmic phase is self-explanatory. It is those few seconds during which the sexual desire and the sexual tensions culminate in an involuntary climax. It is a time of great vulnerability, for all of the individual's sensations are concentrated in the pelvis, to the exclusion of all other sensory inputs. The earth may shake, lightning may strike, a stranger may enter the room, but these events will make little or no impact, as the involuntary muscle contractions of orgasm recur, and a man ejaculates. The whole of the man's sensations are concentrated in his penis, his prostate, and his seminal vesicles during the few seconds of orgasm. And with orgasm all the sexual desire and all the sexual tensions which were raised during the excitement and plateau phases are suddenly, warmly, and explosively released.

Orgasm can be defined as an intense pleasure felt first deep in the pelvis, which spreads in a powerful sensation of well-being, tingling, and warmth of the whole body, to the exclusion of all other sensations. From this definition it is obvious that orgasm is both a physical and emotional (psychological) pleasurable response to sensual stimuli.

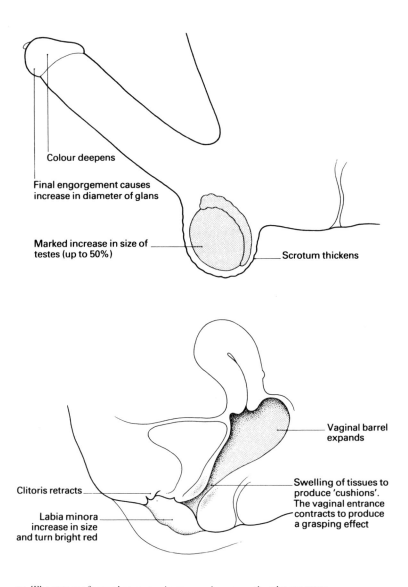

Colour deepens

Final engorgement causes
increase in diameter of glans

Marked increase in size of
testes (up to 50%)

Scrotum thickens

Vaginal barrel
expands

Clitoris retracts

Labia minora
increase in size
and turn bright red

Swelling of tissues to
produce 'cushions'.
The vaginal entrance
contracts to produce
a grasping effect

15 The stages of sexual response in men and women: the plateau stage

In a man, orgasm has two separate stages. In the first, which is called the emission phase, contractions of the muscles of his inner pelvis massage seminal fluid from his prostatic area along his urethra. In the second, or ejaculation, stage, the man ejaculates semen from his penis. The muscle contractions are triggered by the sensations from the base of the glans of the penis and from its shaft, caused by the touch of the woman's vagina as he thrusts in the warm, moist space, or by her hand or mouth, and are relayed to his lower spine where the ejaculation centre is situated. It appears that this is different from the erection centre, as the nerves which lead to ejaculation are sympathetic nerves.

From the ejaculation centre, messages pass along nerves to the muscles of the man's inner pelvis which surround his prostate and the deeper parts of the shaft of his penis. Stimulated by the messages passing along the sympathetic nerves, the muscles contract rhythmically.

The ejaculatory reflex can occur without the involvement of the brain, as has been proved by stimulating a paraplegic man electrically to obtain semen so that his wife could be impregnated. But in most men, the ejaculation centre is under the control of the brain and ejaculation can be delayed so that a man can 'last longer' or, in men who have only poor control, it is precipitated.

Once the contractions of the emission phase begin, ejaculation is inevitable; during the second or so of the emission phase the man knows that he is going to ejaculate and nothing can stop him. As the seminal fluid is massaged along the urethra, pleasurable sensations are sent to the sex centre in his brain. The pleasure is increased as the powerful contractions of his outer pelvic muscles start, at 0.8 second intervals, and with each contraction sperm spurts out of his penis.

The man also loses control of other muscle groups – the muscle at the lowest part of his bowel contracts, as do the muscles of his back, abdomen, and pelvis. His heart rate increases still more, his blood pressure rises more, and he breathes quickly and heavily.

Similar changes occur in a woman during orgasm, which is set off by sensations from her clitoris (and perhaps to a small extent from her vagina). During orgasm the muscles of the pelvis at the lower end of her vagina contract between five and twelve times at the same rate of 0.8 of a second that occurs in a man. At the same time other groups of muscles of her pelvis, her back, and her abdomen

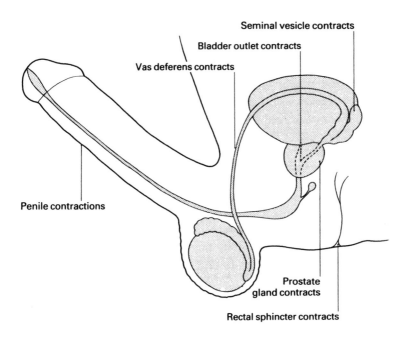

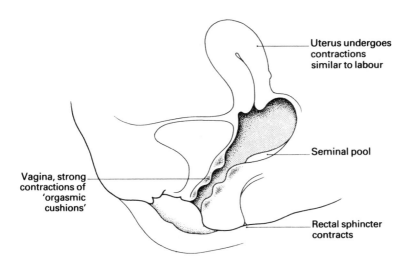

16 The stages of sexual response in men and women: the orgasmic stage

contract. As in a man, a woman's heart rate, her blood pressure, and her breathing increase, and her sex flush (if she has one) increases, paralleling the intensity of her orgasm.

The fourth phase, the resolution phase, is the period during which the individual's response resolves from the climactic peak of orgasm, and returns rapidly to the unstimulated state. During the first few seconds of this phase the glans of the penis is extremely sensitive to touch, and the man is unable to respond to any sexual stimuli. This phase usually merges into a phase of contentment, of love, of relaxation, of warmth, of well-being, and usually of sleep. The old adage that the sleep of the just is not as good as the sleep of the just-after is all too true! This can cause sexual conflict if the man's partner, having failed to obtain sexual release, finds at best a sleeping man holding her in his arms, and at worst, the inert, snoring mass of a satiated man lying beside her. Yet in fairness to the man, his pleasure in sexual intercourse may be reduced if he is unable to enjoy the short period of complete relaxation which characterizes the later part of the resolution phase. In fairness to the woman, it can be remarkably frustrating to be sexually stimulated but not helped to orgasm. The solution must be for the couple to talk to each other about the problem and reach a compromise. If the woman does not reach orgasm during sexual intercourse, the man can help her reach orgasm by stimulating her clitoris with his finger or his tongue either before he ejaculates or afterwards. The couple may decide to vary their technique from time to time, so that the man can enjoy the relaxation of the resolution phase more fully.

There is a difference in the response of men and women during the resolution phase. Men, with few exceptions, need a period of rest before they are able to respond again to sexual stimuli and to re-enter the excitement phase. This is called the refractory period. After orgasm, a man's penis, at first painfully sensitive to touch, becomes flaccid and droops. The detumescence occurs in two stages. In the first, which is rapid, the penis becomes smaller, until it is only about half as big as when stimulated. The second stage, which lasts much longer, reduces the penis to its non-aroused size. An interval of time must pass before sexual stimulation will produce a new erection. This time interval varies in duration in different men and there is no 'normal' time during which no response will occur. In general, men under the age of 30 have a shorter interval than men over the age of 50. Many men aged less than 30 have the ability to reach orgasm again within five minutes of ejaculation. Few men over the age of 50 can achieve this performance level, and most are only able to ejaculate once in a 24-hour period.

Many women, of all ages, by contrast, are able to enjoy multiple orgasms occurring in rapid succession, if adequately stimulated, with only a very brief resolution phase.

As the penis gets smaller, the congestion of the man's scrotum diminishes and his testes become smaller, dropping away from his crutch.

Changes in women during the resolution phase parallel those in men. The congestion-cushions around her lower vagina disappear; the 'tenting' of the upper vagina disappears; the swollen labia diminish in size, and its purplish-red colour fades; the clitoris returns to its non-stimulated state; and the nipples flatten and become smaller.

In both sexes, a film of perspiration may appear, which is not related to the physical activity in which they have engaged.

*

To reinforce what I have written, let us look at the sexual response in the male in a different way, ignoring the phases of the sexual response. In this approach we look at his sexual response in the terms of the changes which occur in his body.

Two generalizations can be made, as two responses occur in all men who are sexually stimulated. The first is that there is a widespread increase in the size of small blood-vessels, and congestion due to the increased quantity of blood within them. Although the congestion is widespread, it is most obviously concentrated in the genitals, particularly in the penis. The congestion increases through sexual stimulation, as sexual tension rises, and is most marked in the late plateau and the orgasmic phases of the sexual cycle.

The second response is a general increase in the tension in the man's muscles, so that a slight stimulus produces a larger response than usual. This reaction also increases in intensity as sexual tension rises. It culminates in the involuntary muscle contractions which accompany orgasm.

This makes it clear that a man's response to sexual stimulation is both general and genital. The general changes which occur include an increase in the heart rate from its non-stimulated rate of 70–80

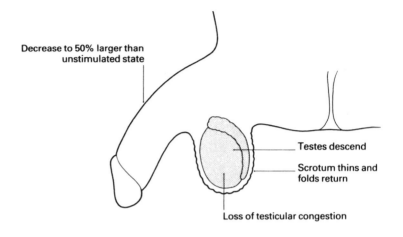

Decrease to 50% larger than
unstimulated state

Testes descend

Scrotum thins and
folds return

Loss of testicular congestion

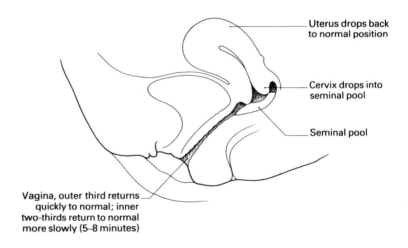

Uterus drops back
to normal position

Cervix drops into
seminal pool

Seminal pool

Vagina, outer third returns
quickly to normal; inner
two-thirds return to normal
more slowly (5–8 minutes)

17 The stages of sexual response in men and women: the early resolution stage

beats a minute to between 100–50 beats a minute in the late plateau and orgasmic phases. This increase in the heart rate is not solely due to sexual exertion or sexual gymnastics, and is not reduced by training, as is the increase in the heart rate of an athlete.

Another change is in a man's blood pressure. As sexual tension rises, so does the blood pressure, reaching the peak at orgasm. At the peak, the man's blood pressure may be one and a half times as high as in his sexually unstimulated state.

The finding that both a man's heart rate and his blood pressure rise during sexual intercourse has occasioned some anxiety about the effect of sex on a man recovering from a heart attack or from a mild stroke. The problem has been investigated in some detail by Dr Hellerstein and Dr Friedman.

They have found that the increased heart rate, the raised blood pressure, and the increased rate of breathing put an extra strain on the heart of a man who has had a heart attack, but it is not more than that caused by mild exertion. When a man who has had a heart attack is able to take mild exertion, such as walking up a flight of stairs, without any problems, he can enjoy sex without any anxiety.

It is part of popular belief that a man pants during sexual intercourse, and that this is due to his sexual exertions. The belief is true, but the reason is wrong. The St. Louis study showed that in the plateau stage and especially in the orgasmic stage men breathe more rapidly but usually less deeply. The increase in the rate of breathing – and during orgasm a man may take in breaths at a rate of as many as forty a minute – is not related to his sexual exertions, but to the degree to which he is sexually stimulated.

These three findings – a raised heart rate, a raised blood pressure, and an increase in his rate of breathing – are a man's principal general reactions to sexual stimulation. In addition, a number of men find that their nipples become erect and somewhat swollen. This is a normal reaction to sexual stimulation in women, whose breasts also become more congested with blood and heavier in the plateau and orgasmic phases. The breasts may increase their size and weight by as much as one-quarter in women who have never breast-fed, but among women who have suckled the increase is less. By contrast, only about one man in three experiences any effect on his breasts. It is also unrelated to the physical type of man – a 'he-man' may experience nipple-swelling and erection as frequently as a mild-mannered, 'feminine' type of man.

The general responses to sexual stimulation pale when compared with the response in a man's genitals. The principal response is obvious. It is the enlargement in the length and circumference of his penis as the empty compartments in the three cylinders, which make up the penis, fill with blood.

Erection of the penis occurs in response to sexual stimuli, but it occurs even more often without sexual stimulation. Babies frequently have erections. Most adolescent boys and mature men have transient erections during sleep, and most wake up with an erection. Diseases, such as a chronic enlargement of the prostate gland, may cause erections, and there is a particularly distressing condition called priapism in which a painful erection persists for a long period. Priapism is usually due to clots forming in the veins which drain the penis. Treatment is often difficult. Rest and sedation may cure the disorder, but surgery is usually required. The surgeon tries to remove the clot, or failing that incises the cylinders of the penis to let the blood escape and so reduce the size of the penis to normal.

During sexual arousal, penile erection may occur with a minimum of sexual stimulation or it may not occur until the stimulation is considerable. Most men observe that a variety of matters can influence the speed with which an erection occurs. An exceptionally erotic experience leads to a rapid erection, while anxiety, tiredness, overwork, and alcohol increase the time it takes for an erection to occur. Indeed, alcohol is a major deterrent to sexual activity, at least in excess. This is because, in excess, alcohol slows the reaction time and induces sleepiness. Shakespeare observed the reaction with singular accuracy. The Porter in *Macbeth*, woken early in the morning to open the castle gate to Macduff and Lennox, remarks to Macduff, who has asked him why he was not up: 'Faith, sir, we were carousing till the second cock; and drink, sir, is a great provoker of three things.' When Macduff asks what are the three things which drink especially provokes, the Porter replies,

Marry, sir, nose painting, sleep and urine. Lechery, sir, it provokes and unprovokes; it provokes the desire but takes away the performance: therefore much drink may be said to be an equivocator with lechery. It makes him and it mars him, it sets him on and it takes him off; it persuades him and disheartens him; it makes him stand to and not stand to; in conclusion, equivocates him in a sleep, and giving him the lie, leaves him.

Most men respond to sexual stimuli by entering the excitement phase and rapidly getting an erection. If sexual pleasuring is prolonged and the man remains in the excitement stage, the erection may be partially or completely lost and then regained. This can occur several times. In this phase, too, a diversion such as a sudden loud noise, a telephone ringing, the arrival of a stranger can result, despite continuing sexual stimulation, in the partial or complete loss of the erection.

As the degree of sexual stimulation increases, the diameter of the shaft of the penis increases and, more particularly, the lower edge of the glans of the penis gets bigger and becomes dusky-red in colour. At this stage a man can still voluntarily suppress the urge to ejaculate, although this is becoming much more insistent with the passing moments.

It is at this time of high sexual arousal that a man who suffers from premature ejaculation often knows he is unable to prevent himself from coming. The knowledge that he has reached this stage is of particular importance to a man who is being treated for premature ejaculation. At this precise time he must withdraw his penis from his partner's vagina – or more accurately, since she is sitting over him, she lifts herself off his penis, and squeezes it in a special way. This retraining process, with the loving help of his partner, is usually effective in curing the disorder.

During sexual arousal, the penis has served two functions. First, it has been the main receptor of sexual stimuli which, acting through the higher centres of the brain, have been focused upon the genital area, particularly on the tense erect penis, so that the whole being of the man, mental and physical, is directed to the pleasurable aspects of sexuality.

Second, by its thrusting within the vagina, and by its indirect stimulation of the woman's clitoris through the movement of her labia minora, the penis provides the woman with sexual stimulation. If the man is a considerate lover, he will not neglect this aspect of the function of his penis in his desire to reach orgasm. This demands that he detaches himself to some extent from his own pleasure, in order to give pleasure to his partner, at a time when he can voluntarily prevent orgasm.

There is a false belief that the peak of sexuality is only achieved if both male and female reach orgasm simultaneously. When this does occur both partners can be happy that they have achieved a joyous sexual experience, but simultaneous orgasm is not necessary for sexual joy. Provided the man is prepared to help his partner to orgasm, should she desire it, either by gently stroking the shaft, or head, of her clitoris, or by stimulating her clitoris with his tongue, depending on her wishes, either before or after his orgasm, their sexual compatibility and enjoyment are as great as if they have an orgasm simultaneously. In fact, the anxiety engendered by both partners struggling to reach orgasm against a mental clock can mar their relationship. The man who believes that his sexual potency is less than normal if he fails to achieve this desired end becomes anxious, frustrated, and tense. The woman, seeing her man so distressed, often fakes an orgasm. Since she does not tell her partner that it was faked, for fear of hurting his pride, she does not obtain the needed sexual relief and, in her turn, becomes frustrated and anxious.

In the late part of sexual arousal (the plateau phase) a man's testes are drawn up close to his body, and they increase in size. Masters and Johnson believe that the more the testes are drawn up, the more explosive is ejaculation and the greater the intensity of orgasm. They have also observed that the shorter the time the man stays in the plateau phase, the less is the movement upwards and the increase in the size of the testes. This argues that a man should 'give to receive'; if he pleasures his partner in this phase, so that it lasts longer, he will receive more pleasure when he reaches orgasm.

The third and shortest phase of the sexual cycle is the orgasmic phase. Once a man has reached this phase there is no way of stopping. Come what may, he is going to ejaculate. Although the higher brain centres are involved in orgasm, no voluntary control can prevent a man from ejaculating once he has reached this stage, so that orgasm resembles a reflex.

The first part of the orgasmic phase is one which lasts less than 3 seconds, during which the man knows that he is going to ejaculate. Inside his genital tract, his prostate gland, and perhaps his seminal vesicles, have begun to contract, forcing seminal fluid into the deepest part of his urethra, which stretches to accommodate the 2 to 5 ml of seminal fluid and the added secretions from his prostate gland. At the same time the entrance from the urethra to the bladder has been closed, so that the seminal fluid cannot escape backwards into it.

The second phase of orgasm quickly follows the first. The

muscles which surround and support the urethra and the base of the penis begin to contract in a rhythmic, regular, co-ordinated way forcing the seminal fluid, under considerable pressure, along the urethra until it is ejected from the eye of the penis. The pressure is such that the ejaculated seminal fluid may spurt a distance of 25 to 50 centimetres (10 to 20 inches) from the penis. At the same time the whole of the man's pelvic muscles and those of his abdomen and buttocks contract rhythmically. The stretching of the man's urethra, the rhythmic contraction of its surrounding muscles, and the expulsion of the seminal fluid along the urethra are interpreted in his brain as the pleasurable response of orgasm. The first two or three contractions of the pelvic muscles are strongest and it is at this time that the pleasure of the orgasm is the greatest. As they occur at intervals of 0.8 seconds, the maximum duration of intense pleasure is 2 seconds. The later contractions of the muscles surrounding the deep urethra are less strong and are associated with less pleasure. They rarely last for more than 2 seconds.

This observation is probably the origin of the statement, attributed to the 4th Earl of Chesterfield, that 'the pleasure is momentary, the position ridiculous and the expense damnable'. However, for this momentary pleasure many a man has travelled many a mile.

Orgasm, as should be obvious, is not all there is to sexual intercourse, although it seems to be all that many men seek. Sexuality is more than a quick orgasm. It is the mutual touching and pleasuring which enhance each partner's awareness of the other, it is the multiple physical changes which precede the climactic explosion of spermatic fluid, it is the psychological closeness of mutual enjoyment, and it is the post-orgasmic relaxation of mind and body.

The sequence of events occurs at a different speed and with a different intensity in different men or in the same man in different situations and at different times of his life. The duration of the excitement and plateau phases can vary considerably. From time to time, a man will be aroused, reach the plateau phase, but not reach orgasm. At other times, a man may be able to have orgasms at short intervals. Sometimes a man may find he gets an erection quickly, at other times it takes a long time; occasionally he will not get an erection despite stimulation. These variations in the human sexual response do not mean that a man is sexually inadequate. They are normal variations of a response which is different at different times.

Nevertheless, it is important for a man to understand the physical changes which occur during sexual arousal. With this knowledge of what normally happens, it is possible to identify patterns of sexual activity which may diminish sexual pleasure and lead to disharmony between the partners. These are the sexual dysfunctions, which I will discuss in later chapters.

5

How to become
a better lover

I wish he would be more experimental. He always wants
sex at night. We get into bed, he turns to me, then he turns
off the light and makes love to me. When he has come he
goes to the bathroom and washes himself. Where's the
romance in that?

English woman (1978)

Men like sex play as much as women do – so long as they
are the ones being played with.

American woman in *The Hite Report* (1976)

'I can't think what is wrong with her since the baby was
born. I spend a lot of time getting her ready. I don't mind
if I have to give her longer foreplay even though I'm ready.
I work on her breasts without even touching her genitals.
She doesn't seem to react properly. It's not me. My
technique is as good as ever.'

Australian man (1978)

SOMETHING MUST BE WRONG WITH THE SEXUAL relationships between men and women judged by the number of articles on 'How to become a better lover' which appear in magazines, or by the increasingly large number of sex manuals which are in circulation. Even more cogent to the belief that all is not well with our sexual relationships is the information that sexual problems occur in over 50 per cent of marriages. In many instances the problem is minor and easily solved, but in some the problem, and a lack of communication between the partners, can destroy the relationship, leaving bitterness and misery instead of love. This statement is supported by a recent survey of 100 middle-class marriages in the U.S.A. by Ellen Frank. All the couples believed their marriages to be happy yet, on questioning, nearly half the women had difficulty in reaching orgasm and more than half had difficulty in becoming sexually excited or, once aroused, of maintaining their excitement. The investigators found that more wives than husbands complained about sexual problems, and the women had far more sexual 'difficulties' than the men: 47 per cent found it difficult to relax, 35 per cent said that they were 'disinterested' sexually, 38 per cent said there was 'too little foreplay before intercourse', and 31 per cent said that their partner often chose 'an inconvenient time'.

These findings seem 'consistent with the typical American pattern of sexual interaction in which, as long as the wife neither complains nor refuses to have intercourse, the husband assumes that all is well', Ms Frank writes. The husbands seemed to be unaware of, or insensitive to, the need for pleasuring and emotional sensitivity in love-making.

The findings have a further implication. If so many women are not enjoying their sexuality as much as they might, where does the fault lie? Does it lie in the way that women have been brought up to understand their sexuality, or is the main problem the lack of sensitivity of men to women's sexual needs?

It seems that both factors are important, but the lack of sensitivity by men is the more important. One reason why sexual relations are so liable to disturbance is because although we know how the body responds to sexual arousal, we know very much less about the psychological responses.

The teachings of our Judaeo-Christian culture, and even more those of Islam, have emphasized that the principal purpose of sexual intercourse is the perpetuation of the race, the tribe, and the family. It followed that a man's orgasm and the ejaculation of his sperms within 'his' women's vagina was paramount, and that sexual pleasure for his partner was of secondary importance. This led to the double standard of sexual behaviour, because it was essential for the man to know that any child conceived by his wife was his own. He had to be sure that his wife was a virgin before he penetrated her, and on marriage she became his exclusive possession. In the past, he could make certain that she was exclusively his by keeping her separate from other men (as in a harem). Today, many men try to achieve the same thing by equating sex with love and by convincing the woman that if she has sex with any other man she will violate the sacred nature of marriage and of romantic love. The belief that sexual intercourse was mainly for the purpose of procreation also had the effect of condemning any form of sexual release which did not culminate in heterosexual sexual intercourse. This led to the conviction, by many people, that masturbation and homosexual relations were dangerous to the 'fabric of society', and the acceptance of the myth that women had fewer sexual needs, particularly the need to have an orgasm.

A woman's orgasm is not necessary for her to become pregnant, so that it is not necessary for procreation. But a man's orgasm is vital for procreation. If a woman happened to have an orgasm it was obvious (to men) that it should occur during sexual intercourse, and preferably simultaneously with the man's, because this demonstrated his domination and his skill as a lover.

The effect of these cultural values has been to develop stereotypes, which are merely shorthand ways of describing a current 'ideal'.

In Western society, the stereotype of a woman is that she should always be attractive, always available for sex, and always ready to give the man pleasure. In return, he gives her love. She trades sex for love while he trades love for sex. She trades sex for the social and economic security which the man gives her. He gives her money, he looks after her welfare, and he provides shelter and clothing for her. In return, she gives him companionship and sexual relief and provides him with children. And because of the marriage vows she believes that she is legally obliged to give her husband sex whenever he wants it.

Such a sequence inevitably leads to a double standard of sexuality. Women are expected to be passive, less sexually aroused, to have less need for sexual release, and to be relatively ignorant about sex. Men are expected to be sexually aggressive, sexually knowledgeable, to have strong sexual urges (which often need to be satisfied by extra-marital sexual encounters), and to initiate any sexual episode with their wives.

This view of men's and women's sexuality has been shown to be mythical, but it is perpetuated by many women, and even more men, because of their sexual conditioning by parents and peers.

The childhood conditioning and the myths continue to have an influence on sexual relations, usually to the detriment of a woman's sexuality.

Perhaps the most insidious of the myths is that unless a woman has an orgasm during sexual intercourse she is 'sick' or 'under-sexed' or 'neurotic' or 'frigid'. In the investigation of American women's sexuality undertaken by Shere Hite, the women she studied had been conditioned to believe that unless they had an orgasm during intercourse they were abnormal, as 'everyone knows that a woman should orgasm during sex'. Studies in several countries show that only between 40 and 50 per cent of women have an orgasm during the time their lover is thrusting in the woman's vagina, and fewer have an orgasm simultaneously with their lover. In spite of this, some sexual manuals imply, and many women believe, that this is the only 'normal' way for a woman to have an orgasm. Many women, conditioned in this way, blame themselves for failing to reach orgasm during sexual intercourse, instead of accepting that their reaction is not unusual, and that they could be helped to have an orgasm by a concerned partner, either before or after intercourse. They believe, wrongly, that an orgasm comes naturally if a woman loves the man enough.

Because the majority of women do not have orgasms during intercourse, and because of the prevalent male domination in sexuality, a number of women fake orgasm. They do this because they believe that having a faked orgasm, when the natural one does not occur, shows the woman's love for her man. He expects her to have an orgasm, so she fakes one! She believes that if she does not have an orgasm (faked or real) she could lose her man's love, and he might find another more sexually proficient partner. A second reason, which is linked with the first, is that if a woman fails to have an orgasm, the man may desert her as an unsatisfactory wife. A third reason, given by women, is that if they do not fake orgasm they will diminish the man's sexual self-esteem and reduce his masculinity, as good lovers are 'known' always to give their women orgasms.

This is arrant nonsense, but unfortunately it is believed. A man does not give a woman an orgasm, but he can help her reach her own orgasm.

Most men do not know if their sexual partner has a real or a faked orgasm unless they are sufficiently relaxed to be able to talk to each other about their sexuality. A man may agree that other men may not know, but that he knows when his partner comes. He may say that it is easy to tell: as he thrusts urgently with his penis in her vagina, she tightens her legs and pelvic muscles, she scratches his back or bites his lip, she moans ecstatically, she writhes about and arches her back. A few women do this when having an orgasm, but the majority do not moan, and certainly do not writhe about or arch their back. During orgasm, most women, at first, become still and rather rigid, with tense muscles as the intense, deep-felt pleasure of orgasm surges up from the pelvic area to envelop them. Only later in orgasm does movement occur, and then not always. One of Shere Hite's respondents wrote, 'I don't move convulsively the way women in books do. I don't know if anyone does. I just hold on tight. Sometimes it bothers me when a man hasn't been able to tell that I climaxed.'

The myth that, to be normal, a woman must have an orgasm during intercourse has to be destroyed. Although only 40 per cent of women reach orgasm during sexual intercourse, more than 90 per cent can be helped to orgasm by masturbation or by their partner stimulating the clitoral area either with finger or tongue.

Another myth is that women are less easily aroused sexually and take longer to reach orgasm than men. It is true that some women, who have been taught in childhood that sex is something rather shameful, do take longer to reach orgasm than most men, but many women, provided that they are adequately and properly stimulated, can have an orgasm as quickly as a man.

A third myth, which is equally damaging to a woman's sexual pleasure, is that women are less interested in the enjoyment of sexual intercourse itself, and more interested in the feelings of closeness and affection which sexual intercourse brings. In other words, it is enough for a man to have sexual intercourse and ejaculate; that will satisfy a woman and she does not need to be helped to have an orgasm.

Most women want affection and closeness and they obtain great sexual enjoyment if their partner arouses them, by stimulating their erotic areas gently and seductively; but once a woman has experienced an orgasm, she wants that too.

*

Shere Hite, who is an American sociologist, asked over 2000 women to relate their feelings about sex and about their lovers. The men do not come out of the survey very well.

Already, critics have said that *The Hite Report* was not a proper sociological survey. The participants were self-selected, not chosen at random. This is true. Shere Hite invited readers of several women's magazines and members of women's groups to respond to a questionnaire. It is also true that the women who answered did not come from all sections of American society. A disproportionate number (nearly 50 per cent) were unmarried and the women tended to be middle or upper-middle class. However, these women are more likely to be sexually aware and more sexually articulate than their sisters, so that if their answers show that sex is not the dreamy, romantic delight it is believed to be, the majority of American women are likely to be missing a lot of sexual pleasure.

The reduction in sexual pleasure experienced by many women is partly due to the negative attitudes to their bodies and to sex which they obtained in childhood and early adolescence from parents, clergy, teachers, and peers. All too often children are taught that the genitals are dirty or disgusting. Even the medical name for a woman's genitals, the 'pudenda' (from Latin, meaning 'that of which one ought to be ashamed'), is symbolic of the disgust some parents induce in children towards their genitals. Women have a second problem. Unlike a boy's very obvious penis, which he knows is pleasurable to touch and fondle, a girl's genitals are hidden, mysterious, remote. I find it remarkable (and disturbing) that many women have never used a mirror to see what their genitals look like and to find out where their clitoris is.

In addition, many boys, and nearly all girls, are taught that masturbation is evil, that it leads to debility, or even if it does not, should not be 'indulged' in! This is nonsense, of course; masturbation has several very positive values, especially for women. In childhood and adolescence it teaches a girl to explore her body and not to be ashamed of its shape, its texture, and its surfaces. It teaches her, especially, not to be ashamed of touching and playing with her genitals. It does more. It helps a girl become aware of her response to sexual stimuli and to recognize the stages of sexual arousal. And it enables a girl to develop her own sexuality – to know what she enjoys and what she dislikes – which is important if she is to be fulfilled sexually later.

Far more destructive to a woman's sexual fulfilment than her negative conditioning to sexuality is the self-satisfied neglect by many men of a woman's sexual needs. If there is a villain in a woman's unfulfilled sexuality it is her male sexual partner!

The women who responded to Shere Hite's invitation to tell their sexual experiences were, in general, disappointed by their lover's sexual techniques, although they often loved the man deeply. The men seemed largely insensitive to the woman's sexual needs, and often unwilling to experiment. They *knew* that a woman wanted 'foreplay' (by which they meant a cursory kiss, a brief fumbling with her breasts, and a perfunctory caress around her vulva) after which the man could get on with what he really wanted. That was to insert his penis into the woman's vagina, thrust, and ejaculate. And after that? Well, a man feels contented and wants to sleep, which does not help the woman much. One woman wrote, 'Most of the men I've slept with have had absolutely no idea of what I want and no interest in finding out.' Another, 'I find a lot of men care nothing about sex foreplay and are only interested in "getting it off".' Another, 'I've only had sex with my husband . . . he always initiates it. We kiss and he plays with my breasts. He puts one hand down and sticks his finger into my vagina and moves it back and forth like a penis would go . . . When he's ready . . . he sticks his penis into me and moves it back and forth until he finishes.' Another, 'Some men just feel, finger and fuck. Then come and light a cigarette.'

These comments are multiplied, with variations, in *The Hite Report,* and from them it seems that many American men are insensitive to a woman's sexual needs, while most women are inarticulate in asking their lover to satisfy those needs. Sex is more than friction and fantasy! Sex means communication. Sex means mutual pleasuring. Sex means closeness and body contact.

At present, sex lacks a lot for many women. This is not because women are under-sexed, as those very women who miss out on full sexual pleasure during intercourse are usually able to enjoy sexual pleasure by masturbating. It is because many women do not say what they want sexually and many men are too embarrassed, or too insensitive, to find out.

*

How can you become a better lover? Well, there are the sex manuals. Unfortunately, they are mainly written by men, who have not had the opportunity to know what women really want. In the U.S.A. there are over fifty sex manuals in circulation, and twelve of them claim to have each sold over one million copies. Most of them are also available in other English-speaking countries.

Perhaps because they are written by Americans who seem to be devoted to the ethic of work, competition, and success, you will learn that to succeed in sex you need to prepare seriously for it and work at it. It is not a frivolous subject, but one deserving serious concentration, arduous preparation, and a good deal of effort. The manuals suggest that sex is mainly a task for young, healthy, beautiful people, because you are cautioned that some of the 'sexercises' are not suitable (too arduous, perhaps) for older people.

Naturally, say the books, you have to work towards an objective and that seems to be the achievement of simultaneous orgasm during sexual intercourse. This is because simultaneous orgasm puts the seal of successful achievement on you as a lover. The books suggest that this is the *raison d'être* of sexual relationships. One manual goes even further, suggesting that ejaculation is the summit *and the end* of the sexual act! In fairness, a number of the manuals do observe that the woman may not reach orgasm during sexual intercourse but can be 'pushed to climax' after the man has ejaculated. One observes that if a woman 'conscientiously works at being available' (again the work ethic) she may find her role satisfying, even if she does not have any sexual desire at the time. Most manuals give instructions, in a number of separate steps or techniques, which will permit simultaneous orgasm.

Obviously to achieve this degree of sexual competence the couple must read, study, and discuss sex. This is sensible, of course, but in most of the manuals the emphasis is on the man instructing the women in the 'right' way, of being the guide whom she should follow, if she is to achieve 'good sex'. Few suggest that she should tell her man what pleasures her most. The manuals imply that the man knows, and can tell her.

The books agree that both partners must understand the anatomy and physiology of sex (which is reasonable) and they imply that, guided by the man, a woman will learn to develop specific sexual techniques, which will eventually enable her to have a voluptuous orgasm, and to give her man an earth-shattering climax.

To achieve this desired state demands not only mental but physical training in sex. You need to learn sex exercises. The more recent manuals extend these exercises from the pelvic muscles to the fingers and the tongue, as digital and oral sex are now accepted as normal. The pelvic muscle training, as outlined, is that a woman should learn to tighten muscles around her vagina so that she can 'squeeze the man's penis' as he thrusts. Men have an equivalent exercise which is to 'snap' the muscles at the base of the penis whenever he has a spare moment, so that he can thrust more powerfully.

With the information from the reading and with the appropriate physical training, you should be able to pleasure your partner, provided you have developed the proper techniques. The techniques include the positions for intercourse, duration and length of foreplay, methods of increasing, prolonging, heightening, and sharpening sexual desire, and additional pieces of equipment which may give greater pleasure to sex. The emotional aspects of sex get only a passing mention.

My analysis of sex manuals is an extension of one made in 1968 by Lionel Lewis and Denis Brissett, and published in *Medical Aspects of Human Sexuality*. In their concluding remarks they said:

The kinds of impressions assembled here seem to support the notion that play, at least sexual play in marriage, has indeed been permeated with dimensions of a work ethic. The play of marital sex is presented by the counsellors quite definitely as work . . . This paradox, play as work, may be said to be an almost logical outcome of the peculiar condition of American society. First of all, it seems that in America, most individuals are faced with the problems of justifying and dignifying their play. The American must justify his play. It is our thesis that he has done this by transforming his play into work. This is not to say that he has disguised his play as work; it is instead to propose that his play has become work . . . Thus there seem to be two antagonistic forces operating in American society. On the one hand, there is an emphasis on work and, on the other hand, there is an emphasis on attaining maximum pleasure. These two themes were recurrent in the fifteen manuals which we read, and as one writer put it: '. . . it may be that the whole level of sexual enjoyment of the partners can be stepped up and greatly enriched if the man is able to exercise a greater degree of deliberation and management'.

My re-reading of the sex manuals, some in newer editions, confirms what Lewis and Brissett wrote over ten years ago, and also suggests that men are still believed to be the sexual experts, who should be able to guide, instruct, and educate their women into better sex, provided the woman is complaisant, relatively receptive, and ready to be instructed.

They also imply that although sex can be seen as work it is also pleasurable, which most work often is not. This creates a dilemma in the mind of some men who place a high value on work and a lower value on pleasure. It seems morally wrong to them to devote much time to a pleasurable activity, when so much 'real' work needs to be done. The files brought home from the office have to be read; the boat has to be painted; the car has to be washed; the lawn has to be cut; the rubbish has to be put out; exercise – golf, tennis, squash, or jogging – has to be taken; the children have to be watched playing organized sport; and sex is relegated to something done when all these important matters have been completed. The result may be that the man only reaches sex when he is tired, or has other things on his mind. He does not want sex for mutual enjoyment but only to get rid of his sexual tension and if necessary to satisfy his partner as quickly as possible.

This is not to say that sex manuals are without value. They have considerable value, and are a source of information for those who are concerned that they know too little about sex. My real complaint is that they make sexual success too pat, too easy. Provided you follow the instructions, you can be a successful lover within a few days or weeks: and the 'you' is usually a man.

It is instructive to read what the women who responded to Shere Hite wanted from their lovers to make sex a more enjoyable experience for them, because if you know what a woman wants and are able to respond you will certainly be a better lover.

*

The women in *The Hite Report* had five main complaints about their lovers. First, many women enjoyed touching and caressing for the pleasure of the activity itself and not necessarily only as a prelude to intercourse. The touching could be from lying pressed close together; or gentle and passionate kissing; or sleeping together in a close embrace. Second, many women complained about the dull routine of sexual intercourse. Inevitably, sex began with kisses, then the woman's breasts were explored, then her clitoral area, while she fondled the man's penis, then, and rather too rapidly, sexual intercourse started and when the man had come it was all over. This is an exaggerated version of the man's lack of sensitivity to his partner's needs, but it seems to have been a 'consistent' pattern of sex for many of the women. Third, many women complained that their lover did not really care about arousing them in a passionate way. Many of the men spent too little time in trying to arouse their partner, or did it in the wrong way, and, worse, having aroused her, did not help her to orgasm. The man either expected the woman to reach orgasm simultaneously with his orgasm, or tried to give her an orgasm when he decided the time was right. Fourth, in spite of the so-called sexual revolution, which is said to have liberated women sexually, many women complained that the men they knew still 'wanted to play games', and were unable to accept the woman as an independent person, were unable to treat her as anything but a sex object, and felt threatened by a sexually 'aggressive' woman. In other words, they still believed in the double standard of sexual behaviour. Fifth, most women wanted sex as part of a warm, affectionate, mutually respecting relationship, and not just as a pleasurable genital sensation. British and Australian women make similar complaints about their partner's sexual behaviour and performance, judging by letters in magazines and by surveys, similar to that made by Shere Hite in the U.S.A.

It is obvious, to me at least, on reading the many comments of the women, and relating their views to what is written in the sex manuals, that two conditions will have to be met before women can enjoy sex to the full, and before men (and women) become better, more considerate, more sensitive lovers.

The first condition is the need for each partner to be able to speak openly about what stimulated him, or her, sexually, and what stops sexual arousal. Sex is communication! Because of our upbringing, during which we have been taught that sex is some 'special' function, that the genitals are to be hidden because they are 'dirty', and that sex is 'indulged' in and not enjoyed, we find it difficult to talk about our sexual needs and what we want. Since women are disadvantaged sexually in our culture, it is even harder for many women to tell their partners what they want.

A man can help, by telling his partner what he wants sexually and by asking her what stimulates her sexually. Once he can communicate openly and comfortably about sex, his sex life will be much more enjoyable.

The second condition is for him to understand that he is not the sex expert, the innovator, the one who initiates sex. Sex is a shared experience. On occasions he may be the initiator; on other occasions his partner should initiate sex, knowing that he will neither be threatened nor embarrassed by this.

When men can accept these conditions, they will be able to understand the complaints the women make, each of which requires further consideration.

Touching

Most women get great sensual pleasure from touching and being touched. Women find body contact and closeness are more important to them than they are to men, but they are not substitutes for orgasms. Women want both physical and emotional closeness *and* orgasms.

Many Western men are unable to enjoy touching, body contact, and caressing, and this is largely a fault of our upbringing. Small boys are taught that to show emotions, to show affection, and to enjoy touching other people diminishes their male identity. Real men – red-blooded masculine men – are taught to hide their emotions. It is weak and feminine to cry. Affection can only be shown in private: to show open affection makes a man's masculinity suspect. Touching is something only women and homosexuals do. By contrast, girls are taught that women can show emotions: they can cry, they can show open affection, and they may touch people without diminishing their femininity.

It is a sad commentary on our culture that this is so. There is no biological difference between men and women in the need for bodily contact – but men are trained to ignore the important psychological values of touching and this can reduce their sexual enjoyment.

To many women, touching is an important part of sex. One

woman wrote to Shere Hite: 'You can't love sex without loving to touch and to be touched. It's the very physical closeness of sex that is the main pleasure.' A British woman wrote: 'I can't understand why most men don't seem to enjoy touching. Perhaps it's the way we bring boys up to believe touching is "sissy". The closeness of our bodies, before and after we have sex, means so much to me. It doesn't replace the marvellous sensation of having my husband inside me but it adds so much to it.'

The evidence, scanty as it is, indicates that many women want to be touched and to touch more during sexual pleasuring. They want closeness and body contact with their lovers, not necessarily as a way of arousing them as a prelude to sexual intercourse, but for its own pleasure. Mutual pleasuring means mutual touching, exploring each other's body, and enjoying each other's shape, smell, and skin texture.

Unfortunately, the women were disappointed by the lack of touching and caressing given by their lovers, except briefly, before the man moved on to intercourse. To touch and cuddle one's lover, except briefly before intercourse, seems to be perceived by many men as inappropriate behaviour. 'I only wish men could do this without it always and only being a lead-in to sex,' wrote one woman.

There is no reason to believe that men do not enjoy physical affection and body contact, but their childhood training has conditioned them to avoid it, and to suppress their feelings.

As a first step to being a better lover find out if your partner would like to be touched and how she would like to be cuddled. Find out if she would enjoy bathing or showering with you, if she would enjoy having her body massaged. And if she does, overcome your fear of expressing your feelings and touch, touch, touch.

Sex as a routine

Have you ever thought how much your sexual activity has become routine? When you want sex, do you indicate this to your partner by word or gesture and expect her to want sex too? Is this what you do? You get undressed, you go to bed (and perhaps turn out the light), you kiss – a little – you caress her breasts – a little. Your hand wanders to her genitals and you finger a bit, meanwhile expecting her to stroke your penis. And when you are aroused, you assume she is ready for sexual intercourse. You mount her, insert your penis in her vagina, you thrust, and after a shorter or longer time you reach orgasm and ejaculate. Then you relax, doze, or sleep – and it is all over.

If you haven't noticed it, your partner probably has! An Australian woman wrote: 'Sex to my husband is a routine. There is no novelty. It's always the same. He kisses, I kiss. He fondles my breasts and expects me to fondle his penis. He puts his finger in my vagina, and then he thinks I'm ready. He knows he is. It's so dull.'

There is no need for sex to be followed to a fixed routine. Why not be innovative? Have sex at different times, in different ways, and in different places. Talk with your partner, you may be surprised to find that she has wanted this for ages but has been shy to ask you and afraid she might be rebuffed.

The fallacy of foreplay

A significant number of women believe that most men do not get much pleasure from 'foreplay'. They only use 'foreplay' to arouse their partner so that she is ready for what they really want, and that is to put their penis in the woman's vagina. Many men see foreplay as a necessary nuisance. not as an integral part of love-making.

The word 'foreplay' is a bad one. It usually means what you do, by touch, to arouse your partner before you have sexual intercourse. In other words, you cannot have foreplay unless it leads to sexual intercourse and ejaculation. It makes sex the routine women complain of . . . foreplay (kisses, breast stimulation, genital touching) then sexual intercourse. This debases the reason for foreplay, which is to pleasure each partner so that each becomes sexually aroused and enjoys the arousal as much as the intercourse. A better term to describe this part of sexuality is 'mutual pleasuring'. 'Mutual' because it is done to each other, 'pleasuring' because the whole purpose of the touching is to increase the emotional and physical pleasure of the encounter. Besides, pleasuring is an old English word for enjoyable sex. Pepys used it in 1666.

Mutual pleasuring is good sex, but for its full enjoyment it must be done at the direction of each partner. No man can know what a woman should want and feel, or what her sexuality requires. For example, most men believe that women are invariably 'turned on' sexually if the man caresses the woman's breasts, and later sucks her nipples.

This belief is reinforced in our culture because a woman's breasts are highly erotic for most men. Men therefore believe that a woman is also aroused if the man 'plays' with her breasts during sexual pleasuring. Most women are erotically aroused by breast stimulation, but some are not. Some get no arousal, and a few dislike their breasts being manipulated. Those women whose breasts are not stimulated may be anxious that they are lacking in sexuality. They are not. They should tell their partner what does arouse them sexually. In mutual pleasuring you find out what your partner wants (as she does for you) and how she is best helped to have it.

If after kissing and cuddling she wishes to have her clitoris stimulated, only she can tell you how she wants it done to pleasure her the most. Most women like clitoral stimulation to start slowly and softly, the shaft of the clitoris being stroked rather than the end, or glans. Gradually the stroking pressure is increased and the stroking quickened. But it is impossible for anyone, especially writers of sex manuals, to tell you how your partner will respond. Only she can do that by putting your fingers where she wants them, and telling you how to caress her as she wants to be caressed. As I have said, sex is communication.

The same directions apply if she wishes you to caress her clitoral area with your tongue or lips. Because of our upbringing, this action, called cunnilingus, is often thought improper and 'dirty'. In fact, a woman's genitals are less 'dirty' than her mouth; that is, there are fewer bacteria in her vagina than in her mouth. The 'dirt' is in the mind, not in the organ, but enterprising manufacturers play on the fear that a woman's genitals are dirty, or smell, and advise women to use an astonishing variety of deodorants and 'hygienic' douches. They are all unnecessary.

Of course, a woman's genitals do have an odour – so does a man's penis, so do our bodies. But the odours of the genitals are good odours, and nothing to be ashamed of. No man can tell how a woman wants cunnilingus done. A man can only do what his partner enjoys best, and do it at her direction. She will have to tell him.

You can't give a woman an orgasm!

You don't *give* a woman an orgasm any more than she gives you an orgasm. But if you are a considerate lover you can help your partner create her own orgasm – if and when she wants you to. She may be one of the 40 per cent of women who reach orgasm during intercourse. If she is, she can tell you which movements of yours give her increased sexual feeling, and which damp her feelings down. If she is one of the 60 per cent of women who do not reach orgasm during intercourse, she can almost certainly have an orgasm if you help her by caressing her clitoral area with your finger or tongue, or if she masturbates. If she chooses to masturbate it is not an insult to your skill as a lover: it is what she wants. Some women enjoy masturbating to orgasm during sexual intercourse, others prefer to be helped to orgasm by finger or tongue before sexual intercourse, or after you have had your orgasm. Unfortunately, many women who are left sexually aroused, but frustrated, because they do not reach orgasm during intercourse are ashamed to masturbate (although they desperately want to have an orgasm) for fear of embarrassing or revolting their partner, or because of their own sexual inhibitions.

Other women, who have a great desire to be helped to orgasm by cunnilingus, are reluctant to ask their sexual partner to do this, as they feel he will find the taste, or the smell, or the position offensive and indecent.

You should tell your partner that you are neither embarrassed nor revolted if she wants to masturbate, that you are not disgusted by cunnilingus and she should not be ashamed to ask you to help her reach orgasm, whichever way pleasures her most.

If you are sufficiently sexually liberated to do that, you are well on the way to being a better lover. The choice of the way a woman wants to be sexually stimulated can only be hers. Only she knows what pleasures her most, and you, as a considerate lover, should help. And you should show that you enjoy helping, or the experience of one woman may be repeated. She wrote: 'I wonder sometimes if my partner is enjoying it or if he is only doing it to please me, especially when I like to take a long time. The feeling that he is not enjoying it reduces my pleasure and I get self-conscious about coming.'

Distrust of the sexual double standard

Many women who are now able to talk about sex and to initiate sex in new and pleasurable ways are still hurt by the attitude of their partner, who has not escaped from the sexual double standard. These men show their hostility to women by castigating them as nymphomaniacs, or over-sexed, or by treating them as 'loose women'. The men themselves want sex for the physical pleasure it gives them, but expect the woman only to 'give' sex because of their love for the man. The man remains the 'sexpert' – the conqueror. Such men do not treat women as real persons but as sex objects, to be enjoyed, and then neglected. A bitter Australian woman wrote: 'Maybe I keep picking the wrong men, but it keeps on happening. Once they think I'm going to let them fuck me, they seem to let me know that I'm a "nothing". I'm not a person, just a vagina to be used, a breast to be pulled, a mouth to put their tongue in.'

The double standard is alive and well in most, if not all, countries!

Emotion and sex

Whatever men may feel, most women want the sexual experience to be an emotional as well as a physical bond. These women perceive sex not merely as brief genital contact, pleasurable though it may be, but also as sharing an emotional, intimate part of each other. They perceive sex as the happiness of sharing experiences, the fun of doing things – sexual and other – together. They believe that pleasure is obtained by giving pleasure. Many accept that the relationship may last for a long time, or may be short lived, but that during it emotional involvement is essential, or much of the joy of sex is reduced.

Of course, this means that both partners have to be emotionally involved. To be a better lover you need to be involved, or to you sex is just intravaginal masturbation. One woman quoted in *The Hite Report* said that her greatest displeasure in sex was the feeling that she was 'simply a substitute for his hand, a dish of mashed potatoes, or any warm place he can stick it into and come'.

Harsh words, perhaps, but how does your partner feel about you? Have you asked her?

The extent to which a man can abandon himself to the joy of sex varies. It depends on the presence or absence of the inhibitions to sex he has acquired during childhood and adolescence. It depends on his acceptance or rejection of the sexual double standard. It depends on his ability to communicate with his partner. It depends on his partner's sexual inhibitions, and on her ability to communicate with him.

In the final analysis it depends on how the couple perceive sexual pleasure, and on their knowledge that the degree of pleasure can be increased by communicating their needs to each other. Some people obtain great sexual pleasure from 'fun sex', that is a sexual encounter between two people who are urgently attracted to each other physically, but who have no deep emotional bond. Others reject this form of sexual pleasuring, claiming that unless the emotions are involved, sexual pleasure is inevitably diminished, and 'fun sex' can never equal 'love sex'. Unfortunately, what some couples believe to be 'love sex' is sterile, in reality, and is associated with minimal surrender by one or both partners during the experience. Other couples enjoy group sex, either as a novelty or as a way of sexual life.

The variations of what produces sexual pleasure seem infinite, and until you find out what your partner wants and are comfortable in helping her realize those needs, you will not be a good lover.

If you are able to find out, by asking, what gives your partner the most sexual pleasure and are able to enjoy sharing the experience, you will become a better lover.

*

There is an increasing amount of evidence that a man's (and a woman's) ability to be a good lover is affected by the attitudes to sexuality acquired during infancy and childhood.

In our type of society, childhood interest in sexuality, and a child's curiosity about its own body and that of others, is discouraged, often punished. At the same time we do nothing to discourage children from seeing violence, greed, and deceit in life and, more particularly, on television screens. We are assured that children are sufficiently discriminating to know that the violence is not real. We are told, by experts, that the violence will not serve as a model for behaviour and that the children will not become violent, greedy, or deceitful by imitation.

We may witness violence to the human body, but we may not see the touching and the loving nature of human sexuality. We can see (all too often) the human body being threatened and brutalized in plays, documentaries, and news films but we are prevented from seeing the human body in loving situations, except when at least partially clothed and, even then, certain activities are proscribed. We may only see a woman's body provided the genital area (and preferably her breasts) are hidden. We may see a man's body, muscular, sweaty, and bare to the waist, but we may not see a man's genitals, and the idea of seeing his erect penis is scandalous.

We permit our children to see violence which leads to death, but we bar our children from seeing sexuality which leads to life. We permit our children to witness greed, competition, and deceit, but we prohibit our children from learning that sexuality is a warm, sharing, harmonious, co-operative, pleasurable activity.

Because of our own inhibitions about sexuality we are silent. We fail to stress the sharing nature of sex, and, by default, the child learns from his age-mates, by hearing whispered confidences and 'dirty jokes', that sex is merely genital contact.

We encourage our male children to be aggressive, competitive, and insensitive to others. We praise them when they 'win', beating the others, but we bar them from learning about the sharing nature of sexuality. Perhaps because we are so fearful of the different shapes of male and female bodies, we emphasize the false attributes of men and women: 'Daddy cuts the lawn, Mummy bakes the cakes', or 'Daddy isn't very good about the house, and Mummy is useless if an appliance goes wrong', and we omit the real attributes of the two sexes.

Many parents are uncomfortable about their own bodies and about their own sexuality, and their children learn early in life that sex is something 'special', usually not mentioned, except obliquely.

Human sexuality is more than human reproduction – it involves all the senses and the emotions, but most parents are unable to handle their sexuality and are uncomfortable, or unwilling, to talk about sexuality with their children.

You will be a better lover if you have been brought up to be honest about sexuality, and to enjoy your body. If you have been punished for 'playing with your privates', you will associate them with naughtiness, and you will associate sex with guilt.

You may have escaped your upbringing to some extent, or you may be rigid in your 'sex is dirty' attitudes. But you can help your children to have a more appropriate, sharing attitude to sexuality if you go about it the right way.

This is what education in human sexuality is all about. It is to give children an understanding of the nature of sexuality. In today's world, we need more sexual understanding and better, more explicit, sex education. You can start helping, by doing as many of the following as you are able to do comfortably.

● Don't be ashamed of your body or your partner's. Let your children see that neither of you is ashamed, by walking about your house naked.

• If you admire and encourage your son when he plays war games or competitive sport, and your daughter when she plays with her dolls or 'helps Mummy', don't show your disapproval when they find out their genitals are different, and when they play with them.

• Answer, as best you can, every question your child asks about sex. Don't be coy or embarrassed. Your child will only become embarrassed if he or she finds that you are. The time to satisfy a child's curiosity is now!

• Don't be evasive if a child asks how babies are made. Explain simply, and let the child see the anatomical differences between its parents. You can obtain books which are illustrated in a way that even small children can understand. Most children should learn about sex and its consequences before the hormonal tides of puberty cause problems. The pictures may be erotic, even to a small child, but they become accepted quickly. Later, with the emotional stress of puberty, the same pictures can cause anxiety which need never occur if they are shown and discussed in a sensible, unembarrassed way. All children need to understand how sexual intercourse takes place, and how a baby is born through its mother's vagina. If you don't explain, the child will make up fanciful explanations which can be damaging to its future sex life.

• Don't be evasive when a child asks questions about sexuality or sexual behaviour. If you are evasive or, worse, if you punish the child for asking, you will give it the message that sex is something unpleasant. Because children are curious they will find out from their age-mates, who generally have rather inaccurate information.

• Don't try to stop sex-play. You won't; all you will do is drive it into another room, or under the bedclothes. Sex play is learning. The child learns how it responds to sexual stimulation, which will be helpful to it later. But if it learns that it is bad, or naughty, or evil, to play with its genitals or to masturbate, you are helping to spoil your son's (or daughter's) later enjoyment of sex.

Unfortunately, all too few parents are sufficiently comfortable with their own bodies and sufficiently secure in their own sexuality to be helpful to their young children. Few are able to let their children see them naked, fewer still are able to talk about sexuality and to respond to the child's curiosity about sex. Because of this, better and more explicit sexual education is needed both for children and for their parents. This education will not lead to a breakdown in the 'fabric of society'; on the contrary, it will improve the relationships between people and will help men to become better, more considerate lovers.

In adolescence and adulthood, our attitudes to our sexuality continue to be distorted by the fantasy world induced by the cinema, by many best-selling novels, and by 'locker-room' discussions between men. The mythology of male sexuality is emphasized in these experiences. It has recently been explored by Bernie Zilbergeld in his book *Male Sexuality*. American men, and many European men, continue to believe in myths about their sexuality in spite of the more open discussion about sexuality which has become permissible in the past decade or so.

Some of the myths have been mentioned earlier in this chapter, for instance, the myth that men should not have or express emotions, such as tenderness, crying, and touching, or the myth that a man should be 'performance oriented' in sex. This myth encourages men to believe that a man's performance in sex is all important as, through his prowess, he 'gives' the woman an orgasm. It encourages the belief that it is a man's responsibility to initiate sex, to arouse the woman, to lead her to her orgasm and then to have his orgasm.

Other myths are equally destructive to a relationship. One of these is that women expect men to have a large penis which, when erect, is 'as hard as steel', and that sex can only take place if a man has an erection. This myth has led to the concern of men who have erectile impotence and to the development of 'implants' in the penis to make it erect (see Chapter 10). Sex can be enjoyable without a steel-hard erection although it is enjoyable when a man has one. The star in the performance is not the man's penis but the man – and the woman. Sex is more than just genital contact. Good sex includes exploring all parts of the body which a person perceives as erotically stimulating.

Another myth is that unless a man has sexual intercourse during an encounter, the experience is inadequate and the man a sexual failure. This myth echoes the complaint of women that all men think about is 'getting it in and having an orgasm', and that mutual pleasuring is a useful means of achieving that goal, but of little value in itself. Men who accept this myth become 'performance oriented' and may diminish the pleasure they and their partner can get from exploring, touching, and caressing each other's body. The myth also puts great psychological pressure on the woman. If she believes that to make a man feel sexually successful she has to have an orgasm simultaneously with his orgasm, she may feel that she is a sexual failure when she doesn't. As I have said, fewer than half of women have orgasms during penile thrusting. This is not to say that sexual intercourse is not enjoyable for them: it is, of course, but it is not the only way, or at times the best, or most appropriate way of enjoying sex.

Many men accept the myth that sex should always be aggressive, and that women when aroused sexually become abandoned in behaviour, shriek in ecstasy at the thrust of the man's penis, are inexhaustible in their demands, enjoy the pain – the agony – of a steel-like penis 'penetrating' them to achieve the ecstasy of orgasm. If men believe that this is how women respond, they may also believe that if a woman says no, she means yes – if only the man can arouse her sufficiently. And if he does, the myth says she will respond increasingly until the excitement is such that it becomes explosive and culminates in the woman's wild abandon and simultaneous orgasm with the man.

Men who accept the myths of male sexuality rarely become good lovers. Men who are unable to find out what pleasures their partner, and to talk with their partner about what gives them pleasure, are likely to be poorer lovers than men who can communicate with their partner. You will become a better lover when you become aware of the conditions under which you are best able to become sexually aroused, and take the trouble to find out the conditions under which your partner is best able to become sexually aroused. Sexuality is a shared experience. The more you and your partner can share the pleasurable feelings of sexuality, uncluttered by anxiety about your 'performance' and relieved of the accumulated cultural myths about male and female sexuality, the better a lover you will be.

Table 4 What women want in a sexual relationship: I

- That men are more sensitive to a woman's needs.
- More love, consideration, emotion, gentleness, and above all more communication (tell me what you want, what turns you on).
- More and longer body stimulation, kissing, hugging, exploration, cuddling – much more innovation and imagination which will arouse her whole body (not just titillate her genitals) so that she is aroused to abandonment.

Table 5 What women want in a sexual relationship: II

- More spontaneity: all too often the sexual pattern is routine, preordained, expected.
- More passion – and less urgency to have intercourse quickly.
- Their man to have less preoccupation with his own penis.

Table 6 What women want in a sexual relationship: III

- That men stop thinking of 'foreplay' as a favour to the woman – a contribution to her enjoyment – so that she will soon be ready for them to have sex.
- To feel that the man wants the woman for what she is, a special person, not just as a receptacle for an erect penis.
- That men remember that women have as strong sexual needs and desires as men, and that they too enjoy having orgasms – provided the man helps the woman to have an orgasm at her direction.

6

The choice of children

The fact itself of causing the existence of a human being, is one of the most responsible actions in the range of human life. To understand this responsibility – to bestow life which may either be a curse or a blessing – unless the being on whom it is to be bestowed will have at least the ordinary chances of desirable existence, is a crime against that being.

J. S. Mill, 'On Liberty'

Today we are better able to plan and prevent pregnancy than at any other time in human history, yet we often get pregnant when we didn't want to or mean to.

Boston Women's Health Book Collective,
Our Bodies, Ourselves (1976)

FOR MANY REASONS, PARTICULARLY SINCE THE development of the highly efficient hormonal contraceptives, the main responsibility for the prevention of an unwanted pregnancy rests with women. While many women resent this as another example of sexism, the reasons are strong.

Pregnancy occurs because a woman makes an egg (ovum) in her ovary, which develops and escapes at ovulation, to be taken into the oviduct. If a man ejaculates into the woman's vagina within twenty-four hours of ovulation, the spermatozoa travel up through her uterus towards the oviduct, and should one reach the ovum it may penetrate its shell. This fertilizes the ovum: and pregnancy is likely.

The ejaculated spermatozoa are about eighty days old, as it has taken this time for them to be available. They are formed in 'nests' in the testes, and undergo several changes of shape before they enter the muscular tubes (or ducts) which connect the testes to the prostate gland. In the ducts, called the epididymis and the vas deferens, the spermatozoa become 'mature', and only when they are, can they fertilize the egg. The mature spermatozoa are stored in the prostate and in the seminal vesicles before being ejaculated during orgasm.

This complex process makes the development of an effective male contraceptive difficult. It must either prevent the spermatozoa from being formed in the testes, or prevent them maturing and moving along the ducts (especially the vas), or kill them before they are ejaculated, or prevent them entering the woman's uterus.

The most effective way would be to develop a drug which prevented the sperms from being formed. Unfortunately, the problem is far more complex than that which led to the development of the hormonal contraceptive pill used by women. A woman produces only one ovum in each menstrual cycle, and ovulation can be suppressed fairly easily, using hormones. In contrast, a man ejaculates several hundred million spermatozoa each time he has an orgasm, and these spermatozoa are eighty days old when they are ejaculated. This means that a male contraceptive pill has to stop *all* sperm formation and it would not be effective until all the sperms already formed had been ejaculated.

Currently several drugs are under investigation to achieve this objective. The first of these is to use a long-acting, powerful gestagen (a synthetic form of the female sex hormone, pro-gesterone). This hormone effectively prevents spermatozoa from being formed, but usually reduces the man's libido to an unacceptably low level. In order to overcome this problem, the gestagen, medroxyprogesterone acetate, is being given together with injections of a long-acting testosterone. The clinical trials with this combination suggest that the drugs effectively suppress sperm formation, without any loss of libido, but a good deal of work is needed before the combination will be generally available, and even then the combination may be unacceptable to most men because of the need for injections every 10 to 14 days.

Another approach has been developed in the People's Republic of China. Scientists have developed a male contraceptive using a substance called gossypol extracted from the roots, stems, and seeds of the cotton plant. In early trials involving over 10,000 men a gossypol pill taken every day reduced sperm counts to safe contraceptive levels without any alteration of the man's sexual desire or performance. Studies are now starting in other nations to determine if gossypol is safe for general use, but it may be some time before this is established.

Initial animal studies in the U.S.A. are not very encouraging. Many of the animals accumulated gossypol in their tissues and toxic actions on the liver, spleen, and heart muscle have been demonstrated.

Until an effective male contraceptive is developed men must play their part in preventing unwanted pregnancies, after discussion with their sexual partner, so that the choice most suitable for the couple's needs can be made.

Which partner uses the contraceptive method, and which method is chosen, depends on a complicated mixture of social, cultural, and psychological influences. Today for the first time in history, men and women have reliable methods to enable them to make that choice freely and relatively easily.

The principle of choice is important, as it includes not only the choice of using family planning, but the choice of the birth control method most suited to the particular circumstances of the couple. Neither the man nor the woman can make a real choice until each has the basic knowledge of the different methods available, their efficiency in protecting against pregnancy, and their advantages and disadvantages. A measure of contraceptive efficiency used by many people is the pregnancy index which is calculated in the following way:

$$\frac{\text{The number of pregnancies} \times 1200}{\text{Total months of exposure to pregnancy}}$$

The result is expressed as the number of pregnancies per 1200 months of exposure, or preferably as the number of pregnancies per hundred woman-years. This shows how many of every 100 women making use of the particular method chosen will become pregnant if the method is used for one year.

In calculating the efficiency of the contraceptive method chosen, the couple have to take several factors into account.

Most sexually active people use contraceptive measures to enable them to enjoy the mutual pleasuring of sexual intercourse, without the fear of a pregnancy occurring at an inappropriate time.

In her reproductive years, a woman may spend periods of time using one form of contraceptive; periods when she uses no contraceptives; periods when she is pregnant; and periods when she returns to contraceptive use. At some times the couple may have sexual intercourse frequently and, at other times, not so often.

The couple will want to know which of the contraceptive measures available is the most efficient in preventing a pregnancy for their particular pattern of sexuality. It may be that the woman will choose one of the most reliable methods (such as the hormonal contraceptives or the I.U.D.) despite the side-effects. It may be that she will choose a slightly less efficient method (such as the vaginal diaphragm) which has few or no side-effects. This choice may be made as a woman grows older, when her fertility is reduced, secure in the knowledge that should an unwanted pregnancy occur she can obtain an abortion with safety.

But it would be irresponsible for a woman to choose not to use any form of contraception and rely on repeated abortions to end her unwanted pregnancies. A single abortion poses little danger to a woman, but repeated abortions increase the danger of damage to her body. This is why abortion cannot replace contraceptive use and should remain as a 'backstop' for contraceptive failure.

On the other hand, the couple may decide that it is more appropriate for them if the man uses a condom. It may be that the woman does not want to, or cannot, use oral contraceptives, and does not like the idea of using an I.U.D., or perhaps there is a medical reason why she should not use either of these methods. After considering the choices the couple may agree that they would prefer it if the man prevented the pregnancy by using a condom or practising withdrawal.

The couple may decide that they have completed their family and want no more children. In this case they may choose a permanent method. The woman can have a tubal ligation, or the man can have a vasectomy. Again, after considering the information available, they may agree that the man should have a vasectomy as this is a simpler operation than tubal ligation and is as effective.

At present, two temporary contraceptive measures are available for men to use. These are coitus interruptus (withdrawal) and the condom. One excellent permanent method is currently available. This is vasectomy.

Coitus interruptus

For many years withdrawal of the penis from the vagina just before ejaculation has been used to avoid pregnancy. In several investigations, made in the days before the pill became available, it was found to be the most usual method adopted. It relies, of course, on the ability of the man to recognize the sensations which occur in his genitals just before ejaculation, and for him rapidly to withdraw his penis from the vagina and ejaculate outside. This requires great self-control, as the man will often want to keep his penis in the woman's vagina for as long as possible to obtain the greatest amount of pleasure. As the first spurt of semen, which contains the most spermatozoa, may either be ejaculated during withdrawal or may spurt into the vaginal entrance, the risk of pregnancy is high, and the pregnancy index is 35 per 100 woman-years.

Coitus interruptus has been said to lead to pelvic discomfort in the woman, who is stimulated but not relieved, and in the man, who has to withdraw at a moment when he would penetrate more deeply. Over long periods it was said to cause mental disorders. There is no evidence that coitus interruptus leads to either of these diseases, or indeed to any disease at all, but it is not a very satisfying method for men or women. If a couple have used coitus interruptus successfully for years and it suits their particular sexual needs, there is no reason for them to change, but they should remember that the method is not very efficient, because spermatozoa are often found in the secretions which seep out of the penis before ejaculation occurs.

The condom

If the male covers his penis with a sheath, which is so thin that it is not noticed by either partner, but so strong that neither the movement of the penis in the vagina nor the ejaculation of semen tears it, pregnancy will be prevented, as no spermatozoa will be deposited near the cervix. The sheath (or condom), which is today made of fine latex rubber, has been used since Roman times.

Modern condoms are prelubricated by adding silicone, and are individually packed in hermetically sealed aluminium foil sachets which enables them to be kept for a long period. Because of the quality of the condom and its prelubrication it can be easily unrolled on to the man's penis. Provided the man (or his partner, who may choose to put it on his penis) makes sure that no bubble of air is left in the closed end, and unrolls the condom to cover the shaft of his penis fully, it is very efficient. Air, together with the ejaculated semen, can lead to the condom bursting or, if it is not put on properly, it may come off, as the man's penis shrinks after orgasm. Because of these small risks, most doctors recommend that a woman puts some spermicidal cream in her vagina if her partner uses a condom.

A condom is probably the most suitable contraceptive if sexual intercourse takes place infrequently and unpredictably. In such circumstances a man may choose always to carry a condom, and a woman may have either a condom or a vaginal diaphragm available, should she and her partner want sexual intercourse and he has no condom available.

Condoms have several other advantages compared with other contraceptives. For example, condoms have no side-effects, because no hormones or chemicals are used; the condom protects by making a mechanical barrier which prevents the spermatozoa reaching the cervix.

A condom helps to prevent the spread of venereal disease, particularly if the man has casual sex with multiple partners, one or more of whom may have gonorrhoea. If the penis is 'protected' by a condom, the germs of gonorrhoea, which live silently in the genital tract of some women, are unable to get into the delicate tissues of the opening of the eye of the penis, and the chance of getting a sexually transmitted disease is reduced.

The advantages of the condom, which make it the most

commonly used male contraceptive, are reduced in the minds of some men by its supposed disadvantages. The first is that until a man's penis is erect, it is difficult to put on a condom properly. Some men think that this interferes with the spontaneity of love-making and decide to 'take a chance'. This can be avoided if the woman puts the condom on to the man's erect penis during sex-play.

Some men believe that a condom reduces that sexual pleasure by reducing the sensitivity of the glans of the penis. There is no evidence that this is so. The reduction in sexual pleasure is not due to the physical presence of the condom but to psychological hang-ups about its use, particularly its use as a 'prophylactic' (the name sometimes used for condoms) against venereal disease.

Its reliability in protecting the woman against an unwanted pregnancy is more difficult to estimate and depends on the integrity of the man, and the motivation of the couple, not to take a chance. Among motivated couples a pregnancy rate of less than 5 per 100 woman-years is reported, and highly motivated couples will have a pregnancy rate of less than 3 per 100 woman-years.

Vasectomy

The interest in vasectomy is increasing, as the operation provides an easy, relatively painless method of making a man sterile without interfering with the couple's sexual enjoyment.

The operation is relatively simple. The principle is to cut a small segment out of the vas deferens, the narrow tube which carries the spermatozoa from the testicles, where they are made, to the area of the prostate gland where they mature. If you gently palpate a man's scrotum, at the level where it joins his body, by putting your thumb in front and your index finger behind and rolling the folds of skin between them, you will feel a cord-like tube. This is the vas. There is a vas from each testicle, so you will feel one on each side.

The operation is made through a tiny cut into the skin of the scrotum, and can be done under local anaesthesia or using a general anaesthetic. Each vas is identified and a small segment is cut out, after which the cut in the skin is closed. The operation takes about 15 minutes, and about ten million operations are done each year.

Sexual intercourse can be resumed as soon as the man wishes, but the couple must continue using some form of contraception until the man has had about twelve ejaculations. This is because he has to ejaculate all the spermatozoa which have been stored in the prostate.

Once all these sperms have been ejaculated, the man is sterile, although he continues to ejaculate fluid which is made in the prostate gland so that neither he nor his partner notices any difference in their sexual pleasure.

What happens to the spermatozoa which are produced in the testicles but cannot escape because of the cut vas?

Although they continue to be produced at the rate of 50,000 every minute, an increase in the blood supply to the testes helps to dispose of them quickly and efficiently, and there is no need to be anxious that the testicles will become swollen, bloated with sperms!

Some men who are thinking of having a vasectomy worry that the sperms, being prevented from escaping, may be absorbed into the body and will produce a group of diseases called auto-immune diseases. Investigations have shown that, although some men form antibodies in their blood to sperm, none of the other indicators of auto-immune disease is produced, and vasectomy does not lead to this type of disease.

The effect of the operation on the sexual pleasure of a couple has been investigated sufficiently to establish that over 70 per cent of men find that after vasectomy their sex life is improved, in 28 per cent it is unaltered, and only 2 per cent of men find it to be worse.

What are the advantages of the man having a vasectomy rather than his wife having a tubal ligation, when their family is complete?

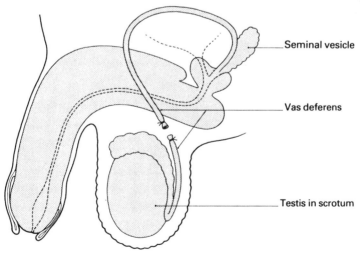

Seminal vesicle

Vas deferens

Testis in scrotum

18 Vasectomy

The main advantage is that a vasectomy is an easier operation, which is nearly painless and which can be done without admission to hospital. Tubal ligation, whether this is done by a small incision in the abdomen, or by pushing an instrument like a narrow telescope into the abdomen, is a much more complicated procedure.

Neither operation should be contemplated unless the couple are certain in their minds that they will never want any more children because operations to restore fertility are complicated and not always successful. Recent experience in Australia and Britain has shown that if a microsurgical technique is used, no more than half the men treated are able to impregnate their partner within two years of the operation.

The barren man

In an over-populated world, it may come as a surprise to learn that between 10 and 15 per cent of couples who desire to have a child are unable to do so. They are barren, sterile, or infertile. The terms are interchangeable.

Until about thirty years ago, the fault was thought to be due to the woman's inability to conceive. If a man could obtain an erection and could ejaculate within the woman's vagina, it was believed that he could not be sterile. It is now known that this belief was wrong. In most investigations of infertility, the man is at fault in nearly one-third of cases. Although he can get an erection and can ejaculate, he has few or no spermatozoa in his seminal fluid. The absence of sperm obviously prevents him having children, although his sexuality is not affected.

A fertile man ejaculates between 200 and 500 million sperms each time he comes. These are formed in a very complex way in small blind 'nests' in his testicles. The blind pockets are lined by cells from which the sperms develop. The cells are pushed inwards into the centre of the nests as new cells are formed, so that the lining of the nest is several cells deep. And each layer of cells is made up of spermatozoa in various stages of development. In the nests the sperms undergo at least twelve phases of maturation until they are discharged into the cavity of the nest. This takes about 74 days. The cavities of the many nests join together to form tiny ducts, or tubes, along which the spermatozoa are pushed by the movement of tiny 'hairs' on the inner surface of the cells which line the ducts, because at this stage they have no movement of their own. The process goes on continuously: 50,000 or more sperms being produced each minute.

The ducts join together to form about twelve larger collecting tubules, which then join to form a tube which lies coiled and twisted alongside the testis and reaches to the vas deferens. The coiled tube is called the epididymis. If it is uncoiled it is nearly 6 metres (20 feet) long. If a man has regular sexual stimulation and ejaculates, the spermatozoa move quite quickly along the epididymis, taking from 2 to 21 days for the journey, but if he does not, they can live in the epididymis for about 70 days. The more frequently a man ejaculates the more quickly the spermatozoa pass along the epididymis.

The end of the epididymis joins the vas deferens. As I mentioned earlier, you can identify the vas deferens if you put your thumb and forefinger on each side of the scrotum where it reaches the crutch, and then roll the tissues between your fingers. The vas reaches from the end of the epididymis, up through the scrotum, and enters the abdomen through a weakened oval area just above the pubic bone on each side – called the inguinal canal. Inside the abdomen it lies close to the prostate gland, where it joins the vas from the other side. Together they enter the urethra, the tube which extends from the bladder to the eye of the penis.

Inside the epididymis, the sperms mature and are stored in the last part of the epididymis and in the vas, especially in the widened end just before it joins the urethra. The mature spermatozoa are ready to be ejaculated, mixed with secretions from two outgrowths from the widened end of the vas, called the seminal vesicles. You can see that seminal fluid is made up of millions of spermatozoa mixed in a much larger amount of secretions from the seminal vesicles and some from the prostate gland. The average amount of seminal fluid which is ejaculated is 3 millilitres, and the secretions make up 90 per cent of it.

About 60 per cent of the secretions come from the seminal vesicles. They contain a sugar (fructose) which gives the spermatozoa energy. Nearly all the remaining secretions come from the prostate gland. These secretions contain various enzymes which can be measured. It has been found that if the level of one of them, acid phosphatase, is high, and the man's sperm count is low, he probably has a low-grade infection of his prostate gland. This infection may be cleared up using antibiotics, with improvement in his sperm count.

The secretions, which make up so much of the semen volume, are important because they provide nourishment and energy for the millions of spermatozoa and permit the sperm to exercise their tails.

Looked at under a microscope, spermatozoa are seen to be complex. Each sperm has a head, a middle piece, and a tail. The head of the sperm is shaped like the head of a snake. The head carries all the genetic material to form a new human if it combines with the genetic material in the ovum. Covering the front of the head is a thickened cap. Behind the head is a cylindrical body or midpiece which contains the 'engine' of the sperm. The energy which is needed to enable the tail of the sperm to propel it through the uterus is produced here. The tail of the sperm is three times as long as the head and body. It propels the sperm by a thrashing, twisting movement.

Scattered all over the surface of the head and midpiece of the sperm are small spots which, as it were, 'squirt out' substances, called antigens. If enough of the substances are extruded, when the spermatozoa have been ejaculated in a woman's vagina, some may enter her tissues and then her blood. If she is especially sensitive to the antigens, special cells 'recognize' the antigen as 'foreign' and rush to surround it and cover it, so that it is no longer recognized. If they fail to do this, the woman's body produces substances called antibodies which combine with the antigen and make it innocuous. But her body is then sensitized to the sperm antigen and the cells which line her cervix may start secreting the antibodies. They then seek and cover the antigen-secreting spots on the sperm. If this happens they may make the spermatozoa stick together, or stop their tails thrashing so that they are unable to make the journey through the uterus and fertilize the egg.

During the first part of a man's orgasm, the muscles surrounding the widened ends of his two vas deferens, and his seminal vesicles, contract and force the mixture of spermatozoa and secretions along the urethra towards and up along his penis. Then the other muscles around the base of his penis start contracting and he ejaculates the seminal fluid in short spurts – and feels the intense pleasure of orgasm.

*

There are several ways in which a man may contribute to, or be responsible for, the couple's inability to conceive a baby.

In most cases the problem is that he is unable
to make sufficient sperms, but in a few cases the
problem is that he is unable to obtain or maintain
an erection. In other words, he is impotent,
which is discussed in Chapter 10.

A few men make normal amounts of spermatozoa, and obtain firm erections, but no matter
how long they thrust in their partner's vagina,
they are unable to reach orgasm or to ejaculate.
Most of them are unable to reach orgasm
when they masturbate, although they have
'wet dreams'. The men are of all ages, are
healthy, and do not take drugs. The only finding common to all of them is that they have usually
had stern parents who have conditioned them to
believe that sex is evil, unpleasant, and dirty; and have
married a woman who has similar opinions.

The condition, which is an advanced form of retarded ejaculation, is uncommon. But if a man has it, it can be desperately
worrying. The most complete study is from Belgium where
Dr Geboes and his colleagues have treated seventy-
five men with the problem. They found that most
successful therapy was the use of an electrovibrator.
The vibrator (which is often used to help women
reach orgasm) is placed against the glans of the
penis. Within five or six minutes the man has
his first conscious orgasm. A few of these
vibrator-induced orgasms, with ejaculations, convince the man that he is normal.
Many men will then be able to reach orgasm
and ejaculate during sexual intercourse, but
those who fail and only ejaculate with the aid of
the vibrator can be helped. Their semen can be
collected and their wife artificially inseminated
with it, provided that it is of good quality. These
are uncommon causes of infertility.

19 A spermato-
zoon as shown by
the electron
microscope

In most cases the man ejaculates normally but his
semen contains no spermatozoa or only a few million,
instead of the 200 million or more which are usually
found. In other words the quality is poor.

When it was realized that a man might be the cause of an infertile marriage, it became obvious that his semen needed to be analysed more exactly. Before this time doctors had not examined the man. Instead, they had instructed the woman to arrange to have sexual intercourse, and to attend about six hours later. The doctor examined the woman's vagina and took a sample of the secretions found around her cervix, which he looked at through a microscope. If he saw any spermatozoa, the man was exonerated as the cause of the infertility.

The 'post-coital' test is still made, but has only limited value. Far more information is obtained by examining a specimen of a man's seminal fluid. This can be obtained by asking the man to masturbate or by suggesting he has sexual intercourse, making sure that before he ejaculates, he withdraws his penis from the woman's vagina and comes into a dry wide-mouthed container, such as a small jam jar. The specimen is then taken, within two hours, to a laboratory so that the seminal fluid can be analysed. The alternative method is to produce the specimen by masturbation in the laboratory, a procedure many men find difficult to achieve.

In the laboratory the quality of the seminal fluid is assessed by measuring its volume, the number of spermatozoa in it, how long they remain active, and how many have abnormal shapes or sizes.

Examination of many thousands of specimens, from men who have had children, has enabled scientists to find out what can be considered a 'normal' sperm count.

The results show that a man is fertile if he has more than 2 millilitres of seminal fluid; if each millilitre contains more than twenty million spermatozoa; if, after four hours, more than 40 per cent of the spermatozoa are active – which means that their tails are still thrashing about – and if more than 60 per cent have a normal shape.

If any of these measurements are below normal the man is subfertile; and if he has no spermatozoa at all, he is sterile.

At first it was thought that a single examination enabled a doctor to decide if the man was subfertile or sterile. It quickly became apparent that an examination of a single specimen was not sufficient to make the diagnosis. This is because the quantity of the seminal fluid and the sperm count (which are the two most important measurements as far as male fertility is concerned) can vary considerably. A diagnosis of subfertility, or sterility, is made only after three specimens produced at intervals of at least one week have been examined.

If three seminal analyses show that a man has no spermatozoa, a sample of his blood is taken and a hormone called follicle stimulating hormone (FSH) is measured. The blood level of FSH may be high or normal. A high FSH level indicates that the nests in his testes, where the spermatozoa develop, are so damaged that no treatment is possible. A normal FSH level suggests that he may have a blockage in the twisted epididymis or in the vas deferens. If further investigations prove that there is a blockage, it may be possible for a surgeon to cut out the damaged or blocked part of the tube and rejoin the healthy parts using microsurgery. It is likely that this very delicate surgery will enable some men with damaged tubes to father children.

Some men are found to have sperm counts which average less than five million. The blood level of FSH is measured and may be high or normal. Unfortunately, whatever it is, no treatment is as yet available which will improve the count, and pregnancy is unlikely to occur. A few men with counts as low as this have fathered children but it is rare for this to happen.

However, if a man's sperm count is more than five million (averaging the three tests), and his FSH level is normal, treatment may improve his sperm count, and the quality of his sperm, sufficiently to enable him to become a father. In these cases, the doctor may decide it is advisable to take a biopsy of his testis. A small incision is made, under local anaesthesia, into his scrotum and then into his testicles, to obtain a tiny piece of tissue. The tissue is examined with a microscope to determine whether spermatozoa are being formed properly and how mature they have become.

In some cases of subfertility, the man is found to have varicose veins surrounding one or both of his vas deferens, where his scrotum is attached to his body. Surgery, to cure the varicose veins, is usually followed by an increase in his sperm count and he has a 50 per cent chance of fathering a child.

The only subfertile men whose sperm counts may increase if drugs are used are those men whose count is more than five million sperms per millilitre, whose FSH levels are normal, and who have no varicose veins in their scrotum. This small group of subfertile men are being treated with a drug called clomiphene, in carefully observed trials. As spermatozoa take about eighty days to become mature the drug has to be given for at least this length of time if improvement in the man's sperm count is to be achieved.

Certain general measures may also help to improve a low sperm count. These are for the man to drink and smoke less, to wear loose underpants (so that the testicles are no longer held up close to his crutch), and to know the best time during the woman's menstrual cycle to have intercourse for a pregnancy to occur.

Until about 1970 infertile couples whose inability to have a child was solely due to the husband's very low sperm count or to his complete lack of spermatozoa were able to adopt a child relatively easily. Since 1970 this has changed in most developed nations. The numbers of children available for adoption have dropped very considerably, so that a delay of up to five years is usual before a suitable baby is found. This is because women avoid pregnancy by using efficient contraceptives and because legal abortion is more readily available. Ten years ago a young unmarried woman who became pregnant and did not wish, or was not able, to marry the man who made her pregnant, either sought a dangerous (or a safe, but expensive) illegal abortion, or had the baby. Many women preferred to have the baby and most surrendered it for adoption. Today, with legal, safe abortion, fewer unmarried women continue with the pregnancy and of those who do most keep the baby. Society has ceased to be so censorious about unmarried mothers and the sanctions against them have diminished.

The fact that safe abortions and efficient contraceptives are now more readily available has also reduced the number of babies offered for adoption by married women (or deserted wives), who already have several children.

The changes which have occurred are beneficial socially, but they have made it harder for an infertile couple to adopt a child.

Because of this, the idea of making the woman pregnant with the semen of an unknown donor is becoming increasingly popular. This is called A.I.D. – or Artificial Insemination by Donor.

Before the insemination is attempted, investigations have to be made. There must be no obvious reason why the woman should not become pregnant. She must be healthy and have been investigated to find out that she has patent (open) oviducts and be ovulating. One method of determining if she is ovulating is for her to take her temperature each morning just after she has woken up and before she has eaten or drunk anything. The temperature of a woman who ovulates shows a fall and then a rise.

The time of ovulation can be predicted more accurately by taking a sample of the woman's blood and by measuring a hormone called estradiol. This peaks about twenty-four hours before ovulation occurs.

Once the investigation has established when ovulation is due, the woman goes to the doctor. He has some donor's semen available, which has either been produced within the preceding two hours by masturbation, or has been donated earlier and has been 'snap frozen'. Rather more pregnancies follow insemination with fresh semen, but the organizational problems are greater.

The doctor takes the donor's semen and injects it gently with a syringe into the woman's upper vagina and over her cervix. The woman lies on her back for about thirty minutes and then goes home. The procedure is repeated the next day or the day after that.

About 60 to 65 per cent of women inseminated in this way become pregnant if the method is used over six ovulation times.

The organization of an A.I.D. programme is the problem. Ideally the donor, who provides his semen, should resemble the husband to some extent. This is understandable. A tall, blond Scandinavian man married to a similar woman might be disconcerted if the donor was a short, dark Southern European and the child resembled the donor rather than the mother. For this reason a well-organized Donor Insemination Service has to have a large panel of donors, one

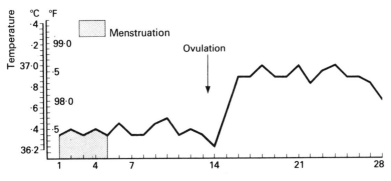

20 Ovulation detected by taking the temperature each day

or more of whom has physical characteristics which can be matched as closely as possible with those of the husband. A donor should be removed from the list when his sperm has produced six pregnancies, to avoid the possibility, however remote, of his progeny mating.

Neither the man nor his wife must have any idea who the donor is: they must never meet him knowing that he provided the semen. Nor may the donor have any idea who has received his semen.

The reason for the security is that confidentiality is essential as the child of the artificial insemination is the 'natural' child, in law, of the couple. It might be argued that by some chance the child might later have a child by its half-sister or half-brother and that this could lead to some genetic defect. This result is so unlikely (about a million to one chance of a genetic defect occurring) that it can be ignored. The couple need have no anxiety about this.

For legal protection both husband and wife must sign a document confirming that they understand and agree without coercion to the artificial insemination by the unknown donor. In some countries the legal status of a child produced by artificial insemination using a donor's semen is unclear, but changes are occurring and A.I.D. has enabled a large and increasing number of infertile couples to enjoy raising a child of their own.

7
The expectant father

Many men have a distorded idea of the amount of blood
and suffering in labour and feel they would hate to witness
it. They do not realize how involved they will feel inside
the room, doing something helpful, rather than pacing the
corridor outside. Many couples feel that sharing this
experience of birth has given a deeper meaning to their
relationship and to their feelings for the child. The vast
majority of husbands rate it one of the most important
experiences of their lives.

Anne Loader (ed.), The National Childbirth Trust,
Pregnancy & Parenthood (1980)

IN MOST CULTURES, PREGNANCY IS STILL A MATTER FOR the woman and her mother or some other female relative. Childbirth is a period for women alone, the man having no part in the process and being expected to keep away. The care of the newborn infant is the woman's responsibility, although the man is happy to receive the congratulations of his neighbours if the child is a boy!

In recent years, in the English-speaking and Scandinavian nations, particularly among better-informed women, there has been a change. These women want to share their experience of pregnancy with their man. They hope that he will become as informed about pregnancy as they are, and that they will both read about pregnancy and attend pre-natal educational classes so that, together, they can learn about the changes which happen to a woman's body and her emotions in pregnancy. The women hope that their men will be there to support them emotionally (and sometimes physically) during labour, and will be able to share with them the wondrous moment of the birth of their baby. They hope that their men will participate in the care of the newborn baby and will share in its upbringing. They argue, quite correctly, that as conception was a jointly pleasurable moment, their relationship will become closer and more intense if they can share the process of pregnancy, labour, and parenthood.

Not all men would agree! Because of their upbringing, which identified certain functions as appropriate for women and others for men, some men are afraid to become involved in this way, feeling it diminishes their masculinity.

Happily, more and more men are sharing with their pregnant partners the experiences, traumas, and joys of pregnancy and parenthood.

To meet the pregnant couple's expectations, many hospitals and concerned organizations provide educational classes at which films of pregnancy and childbirth are shown and at which questions can be asked and answered.* Books are available so that both expectant parents can read about the changes which occur during pregnancy and about the process of labour.

* In Australia, the Childbirth Education Association, the Childbirth and Parenting Association of Victoria, and Parent Centres, Australia. In Britain, the National Childbirth Trust.

Expectant fathers are becoming increasingly supportive during pregnancy. In certain areas their support and understanding can aid their partner considerably and reduce her discomfort or anxiety.

Of many topics, four deserve further discussion in this chapter.

Nausea

In the first weeks of pregnancy many women are nauseated and a few vomit. These uncomfortable conditions are self-limiting and by the 15th week of pregnancy usually have ceased, but during the time they occur, the expectant father can help. Nausea is most common in the morning (hence its other term, 'morning sickness'). Its effects may be reduced if the woman is given some food, such as toast, and a drink before she gets up. The man who expects his wife to make breakfast for him, can, when an expectant father, make breakfast for her, and bring it to her so that she can eat it slowly in bed. Fatty foods and fatty smells aggravate nausea, so that a considerate expectant father will avoid asking for such foods during his wife's early pregnancy. Women with nausea are often advised to eat small meals often, and if the man expects a large meal on his return home, may aggravate the nausea as the woman has to cook it and watch him eat. Be considerate, and adjust your eating habits to hers.

The emotional changes during pregnancy

The effect of pregnancy on the emotions of a woman are very varied. Some women's emotions alter hardly at all, other women become increasingly placid and less reactive to stress; still other women react excessively to upsets which would hardly affect them at all when they were not pregnant.

In the early weeks of pregnancy, most women identify with the tiny foetus; they talk about 'my' pregnancy rather than 'the' pregnancy or 'it'. This is because the foetus is perceived as part of the woman's body and has no separate identity. Between the 15th and 20th weeks of pregnancy a change occurs. The foetus begins to move, and to develop an identity of its own. The woman's enlarging abdomen tells her (and her friends) that she really is pregnant and she now begins to be interested in the foetus as 'her baby'. In late pregnancy from about the 35th week a further change occurs. Now most women become impatient with the pregnancy, bored with their swollen abdomen, anxious to give birth and to see, touch, and care for the newborn baby.

As pregnancy advances, with its attendant minor discomforts, many women are concerned that their increased fatness, lethargy, distended abdomen, and pendulous breasts may adversely affect their man's love. The way a man can reassure his partner is to kiss and cuddle her and to be interested (as he should be) in the continuing pregnancy and the growth, in the mother's uterus, of their baby. After all, the start of pregnancy was a joint pleasure; its continuation should be shared too!

Their shared experiences can be increased if the expectant father goes with the expectant mother for her antenatal appointment from time to time. This enables him to ask the doctor or the nurse questions, and to identify more closely with the pregnancy. It is a good introduction to parenting. Some doctors resent the man being there: if this happens change your doctor! It is important for the expectant father to know what is happening and to be reassured that the pregnancy is progressing normally.

Sex during pregnancy

During pregnancy, changes in a woman's sexual desire and in her response are usual. Most pregnant women have a reduced sexual interest in the first half of pregnancy, which continues, with considerable individual variation, through the second half of pregnancy. Once aroused, however, pregnant women experience an increased amount of swelling around the vagina, so that sexual intercourse itself can be very pleasurable to both partners.

It is not clear why women are less sexually aroused in pregnancy. While it is probably due to the hormones which are produced by the placenta, there is also an emotional factor. Some women find that sexual intercourse is uncomfortable; others fear that the man's thrusting penis may injure the baby; others are embarrassed about their enlarged, droopy breasts and their swollen abdomen, and see themselves as unattractive and not sexy. In contrast, some women enjoy sex more in pregnancy, as they have proved their fertility and are no longer fearful of becoming pregnant.

Because most women find their sexual urge reduced and because so many perceive themselves as sexually unattractive, the expectant father should spend a longer time in body contact with his partner and show his affection and desire for her. Sexual intercourse is safe at all stages of pregnancy, right up to the date the baby is due, unless the woman has had repeated abortions, or has had a series of premature labours, when the couple should seek the advice of their obstetrician as there is some evidence that sexual intercourse may lead to an abortion or to the onset of premature labour. The evidence is not very strong but the couple may choose to adopt other ways of sexual pleasuring. In late pregnancy, because of the growing foetus, the woman may find the male-superior position uncomfortable and be more relaxed, happy, and comfortable if the couple try the side-by-side or rear-entry positions.

Several myths about sexual intercourse in pregnancy need to be exposed, as they are not true. The first is that the penis thrusting in the woman's vagina may cause an abortion. The second is that penile thrusting in late pregnancy may damage the baby, break the 'bag of water', introduce infection, or lead to premature labour. None of these dangers is real. The third is that if a woman has an orgasm when pregnant it will injure the baby or start labour prematurely. This is also untrue, although some obstetricians prohibit sexual intercourse in late pregnancy if the woman has previously had premature labours.

Of course, both partners may choose methods of sexual gratification other than sexual intercourse, and still obtain as much pleasure. A woman who is not particularly aroused may prefer to help her husband to have an orgasm by stimulating his penis with her hand or by sucking it. Or she may prefer to enjoy sex by asking her husband to stimulate her clitoral area with his fingers or tongue, rather than having sexual intercourse. If she prefers cunnilingus, the man should not blow into her vagina (which increases sexual excitement for some women) during pregnancy, as some pregnant women have died after this action. However, cunnilingus, without blowing in the woman's vagina, is safe and enjoyable.

The man's realization of the changes in the woman's sexuality during pregnancy, his enjoyment in cuddling her, his excitement in exploring how their baby is growing, and where it is lying in her uterus, his interest in her reactions to pregnancy, his co-operation in readjusting sexually to each other, can increase the intensity of their relationship and bring the couple closer together, and can increase their shared experience. The involvement of the expectant father in the pregnancy also has the effect of reducing any possible jealousy he may experience after childbirth, when he realizes that his partner has to share her time and her affections. She can no longer give her love exclusively to him.

The father in childbirth

Traditionally the business of childbirth is something done by a woman with the help of other women. During childbirth, the husband was absent, either working, or drinking with his friends, or anxiously pacing the hospital waiting-room! In most European cultures, and in nearly all Asian and African cultures, the man kept away during childbirth, although in a few the husband went to bed and 'suffered' from imaginary labour pains during his wife's real labour. This custom is called 'couvade'.

In English-speaking and Scandinavian nations a change has occurred in recent years. During this time couples have communicated more about sex, and have had a closer relationship. This has extended to the desire, felt by many expectant mothers and fathers, that both should participate in the birth process, both be able to witness the birth of their baby, and to share their mutual joy.

A man can only participate in this way if he and the expectant mother have received training during pregnancy. He can only help his partner if he understands the processes of childbirth, if he has learned how to support and encourage the woman during childbirth. A couple can do this most effectively if they have attended educational classes together, and have read books, so that they are prepared to participate in childbirth.

In the past decade, slowly at first, but now with an increasing momentum, obstetricians, nurse-midwives, and hospital administrators have accepted the change to family-centred, participatory childbirth in which a couple who have been prepared can participate jointly.

Many hospitals now realize that their attitude to a woman in childbirth was too authoritarian and are beginning to review their procedures to make sure that their staff are less officious and that childbirth is made more pleasant for the expectant mother. Most now agree that the child's father (or some other close relative) has a right to be with the expectant mother during labour if she wishes. Increasingly nursing staff are talking with mothers during childbirth, explaining what they are doing and why. Some hospitals have begun to pay attention to their physical surroundings. They have reduced the 'clinical' appearance of the delivery room. A few have introduced 'birthing rooms'. These rooms are furnished like a bedroom in a house, and contain a double bed. The woman stays in this room and, if everything progresses normally, delivers her baby in it; but should a threat to the baby's health or life arise, the room can be converted rapidly into a traditional delivery room, or the woman can be moved to a delivery room.

One of the most important changes is the realization by hospital staff that the child's father (or some close friend) plays an important role in supporting the expectant mother during childbirth. Most women fear being left alone during childbirth, and the presence of a loved one reduces the anxiety of being in a relatively impersonal institution, where the staff seem to be constantly hurried and change often.

The expectant father's support begins when the woman is aware that she is in labour and feels that she should go to hospital. The man takes her there and smooths the administrative details which, for some reason, hospitals insist be completed before a 'patient' can be admitted. Most of these could be completed during pregnancy, but this only occurs in a few hospitals. Once the woman has been admitted to the delivery floor, the man's role increases, provided he has been trained during pregnancy and understands what he has to do. He acts as a spokesman for his partner with the attending staff. He helps the staff by recording the duration of, and the interval between, the uterine contractions, and by generally helping the woman. If she has chosen to have minimal analgesia to dull the pains, he can help her by massaging her back, by stroking her abdomen, and by caressing her. He acts as her helpmate, participating and encouraging her during the hours of childbirth and reinforcing her breathing and relaxation patterns.

In the second stage of labour, during which the baby is pushed out into the world, the man encourages the woman, as she uses her muscles to force the baby lower and lower in her birth canal.

Together, they share the joy at seeing the birth of their baby. First, its head appears, then its shoulders and arms, then its body slips out of the woman's vagina, and it lies crying gently and moving its limbs between its mother's legs, its cord still beating.

They can both share in the pleasure of touching and cuddling their newborn child as it lies naked on its mother's body, being gently stroked by both parents while it searches for her nipple. This early 'bonding' between the child and its parents is thought to be important for the subsequent development of the baby and for the relationship between its parents.

Hospitals which have thought about the shared experience of childbirth leave the mother, the father, and the newborn baby alone as soon after birth as possible, so that they may get to know their baby and may enjoy a quiet time together. Unfortunately, these hospitals are still too few: most do not leave the family alone to celebrate the birth of the baby and to adjust to being parents.

Couples who have shared in and jointly participated in childbirth confirm the intensity of the experience, and speak of their mutual joy in being together during such an important and emotionally charged period of their relationship.

The experience is enhanced if both parents have learnt what happens during pregnancy and labour, if both are prepared to share in the care of their baby, and if they have a warm, sharing relationship with each other.

Adjustment to parenthood

> It suddenly struck me that this tiny dependent creature was utterly dependent on me. His life hung on it and I didn't know how to ensure his comfort.
> The baby altered my life-style dramatically; it didn't seem to alter my husband's life-style very much, which seems unfair.
>
> Australian woman in response to
> Parenting Survey (1979)

The period of adjusting to the changed life-style necessitated by the presence of a small, helpless, demanding, utterly dependent baby can be distressing to both parents. For biological reasons, the mother bears most of the stress. In hospital, after delivery, most mothers are not encouraged to ask the questions which trouble them. Unless the hospital permits the baby to stay all, or nearly all, the time with the mother she may have difficulty in knowing her baby and being able to interpret his cry. She does not know whether the baby is crying because of hunger, the desire for cuddling, or because it is in pain.

When she leaves hospital she may have insufficient confidence to face the demands of an unpredictable baby. In the past, parents and relatives were able to help her. But today, particularly in urban living, the new mother may feel increasingly isolated because distance precludes her mother from visiting and helping her. Even those visitors who come to see her often give her conflicting advice, and tell her of their experiences of caring for a newborn baby. These experiences are usually that the baby always smiled, rarely cried, put on weight, and was no trouble! The harassed mother contrasts this with the reality of her own baby, who wakes frequently, cries often, and seems to demand her constant attention.

Faced with the problems of learning how to mother the infant, often lacking sufficient confidence, and without support, the new mother may begin to feel that her baby's demands are excessive and she is never going to be able to satisfy them.

She is woken at night, and becomes increasingly tired, so that even normal household duties become an effort. As most women are reared to believe that they can be housewives *and* mothers, she feels inadequate if she is unable to care for her child *and* keep the house as clean and tidy as she would wish.

She is also anxious that her relationship with her husband is deteriorating. Previously they could give a good deal of time to each other. Now the baby occupies much of her time.

As the mental tension, strain, and lack of sleep mount, the new mother may become depressed, irritable, have outbursts of anger, and break into floods of tears, for what would normally be a trivial reason.

Adjustment to parenthood is much more of a problem than has been realized, but the stress on the mother can be reduced if her husband is understanding and sympathetic and if the couple jointly care for their child.

To be an effective helper, the man must have some knowledge of the stresses on his wife and should try and reduce them by his compassion and his help. He can share the shopping and do the house-cleaning. He can reassure and cuddle his wife. He can take over the baby and cuddle it when its cry is not for food, but for body comfort.

A large number of women wrote to me in response to a request for information about the problems they had experienced when adjusting to parenthood. Those who had found the adjustment easy had had the help of an informed, co-operative husband or had had a female relative who was close to them. Those who had found the adjustment hardest and who, often, had had quite severe depression, had a husband who had refused to help and who had made selfish demands, expecting the woman to entertain, to be immaculately coiffured and dressed, to have food ready when he wanted it, and to cope with the baby's demands at all times.

The lesson is clear. The pregnancy occurred when you made love jointly, the care of the baby is a joint responsibility, and a loving man would make sure that he knew how to help, and did help.

There is a further point, which is important for the development of the child. If the child sees, from its earliest weeks, that its father and mother have a sharing relationship, it will in turn be able to form such a relationship with others, and the alienization of so many children will be avoided. Anti-social behaviour of children is often modelled on the anti-social behaviour of parents.

Sex after childbirth

A question which many couples would like to ask, but are often too shy to ask, is when can sexual relations resume after childbirth. A couple could and should cuddle immediately after childbirth, and on return home one or other partner may wish to be stimulated sexually by fondling or petting. Sexual intercourse can begin as soon as the woman wishes. Usually a couple of weeks pass after childbirth, because sexual intercourse would be painful or messy before this. During this time other forms of sexual stimulation can be used.

Many women find that their sexual desire and response is less in the first months after childbirth than it was before pregnancy. To a large extent this is because the demands of mothering make the woman tired and less able to respond quickly. A relating partner will realize this and will spend time in body contact and caressing, often without expecting that this is a necessary preliminary to sexual intercourse. Mutual pleasuring and communication will reduce or eliminate many of the sexual problems which can occur after childbirth and are a part of adjusting to parenthood.

8
Sexual problems

The experienced counsellor will not go along with the one
marriage partner who tries to place all the blame for
marital sex problems on the other mate.

Robert A. Harper, *Sexology* (1972)

ACCORDING TO BOOKS ABOUT SEXUALITY AND MARRIAGE, most couples achieve a harmonious, mutually satisfying sexual relationship within a few months.

The reality, it appears, is different. Large numbers of couples fail to achieve a harmonious sexual relationship and others only achieve it for periods of time. The lack of harmony in the relationship may lead either of the couple to form an extramarital relationship, or it may lead to a sexual problem in one or other partner, in other words, a sexual dysfunction. This means that the person is unable to function sexually as well as he or she might.

In the past, it was believed that few women had extramarital sexual relationships, and few men had sexual dysfunctions. These beliefs are known to be incorrect.

Extramarital sex

In 1957 Kinsey reported that 50 per cent of married men and 26 per cent of married women had had a relationship which had included sexual intercourse with a person who was not their marriage partner. More recent studies suggest that, in the last twenty years, the proportion of married men and women who have had at least one episode of extramarital sex is increasing. In the earlier research it was thought that there was a sex difference: men were more likely to have extramarital sex in the earlier years of marriage, women more frequently in their late thirties. Recent research questions if this is so.

The majority of extramarital 'affairs' remain secret from the partner, although suspicions may occur. Middle-aged men often choose (or perhaps are accepted by) younger women as lovers, either as compensation for what the man perceives as dullness within marriage, or because his self-confidence has been diminished in his work, or to reassure himself of his attractiveness and virility. These are important in our youth-oriented, competitive society. In many instances the reason is unclear, and a combination of circumstances leads to a situation in which an affair begins.

These relationships are quite distinct from partner-swapping or 'swinging' in which the couples involved know the identity and personality of each partner and strict rules are enforced to make sure that the permanent relationship persists. The sexual experiences are seen as fulfilling, exciting, and pleasurable, and not as damaging to the permanent relationship.

The effect of an extramarital sexual relationship on the marriage is generally damaging, and usually one or all of the people involved is hurt; although in a few instances the 'affairs' may induce the married partners to communicate with each other, so that after the initial trauma the marriage is enhanced rather than diminished.

In most extramarital relationships the pride of the uninvolved partner is damaged and, if the marriage continues, a period of agonizing readjustment is needed.

In our society, the damage to a man's pride seems greater if he finds his wife is having an extramarital relationship, because many men still perceive their wives as sex-objects, to be possessed by them exclusively.

Although most extramarital affairs are initially exciting because of the novelty, the 'conquest', and the opportunity to relate to another person in an intimate way, with time they often turn out to be less fulfilling and pleasurable. The tensions increase for both participants, as neither seems to be able to extricate him or herself without hurting the other.

This knowledge is unlikely to reduce the frequency of extramarital affairs; and their effect, as Rosenzweig has written, 'must await more extensive knowledge as to the individual and social consequences, than is presently available'.

Sexual dysfunctions

Men and women may have sexual dysfunctions which may cause considerable distress. Women have four main problems. The first is that some women have little or no sexual desire, and consequently fail to become sexually aroused. These women may avoid sexual intercourse or may submit because they feel it their duty, but find it distasteful. Some of the women with this sexual problem are hostile to, or bored with, their partner; others enjoy caring for the man in other ways but avoid any sexual advances he may make. The problem has recently been called 'inhibited sexual desire'. The second sexual problem is that although the woman has a normal sexual desire, she does not become aroused when sexually pleasured. This means that her vagina lubricates poorly and sexual intercourse may be painful or unpleasant. The third problem is that some women are so inhibited about sex that when a man attempts to insert his penis into the woman's vagina, an intense muscular spasm occurs, because of the pain the woman feels. The woman has a normal sexual desire, and becomes sexually aroused but is unable to accept the man's penis in or near her vagina; the condition is called vaginismus. The fourth problem is that the woman has a normal sexual desire, is easily sexually aroused, but is unable to reach orgasm, at least during sexual intercourse.

Men have labelled women with the first and third dysfunctions 'frigid'. The term is pejorative and inaccurate. It implies that, because of some inherent defect, a woman is unable to respond to the man's attempts to arouse her sexually. It absolves the man from any responsibility for his partner's reduced sexuality, and diminishes any guilt he may feel if he has sex with another, more responsive partner.

Dr Robert Dickinson has written, 'it takes two people to make one "frigid" wife'. Given proper counselling and appropriate help, most women with sexual dysfunctions will resolve them.

Men also have four sexual dysfunctions. The first is that the man reaches orgasm and ejaculates too quickly, either very soon after his penis is in the woman's vagina or even before he inserts it. This is premature ejaculation. The second is that the man is able to obtain an erection, but no matter how long he thrusts with his penis in his partner's vagina he is unable to reach orgasm and ejaculate. This is called retarded ejaculation. The third dysfunction is that the man has inhibited sexual desire, consequently is not sexually aroused even if the woman attempts to tease him sexually, and does not achieve an erection. This sexual problem has been confused, until recently, with erectile impotence which is the fourth sexual dysfunction. A man who has erectile impotence has a normal sexual desire, becomes sexually aroused but, in spite of this, is unable to obtain an erection, or if he does it lasts for such a short time that he cannot engage in sexual intercourse.

Men (and women) with sexual dysfunctions can be helped if they are willing to seek help. But in many cases the problem will only be resolved if the partner is willing to help and if the person can obtain appropriate counselling.

*

Of all human behaviour, sex, to achieve its full dimensions, needs the involvement of both partners. To achieve the full sexual potential of the union, the partners must be able to communicate with each other about their sexuality. They must be able to talk to each other about their sexual needs, their sexual attitudes, and the sexual stimulation they prefer. Communication in sex can be by words – by the couple talking to each other – but it can also be non-verbal. Communication, indicating love, affection, and desire, can be by body-language, by smiles and gestures, by touch, by taste, and by smell. When there is failure to communicate, either because of childhood inhibitions about sex, or because of traumatic adolescent sexual experiences, disharmony intensifies. And when sexual inadequacy exists, both partners are involved, since sexual response represents the interaction between two involved people. Transient sexual encounters can occur without emotional involvement, but more lasting sex means the emotional and physical involvement of both partners.

Many people either do not know, or reject, the normalcy of human sexuality. It is as normal as any other physiological response, such as breathing or eating or moving. It also has a marked emotional and psychological element, mainly directed to pleasurable feelings. In one way the sexual response is unique. It can be delayed or denied during a person's entire life. But for most people a functioning, happy sexual relationship is important. Sexual dysfunction mars an important human relationship. While a sexual relationship is not the only form of relationship between two humans, it is an important one.

Because the sexual response is not only a physiological event but has a psychological component, much sexual dysfunction is due to distorted learning about human sexuality or to early, hurried, ill-understood sexual experiences. The correction of sexual dysfunction is largely a matter of directed re-education in human sexuality. The importance of the involvement of the partner in this re-education is paramount.

Such re-education demands that both partners must be able to discard all the myths and misconceptions accumulated during their lives. They must discard the view that sex is sinful, and reject the double standard of human sexuality. They must learn about each other's sexual anatomy and physiology. This knowledge is not only important in itself, but it helps the sexual partners to talk to each other without embarrassment, so that they may achieve a change in their attitudes towards sex. In the various centres which have been established to treat sexual problems the extent of the couple's sexual information, or misinformation, is obtained by the therapist who asks a series of questions.

After talking individually about their sexual knowledge, attitudes, and behaviour, the couple talk together, guided by the therapist, about their sexual attitudes, so that misinformation can be corrected.

While communication in words is important, it is equally important for the couple to learn to communicate without words. Re-education in sexual communication involves touching, smelling, and tasting as much as talking.

Many people know little about their partner's feelings, and some have never explored their partner's body. The therapists invite the couple to begin this exploration privately. One partner touches, fondles, massages, or caresses the other partner's body to try and find what is most stimulating and pleasurable. In the first sessions they are not permitted to touch each other's genital area or breasts. The objective of these sessions is to pleasure the partner and to find and focus his or her mind on pleasurable sensations. This 'sensate focusing' is performed to enable the couple to relax in each other's company, unimpeded by the threat of interruption or the anxiety of sexual failure. It is designed to remind the couple that sexuality is not just a genital connection. Sexuality is, in addition, stimulation of touch and all the other senses. In our culture, and in most others, affection, warmth, love, devotion, and desire are expressed by touch as well as words.

The 'sensate focus' exercises are designed to re-educate the couple in the importance of touch, to which are added smell, by using scented body lotions for the massage, and occasionally taste. In these sessions the giving partner gives, without seeking any return of the favour. The receiving partner receives, without the possible threat of having to give in return, and without the need to explain. All that the pleasured partner has to do is prevent the pleasuring partner from doing anything which distracts from or diminishes the pleasure felt.

With succeeding sessions the partners change roles and, after a while, pleasure each other by exploring, fondling, and caressing each other's genitals, and begin to help each other overcome the specific sexual dysfunction, which requires additional techniques.

Some sexual therapists, notably Dr Masters and Dr Johnson in the U.S.A., find that they are able to get the most successful results in treating sexual dysfunctions if the couple are able to spend at least two weeks in a residential remedial course. This is expensive. Other sexual therapists have found that most sexual dysfunctions can be resolved using less expensive techniques.

In Australia, one sexual therapist has devised a two-week sexual therapy programme of daily 'sexual experiences and exercises' which has helped many couples who have sexual dysfunctions. The couple have to agree to set aside at least 30 minutes each day to carry out the exercises. They have to agree to follow the instructions exactly, even if this may make one or other shy and perhaps uncomfortable. If that occurs, the person who is uncomfortable has to agree to tell his or her partner and to talk it over the next day with the therapist. The couple have to agree to be honest with each other and neither to cheat nor to take short cuts. If one or other gets irritated about an apparent lack of progress, he or she has to agree to talk about it, rather than to 'bottle it up inside'. The exercises are done at home and, before they are started, the atmosphere must be right. The room should be warm, the lights soft, and, if the couple like background music, they should start the cassette- or record-player. A bottle of perfumed skin oil will also help as many of the exercises involve touch.

The exercises are in two parts. For the first three days neither partner is allowed to touch the other's especially erotic zones – the genitals, breasts, and nipples. Only on the fourth day does the genital area become the focus of attention. Then either partner can fondle, play with, and pleasure the other's genitals, but sexual intercourse is prohibited until the second week.

Non-genital pleasuring

For the first fifteen minutes one partner pleasures the other. If the man has the sexual problem (for example, if he is a premature ejaculator) he massages, fondles, and kisses the woman, with the sole objective of making her feel good and of giving her pleasure. He may stroke her hair, nibble her neck, lick her ears, kiss her hands, or massage her back or legs. While he does this, she responds by telling him how she feels, on a five-point scale of 'marvellous', 'good', 'neutral', 'don't like it much', 'hate it'. She also guides him by telling him how to stroke or fondle, so that they can enjoy the feeling of each other's bodies without this being a prelude to be hurried through so that they can have sexual intercourse.

At the end of fifteen minutes they change roles. The woman does the pleasuring and the man tells her how he feels. Even if he gets the most magnificent erection, she must avoid touching his penis. Genital touching is prohibited!

Genital pleasuring
After three non-genital pleasuring sessions, genital pleasuring can begin. The breasts and genital area can now be touched and fondled.

The session starts with five minutes of the non-genital pleasuring the couple practised in the first three days. First one and then the other plays the active role.

Following this they begin genital pleasuring. It has been found that sexual dysfunction appears to resolve more quickly if the person who has the dysfunction is the active partner first. If the man has the sexual dysfunction, he should pleasure the woman first.

He starts by exploring and playing with her breasts and particularly with her nipples. He should find different ways in which they can be caressed – he may lightly flick them, suck them gently or hard, or press them with his fingers or his lips – the choices are wide! As with the non-genital pleasuring exercises, the woman tells the man the pleasure she gets from each experience by relating it to the scale.

Then he begins to pleasure her genitals, particularly her clitoris. Again he has a wide variety of choices. He may look at, stroke, fondle, rub – even pinch – her vulva and clitoris. And all the time she tells him by words, by movements, or by sounds what gives her most pleasure and what she dislikes, so that he can learn what she likes and what she dislikes.

After fifteen minutes or so it is the woman's turn to be the 'pleasurer'. She looks at, fondles, strokes, kisses her partner's penis, scrotum, and testicles, searching for ways which give him the most pleasure. He tells her what he likes best and what he dislikes, using the five-point scale.

These general sexual exercises prepare the couple for undertaking the specific exercises needed to resolve the particular dysfunction, which will be discussed in the next two chapters.

Fantasy
In the treatment of sexual dysfunctions fantasy may play an

important role. Sexual fantasies, even of a bizarre nature, are not unusual in a sexual relationship and are innocuous, unless the person confuses the fantasy with reality, becomes obsessional about the fantasy, or seeks to exploit the partner in acting out the fantasy. Most people do not confuse sexual fantasy and reality, and fantasies are one of the ways in which people express their sexuality.

In sexual dysfunctions many people find that by fantasizing about a sexual exploit which excites them, their sexual arousal is increased. Some people are reluctant to fantasize about themselves in sexual situations with a person or persons other than their permanent sexual partner, because they feel that by doing this they are being unfaithful, and become guilty. However in treating sexual problems, fantasy may be the trigger which starts the cure, and guilt should not be felt, if the fantasy helps to resolve the problem.

9

'Too quickly, too slowly, or not at all'

He gets upon her before she has begun to long for pleasure
and then he introduces, with infinite trouble, a member
soft and nerveless. Scarcely has he commenced when he is
already done for.

Sheik Nefzawi, *The Perfumed Garden* (c. 1400)

'It's hard to be good,' said the good girl.
'It has to be,' said the bad girl.

Old army anecdote

A hurried kiss
Is better than a hurried coitus.

Arab proverb (13th century)

Premature ejaculation

Premature ejaculation is probably the most common form of sexual dysfunction in men. It is difficult to determine the number of men who have this type of sexual problem because many are unaware that there is a problem in their sexual relations or, in the case of other couples, the condition is accepted as normal.

A difficulty in discussing premature ejaculation is that it is poorly defined. About twenty years ago it was said that a premature ejaculator either reached orgasm and ejaculated before his penis entered his partner's vagina, or within 30 seconds of vaginal intromission. This 'stop-watch' definition was not really accurate and led to a variety of 'home treatments' *involving the man only*. These home treatments included mental exercises during intercourse, such as multiplying complex numbers, to take the man's mind off coming; masturbation just before intercourse; the use of thick condoms or anaesthetic ointments on the penis to dull its response to touch; alcohol or sedatives; and methods of causing self-inflicted pain (like lip-biting or nail-digging) during sexual intercourse. None of them was very successful.

Research in recent years has shown the limitations of the 'stop-watch' definition, and another definition has been proposed. This is that premature ejaculation occurs if a man ejaculates either before entering or, more usually, after his penis is in his partner's vagina, so quickly that a normally orgasmic woman gets little or no enjoyment from the episode of sexual intercourse. By avoiding any time-interval, this definition excludes a man who ejaculates soon after entering the woman's vagina, but who has satisfied his partner sexually by helping her to orgasm during an extended period of sex-play, or whose partner reaches her orgasm very quickly. But the definition fails to recognize that many women obtain sexual pleasure from the feel of the man's penis thrusting in her vagina, and from the close body contact which occurs during prolonged sexual intercourse.

A man who ejaculates prematurely has the problem that he is unable to delay his sexual response voluntarily, and he passes rapidly from the late plateau stage (in which many men can remain for long periods) to the stage when ejaculation is inevitable. In other words, a premature ejaculator is the reverse of a woman who cannot reach orgasm. In her case, messages from the sex centre in the brain inhibit the reflex which causes orgasm; in his case, messages from the brain facilitate the reflex which controls orgasm and ejaculation.

It is not too far-fetched to compare premature ejaculation to bed-wetting. A small infant has no control over its bladder. When the urine stretches the bladder, a reflex occurs which makes the bladder contract and the infant urinates. As the infant grows it learns to suppress the reflex, and delays urination until an appropriate time. In some ways, a man with premature ejaculation is like the infant; he has not learned to delay his ejaculation until a more appropriate time.

Premature ejaculation is not only frustrating to a man's sexual partner, but also reduces his full sexual enjoyment. Men who have been cured of premature ejaculation report that when they had the sexual problem, their orgasms were less pleasurable. Some men have said that it was as if their penises were anaesthetized.

In addition to reducing a man's sexual pleasure, premature ejaculation can cause anxiety and distress to both partners. The man feels guilty about his inadequate sexual performance, the woman feels perplexed, rejected, and perhaps hostile to the man who seems to be ignoring her sexual needs.

It is also obvious, from any of the definitions, that premature ejaculation is usually only of concern to a man whose relationship with his partner is a sharing one and who wants to help her have as much sexual pleasure as he is having. If a man's socio-cultural background is a male-dominated one, in which no sharing sexual relationship is expected, or wanted, and in which his own sexual satisfaction, by orgasm, is the sole criterion of sexual enjoyment, he will perceive no problem; nor will his partner. In such cases, sex-play is brief, or absent, communication is unusual, sexual intercourse urgent, brief, and ejaculation is rapid. It is an example of the 'wham, bam, thank you, ma'am' pattern of sexual behaviour.

In such sexual (and marital) partnerships, a double standard of sexuality is usual. The woman may have been told that this is what she should expect in sex. Or she may be so sexually unstimulated that she welcomes her partner's quick ejaculation as rapid relief from a resented 'duty' expected by her partner, irrespective of her feelings. This resentment is aggravated if, after ejaculating, the man rolls off his recumbent partner without offering any tender exchange of words, and falls asleep, snoring, next to a resentful woman, who is wide awake.

But a man who persistently ejaculates prematurely in a sharing sexual partnership may become anxious that he is giving nothing and taking everything sexually; or his partner sooner or later complains. Sexually aroused by mutual pleasuring, expecting a period of enjoyable penile movement within her vagina, hopeful that she may reach orgasm herself, she finds that her partner has ejaculated almost as soon as his penis enters his vagina, leaving her sexually frustrated. When this pattern of sexual activity is repeated over several months, both partners become anxious. The anxiety is aggravated if they are unable to talk to each other about their sexual problems. The woman becomes tense because of her continuing sexual frustration; the man becomes increasingly anxious because he feels that he has failed his partner sexually and so diminished his masculinity. A vicious circle of sexual dysfunction has been established. Help is needed to break it.

What sort of man gets into this problem? What hope has he of escaping from it? The answer to the first question is still unclear. The answer to the second question is that almost every man who is concerned about his premature ejaculation can be cured with the help of a sexual therapist and, more importantly, with the loving help and educated cooperation of his sexual partner.

Studies by several sexual counsellors show that men who are premature ejaculators frequently had sexually inhibited parents, who had taught the boy that sex was something rather shameful. In adolescence or young manhood the man's first sexual encounter was associated with guilt. He may have had his first sexual experience with a prostitute who wanted the man to 'finish it off quickly', or it was in an inappropriate place where the couple could be surprised by parents or passers-by. The anxiety caused by this possible eventuality led to a furtive, speedy, and unsatisfactory sexual experience, which was often repeated.

The theory that most men with premature ejaculation have had stressful initial sexual encounters is not the only one. After all, many men have hurried or unrelaxed sexual encounters; trying to make it with one ear for the steps on the stairs; or one eye on the darkening lane; but only a few appear to become premature ejaculators. Moreover, men who have been cured of premature ejaculation often feel anxious when highly aroused sexually that they are going to ejaculate too soon – but they very rarely do.

Other theories of premature ejaculation include the Freudian belief that premature ejaculators unconsciously hate women. They ejaculate quickly to deprive their sexual partner of any sexual pleasure, to 'use' her as a receptacle for semen, to be 'soiled'. Freudian analysts trace this hostility to a mother-hostility which had to be repressed. Unfortunately for psychoanalysts, only a few men who ejaculate quickly show any hostility to women, and psychoanalytic therapy is costly, time consuming, and usually unsuccessful.

Another idea is that the premature ejaculator is engaged in a 'power game' with his sexual partner. He wants to dominate her, to subjugate her. But he sees her as trying to dominate him, and believes that she tries to do this by expecting him to delay his orgasm until she has climaxed. To show his independence and to punish her, he ejaculates quickly. The theory is fun, but has little evidence to support it, and treatment merely to improve the couple's general relationship, without tackling the specific problem of premature ejaculation, is rather unsuccessful.

None of these theories fits the clinical situation as well as the theory that premature ejaculation is an anxiety-induced response to early unsatisfactory and stressful sexual experiences. Because of these unsatisfactory experiences the man has learned that sex is furtive, quick, and guilt-ridden. It is something which is pleasurable, but also shameful. It is something which should be done quickly and is stressful. He has learned a pattern of response to sexual stimulation, in which he is rapidly aroused and is unable to damp down the arousal, keeping it in the late plateau stage. He has lost his voluntary control over his sexual response because of his anxiety about his sexuality. He has pushed the anxiety into his subconscious where it reinforces his quick response pattern, until it becomes the only way he responds to sexual arousal. His sexual impulse has escaped his brain control.

In other instances, premature ejaculation occurs because the man is over-anxious or over-sensitive about his ability to satisfy his partner sexually. He may be unaware that many women fail to reach orgasm during penile thrusting and may feel that because his partner does not, he is a sexual failure. He may be over-sensitive about his relationship with his partner. This can induce anxiety and lower his self-esteem so that, paradoxically, he loses his own ejaculatory control, and comes increasingly quickly.

During his life nearly every man finds that at times he ejaculates very quickly. This is normal. Stress, a particularly exciting erotic encounter, or tension may result in premature ejaculation, which ceases when the particular stimulus ceases. It is only when a man consistently ejaculates too quickly that he has a real sexual dysfunction.

*

A typical example of this pattern of sexual disability is shown by the case of John.

Most of John's sexual knowledge was obtained by listening to his friends talking and boasting about their real or imagined sexual exploits. When he was 17 he met a girl and a love-affair began.

As the affair developed, John and his girl began petting and this got heavier. They were both inexperienced and both tense. Sometimes after intense kissing, John fondled the girl's breasts while she rubbed his erect penis, through his unzipped trousers. Because both were concerned about the consequences of sexual intercourse, the next step, as sexual tensions rose, was for John to lie upon her, his clothes relatively in place, and to mime sexual intercourse, without any attempt at vaginal penetration. As the purpose of this, both for John and for his partner, was to obtain a rapid release of sexual tension, John was quickly stimulated to ejaculation by the mock-sexual intercourse. He was learning a pattern of sexual behaviour, namely that once his penis was in his partner's vagina, ejaculation was expected to occur at once.

One night in the back seat of his car the girl permitted him to make love to her. He was aroused by the petting, desperate to put his penis in her vagina. This necessitated some fumbling and just when he succeeded, he thought he heard someone coming down the lane towards the car. With extraordinary rapidity he reached orgasm, ejaculated, and withdrew, zipping up his trousers and moving along the back seat of the car away from his partner.

In the next few years, John was sexually active. But each time he had sexual intercourse, he found that he came very quickly: usually two or three thrusts and he had ejaculated. Several times he found he came even before he had inserted his penis into his partner's vagina. Most of the women John knew were as sexually uninformed as he was and accepted this as normal, but one affair ended disastrously when the woman laughed at John's rapid ejaculation and demanded sexual satisfaction herself. John considered her to be an over-sexed woman, unlike the 'nice' girls he usually knew.

When John married, his pattern of sexual behaviour persisted. Sex for him was some foreplay, which both he and his wife enjoyed, and then rapid ejaculation, which satisfied him but left his wife sexually frustrated. Her frustration increased because she thought it wrong to masturbate and the idea of cunnilingus was repellent. Her mother told her that women had to expect a period of adjustment and a child often made it better. John talked with his friends and learned that women were expected to reach orgasm as quickly as men. If they didn't they were frigid.

The couple had a child, and John's wife, deeply involved with the child, dissatisfied with their sexual relationship, found that she wanted sex less and, when it happened, was uninvolved. This proved to John that he had married a frigid woman. His wife, for her part, felt that she was only being used, and that such sexual love as there had been in the marriage had now gone. Neither John nor his wife was able to talk to the other about their mutual sexual problems, and their sexual frustration increased. John found excuses to stay away from home until late. When they were together the couple bickered and nagged each other constantly. The wife became increasingly depressed and visited her doctor. She was given pills to cause a mood-elevation, because her doctor had neither the time, nor had he had the training, to perceive that underlying her depression was sexual frustration.

*

There are several degrees of severity of premature ejaculation, and all can be cured. In the most severe form, which is also the most frustrating to the woman, the man ejaculates as soon as his naked penis is touched, and may even ejaculate in response to the stimulus of looking at photographs of naked women. Luckily, this pattern is unusual. In less severe forms the man ejaculates during foreplay. In most cases, however, premature ejaculation only occurs when the man inserts his penis into his partner's vagina, or after a few thrusts within her vagina.

When a couple, such as John and his wife, are aware that they have a sexual problem, they either accept it or take action to try and correct it. Should they choose the latter course, five scenarios are possible.

The first scenario is that the man tries to correct his problem himself. In his mind, to seek help from another person would force him to admit he was not a good lover and would diminish his image of himself as a man. So instead of seeking help, he tries home remedies in an attempt to delay his ejaculatory response. During sexual pleasuring he tries to disassociate his mind from the sexual activity. He concentrates on what happened during the day at work, the events of a recent holiday, a film or television programme he has seen, or a book he has read, or he may try to do complicated mathematical problems. But he usually finds that the strategies fail to stop him from coming. Then he tries to use physical pain to distract his mind from his problem. He bites his cheek, he pinches himself, he contracts the muscles around his anus in an attempt to delay his urge to ejaculate.

If he is a sensitive lover he realizes that his sexual dysfunction is diminishing his partner's sexual pleasure. To delay his orgasm he asks her to ignore him while he tries to bring her to the edge of orgasm. Then, he reasons, he can insert his penis into her vagina in the hope that she will come before he does. Usually it does not work because her obvious arousal is a signal to him and he cannot stop himself coming prematurely.

This is the essence of his problem. He cannot prevent himself reaching the stage of sexual arousal when an orgasm is inevitable.

The second scenario is for the man to reduce his sexual anxiety by reducing his sexual activity. He argues that if he does not have sex, he will not ejaculate prematurely and will not feel he is a sexual failure.

The third scenario is one in which he becomes increasingly anxious, but he is uncertain what to do and is unable to talk with his sexual partner because of his inhibitions. To avoid increasing his anxiety he becomes impotent.

The fourth scenario is one in which the frustrations increase, hostility appears, and the couple separate.

In the fifth scenario, professional help is sought. The nature of the help varies. The wife may seek psychiatric help as she believes that if only she could reach orgasm rapidly the problem would be solved. Unfortunately, such an approach is palliative at best, damaging at worst. She may suggest, on the other hand, that her husband seeks professional help. This solution, although directed to the main problem, is also a poor one.

Another two choices exist. The first is for the woman to obtain sexual release with another partner, either male or female, which is scarcely conducive to harmony. The second choice is for the *couple* to seek professional help. This is the only solution which will permit the relationship to continue and which offers a guarantee that the man's problem can be corrected.

*

The most reliably reported study of the treatment of premature ejaculation is that of Dr Masters and Dr Johnson in St. Louis. In the past fourteen years they have treated over 200 couples whose main sexual problem was that of premature ejaculation, with only four failures.

The programme initiated by Masters and Johnson at the Reproductive Biology Research Foundation is fairly complex. They believe that as most forms of sexual dysfunction are learned (because of anxiety-provoking sexual experiences), they can be unlearned, and a new and better sexuality, more harmonious and pleasure-giving, can replace the older sexual dysfunction. They are convinced that sexual dysfunction is a problem to be solved by the couple and that it can never be solved by treating only one partner. They are certain that in all sexual problems there is no uninvolved partner. For cure, both partners need to be involved. They believe additionally that, particularly in sexual dysfunction in the male, fear of inadequate sexual performance is not only a threat to his psyche but to his masculinity. Men with premature ejaculation fear that their performance is inadequate compared with that of other men, and that they are 'lousy lovers'. Masters and Johnson also believe that communication on sexual matters between the partners is essential. This communication is both verbal and non-verbal.

In Dr Masters's clinic the first four days are arranged so that the couple can learn about their sexual anatomy and sexual function. They talk to each other about sexual matters. They learn to touch each other and to pleasure each other. Only when these preliminaries have been completed does the specific therapy for the specific problem begin. During the preliminary phase, the time given to 'sensate focus' exploration is especially important. In the later stages of this period, the woman is encouraged to find out which form of genital stimulation the man most appreciates. He may prefer her to caress his penis with her fingers, or with her mouth, or to place his penis between her breasts. If this stimulation leads to ejaculation it does not matter, for the couple are exploring each other's bodies and minds. At this stage, the man is instructed to be selfish and pay no attention to the woman's sexual needs. Instead, he must concentrate exclusively on the pleasurable erotic sensations coming from his stimulated penis. He shuts his eyes, he keeps his hands still, and he concentrates on his erotic fantasies and on what he is feeling. In this way, the threat to his sexuality is reduced, as he knows that the woman is happily helping him to overcome his sexual problem, which will in turn help her to obtain greater sexual joy.

The method described is in direct contrast to that used by earlier therapists who believed that a man with premature ejaculation should not be touched during foreplay, and in intercourse should direct his mind from his sexual performance by thinking about non-erotic matters, Their success rate was low.

The couple are now ready for sex-play and genital stimulation to retrain the man so that he can delay his climax. Masters and Johnson recommend that the woman can best stimulate the man's penis if she sits, her back against the headboard of the bed, her legs spread out, with her husband lying on his back facing her, his body between her legs, his legs over hers, but the couple should use the position they find most pleasing. Whatever position is chosen it must give the woman a free, gentle, and ready access to the man's genital area. First, she stimulates his penis to a good erection and then uses the 'squeeze technique' suggested in 1969 by Dr James Semans. The idea is that as sexual tension mounts in the man and as he feels his climax approaching, he signals the woman to stop stimulating his penis, and to reduce his need to ejaculate by squeezing his penis firmly, just below the glans. The woman's thumb presses on the frenulum, and her first and second finger give counter-pressure just below the coronal ridge. If the woman presses firmly in this way for about 3 to 5 seconds, the man loses the urge to ejaculate, provided he has not reached the phase of inevitable ejaculation. Quite quickly he learns to anticipate this, and is able to signal his partner to start the squeeze technique just before the phase is reached. She must press or squeeze firmly, or it will not stop him ejaculating. She will not hurt her partner's penis; it is much less delicate than many people imagine. This applies equally to stimulating a man's penis. It can be gripped firmly and masturbated vigorously. If the woman believes she is squeezing or manipulating her man's penis too hard, all she has to do is to ask him. He will tell her!

With the squeeze, the urge to ejaculate goes. The woman now waits until the man feels no desire to ejaculate, but still has an erection. Then, at his signal, she again stimulates his penis, again waiting for his signal to stop, and again preventing him from ejaculating by using the squeeze technique at the appropriate time.

The period of stimulation, then squeeze, then restimulation is made over 15 to 20 minutes of sex-play; until the man decides that he would like to go on to orgasm. Most couples manage quite quickly to 'start and stop' for four or five times before the man has an orgasm.

The objective of the stimulation-squeeze-restimulation is to help the man to identify a state of sexual excitement, which he can sustain, without the need to go into the next phase of sexual tension release, namely orgasm and ejaculation. In other words, it helps him to perceive when he reaches the late plateau phase, and to retrain his higher brain centre to re-establish control over the ejaculatory reflex.

Once the couple have found that the man can control his need to

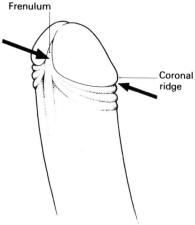

21 The squeeze technique

ejaculate for five stimulations at each session of sex-play, they are ready to try having sexual intercourse. The woman straddles the man and puts his penis in her vagina. Once it is inside she does not move, for the object of this training period is to let the man learn the feeling of his penis in a non-demanding, non-threatening female vagina. The couple are learning to communicate. It is likely, at this early stage of therapy, that if the woman starts thrusting with her pelvis, the man will ejaculate. If he begins to feel he is going to come, he tells her and she gently lifts herself off his penis and uses the squeeze technique to reduce the urge. She can then remount him and sit motionless on him, so that he learns he need not fear he will ejaculate once his penis is in a vagina. Masters and Johnson claim that after three sessions of the female-superior coital position most men will be able to keep their penis in the woman's vagina for 15 minutes without ejaculating. The relearning process is becoming effective.

After a few experiences of motionless vaginal containment, the man learns to thrust just sufficiently to maintain his erection but not to bring him to orgasm.

Alternatively, if the couple get greater pleasure in this way, the woman may thrust gently and in a non-demanding way against her man. Or they can vary the technique, sometimes one being the active partner, sometimes the other.

The couple are now ready for the final phase of the relearning programme. They adopt the lateral position for sexual intercourse instead of the female-superior position. The man is now ready to be the active sexual partner without the fear that he will ejaculate prematurely. In the lateral position he is less dominant and aggressive, and he has better ejaculatory control, so that sexual intercourse can be prolonged. Before they have sex in the new position, they should engage in sexual pleasuring and the woman should use the squeeze technique about three times before she accepts the man's penis in her vagina.

By now – between three and five weeks since they first sought help – the couple are ready to use any sexual position they prefer, but if they choose the male-superior position, the woman may need to use the squeeze technique first, so that the hidden anxiety that premature ejaculation will recur is reduced.

Some therapists recommend that for the next twelve months the woman should use the squeeze technique every third time the couple have sexual intercourse; but at other times they have the freedom to experiment and adopt whichever sexual position most pleases them. A useful time for reinforcing the new sexual learning is during the time the woman is menstruating. At this time, each month, the couple should have one period of 15 to 20 minutes of sex-play when the woman uses the stimulation-squeeze-restimulation technique.

It may seem that throughout the course of remedial sexual exercises the erotic needs of the woman have been ignored. To some extent they have, as the purpose of the exercises is to enable the man to learn 'to last longer'.

But there is no reason why the man should not help his partner reach orgasm before or after he has ejaculated, by stimulating her clitoris with his fingers or tongue, or by whatever method most pleasures her. This is a matter of communication between the partners.

Communication is important, as many men who are premature ejaculators are unwilling (or unable) to bring their sexual partner to orgasm.

The researchers in St. Louis have found that when the couple followed their therapeutic programme, the woman obtained increased sexual satisfaction. The couple were no longer so inhibited when they talked to each other and touched each other, so the tensions were reduced. As the woman became involved in correcting her partner's sexual problem, she obtained psychological pleasure in the obvious improvement, and became less tense about her own sexuality. During the period of immobility when she sat with the man's penis quietly contained in her vagina, she was actively involved in sexual intercourse. Before this, often through the entire relationship, she had been a pressed-upon, inferior, inert, recipient of an urgent, rapidly completed sexual assault. Now, for perhaps the first time, she had sexual freedom and sexual responsibility and, by helping her partner to cure his premature ejaculation, she obtained pleasure because he lasted longer before ejaculating.

Ejaculatory incompetence or retarded ejaculation

In this type of sexual disability, which is not as common as premature ejaculation, the man is sexually aroused, he gets an erection easily, he wants and enjoys sexual intercourse, but he is unable to reach orgasm and ejaculate despite prolonged thrusting in his partner's vagina.

Delay in reaching orgasm, despite vigorous movement of the penis within the vagina, happens to most men at some time or other during their lives, but a man who has ejaculatory incompetence is unable to reach orgasm no matter how hard and how often he tries. He has no difficulty in obtaining and maintaining an erection, but despite fantasy, sweat, and perhaps tears, despite a prolonged period of trying, he just cannot come. During this period, his partner may have one or many orgasms. She might find the sexual experience particularly pleasant, except for her concern about her partner's sexual problem.

Other women interpret the man's inability to reach orgasm and ejaculate differently. The man's failure to climax is perceived by her as rejection, or she believes she is an inadequate lover because she has failed to stimulate him enough.

In some cases both partners 'fake'. The man 'fakes' an ejaculation (which leaves him frustrated, although he can often get an orgasm by masturbating later). The woman 'fakes' that she believes he has ejaculated, although she knows that he has not. Eventually, both are found out, and neither is helped by the deception.

The degree of the ejaculatory incompetence varies. Some men can ejaculate normally with one woman, but fail to climax with another, particularly if the man feels anxiety or guilt about the relationship or is hostile to, or bored with, his partner. Other men, after much effort, get the feeling that they are about to ejaculate, but in place of an intense pleasurable orgasm find that the semen seeps instead of spurting out of the penis, so that the man feels that he had an unsatisfactory climax. This pattern is not unusual if a man is preoccupied, or tired, or in conflict with his partner, although in such cases the inability to ejaculate is usually transient.

Occasional ejaculatory incompetence is of no consequence. It may even make for sexual joy, provided the partners are able to talk to each other about it. Persistent ejaculatory incompetence is a sexual dysfunction, although surprisingly, many of the men can climax if the woman stimulates the penis with her fingers or mouth. In other men, the anxiety about being unable to ejaculate creates such a mental conflict that they either avoid sex or become impotent.

Some men with ejaculatory incompetence have had a particularly rigid upbringing with a dominant mother whose stern religious views that sex is dirty were stressed repeatedly throughout their childhood. This adverse background is usually overcome by later, more realistic attitudes towards sex, but a few men remain frozen in their childhood view of sex. This attitude may be reinforced by a traumatic sexual experience in adult life, which confirms in the man's mind that sex is unpleasant.

A sternly moralistic upbringing may also lead to the man's inability to express any emotions. He has been taught (or has learned) to control his emotions, particularly anger, which he suppresses. He also tends to avoid emotional closeness with his partner,.although he feels an 'obligation' to please her.

A few men with the disorder fear that if they ejaculate within their partner's vagina, she will become pregnant. The man may fear that a pregnancy – and more particularly, a baby – will lead to a conflict in the woman's mind, and reduce her devotion to him. These men are immature in their personal relations and need help to establish better communication with their partners.

A study of case reports shows that a variety of conflicts can cause ejaculatory incompetence. These include the belief, due to a strict religious upbringing, that sex is 'dirty'; conflicts from a real or imagined 'power game' with the partner; conflicts over the fear that the man will be abandoned by his partner unless he is a sexual superman; conflicts from the memory of a traumatic sexual experience; or conflicts from a fear of failure, occasioned by a transient inability to ejaculate, which, as I have mentioned, is normal.

Any of these conflicts can cause a suppressed anxiety about the man's ability to perform sexually which, in turn, stimulates the brain sex centre to send messages which damp down, or inhibit, the ejaculatory reflex in the spine.

Most of the men can ejaculate when they masturbate and some do this to obtain release from sexual tension. This ability is the basis of therapy.

The aim of therapy is for the man's sexual partner to pleasure him and, by masturbation, bring him to orgasm and ejaculation. In this way, with a helpful partner, he is able to escape from his psychological 'fix'.

The first step in correcting the sexual dysfunction is for the couple to learn about normal sexuality. As with premature ejaculators, this is done in joint discussions with trained therapists and by the exercise programme described earlier.

Usually the therapist suggests to the couple that they have sexual intercourse so that the wife reaches orgasm, if she so wishes. Then the couple are instructed that the wife is to pleasure the man, stimulating him sexually, until he wants to be masturbated. She then stimulates his penis and genital area in whichever way pleases him most, either with her hand or mouth or with a vibrator. In this way he is able to reach orgasm and ejaculate in a way which is neither threatening nor causes anxiety.

After a few experiences of this kind, the man usually finds he can ejaculate more quickly, and he is now ready for the next stage of retraining.

In this stage the man is stimulated to a high level of sexual desire, until he reaches the first part of the orgasmic phase when ejaculation is nearly inevitable. At this moment, in the female-superior position, the woman slips his penis into her vagina, continuing to stimulate it manually at the same time. Once his penis is inside her, she thrusts actively against him. Usually this is sufficient to produce his orgasm, but should it fail to occur quickly, she lifts herself off the man and begins to stimulate his penis with her hand once again. As his sexual urge rises to the stage of ejaculatory inevitability, he tells her and she again mounts him. If he ejaculates during the process it does not matter, at least for the first few times, for he is learning that he is able to ejaculate near, if not within, a vagina. His psychological block is beginning to break, and soon he will be able to ejaculate within the woman's vagina. Once he feels confident, he can adopt the man-on-top position, and his problem has ceased.

It will be obvious that ejaculatory incompetence is the obverse of premature ejaculation. In both instances the man gets an erection. In premature ejaculation he comes too quickly, while if he has ejaculatory incompetence he cannot come at all. But, at least, in both types of sexual disorder an erection can be obtained. The impotent man is not so lucky.

10

Lack of sexual desire and erectile failure

Cure of erectile failure is certain when the man:
Abandons himself to the joy of sexual intercourse
Stops worrying about his sexual performance
Stops being overconcerned about satisfying his partner
Stops being obsessive about his problem
Begins to be 'selfish' in love.

A LOSS OF INTEREST IN SEX, OR INHIBITED SEXUAL DESIRE, has recently been identified as a major sexual problem which affects both men and women. In most of the reported cases, the individual is married. Inhibited sexual desire may be general, when the person has no sexual desire for another, or it may be situational. In this form the person has no sexual desire for one person – often the marriage partner – but is sexually aroused by and can perform sexually with other partners.

A man who has inhibited sexual desire no longer desires sexual intercourse and, if his partner seeks to stimulate him, remains sexually unaroused. In most of the reported cases, inhibited sexual desire occurs after some years of marriage, but it may occur early in marriage. Unmarried men are not commonly affected. Many men complaining of the sexual problem are under the age of 40, and some are in their twenties, but the condition can affect men of all ages.

Investigation into inhibited sexual desire suggests that it may be due in some cases to a hidden hostility towards the man's partner and in other cases to boredom, the couple having fallen into a routine pattern of life, in which everything, including sex, is predictable. In some cases, the man may lose his interest in sex with his wife because she seems to be devoting all her time to their children, or to her career; in other cases he may be guilty about an extramarital affair and the guilt may make him lose his desire for the wife he has 'wronged'. An alternative theory is that some men lose interest in sex with their wife because they *want* to have an affair. If they find that they have no sexual desire at home they rationalize that it is justifiable to have extramarital sex.

In a few cases, illnesses, such as diabetes and hepatitis, high blood pressure and drugs used to treat it, or alcoholism, may be the reason for the man's inhibited sexual desire, but most cases are due to a failure in the relationship between the couple. An example of this is the man who complained of inhibited sexual desire. During talks with his therapist, he gave the information that he 'was turned off by his wife because she had stopped bothering about her appearance and had become a slob'. He had failed to notice that he had developed a beer-belly and was spending more time drinking in the pub. He was asked if he had tried to talk with his wife about their problems and replied that it 'wouldn't do any good'. The therapist suggested that the couple should talk, each asking the other to say what annoyed them, and the problem was resolved.

In many cases of inhibited sexual desire such simple techniques, or the 'sensate focus' and pleasuring techniques outlined in Chapter 8, do not work and psychotherapy has to be used. Unfortunately, even psychotherapy fails to help at least half those who have this problem.

Inhibited sexual desire obviously inhibits sexual arousal and consequently a man fails to obtain an erection. Because the man's sexual desire is inhibited, the emotional distress caused is likely to be less than if a man has normal sexual desire, is sexually aroused but, in spite of this, is unable to achieve an erection or to sustain it for long enough for him to insert his erect penis into his partner's vagina. His erectile failure may make him feel that his masculinity is suspect or that he is an incomplete man, a failure. He believes himself to be impotent. When this occurs, his image of himself as a man diminishes and anxieties about his self-image increase.

Impotence is an unfortunate term as it implies that the man is a complete sexual failure. This is not necessarily true, as apart from his inability to achieve an erection, the man may be as sexually successful as previously. He may be able to show affection, to enjoy body contact, and to relate to his partner sexually, except for his particular disability. However, the word impotence has become embedded in the language, and continues to be used. Impotence may affect men of all ages, of all classes, and of all races: it can affect a bishop or a butcher, a doctor or a docker, a lawyer or a lecher.

The degree of impotence and the time when it occurs during sexual arousal are quite variable. At some time or other, under some special condition, most men fail to get an erection, despite sexual arousal. The problem does not last long and should cause no concern. It becomes serious when the man fails to get an erection even with the most sexually arousing pleasuring, or when he gets an erection when sexually aroused, only to lose it when he tries to have intercourse. Some men can get an erection with one woman, and fail to do so with another woman. Some men can get an erection by masturbating, or during oral sex, but cannot when they try to have sexual intercourse. This can be enormously frustrating to both partners.

An impotent man who is unable to get an erection may believe that his sexual partner, who is usually his wife, is disgusted with his diminished masculinity, talks about his masculine inadequacy to her friends, may seek sexual release with other men, and generally belittles him. The vicious circle of failure to achieve an erection causes anxiety, which is increased the harder he tries, and the harder he tries the more he fails.

Table 7 Diseases and drugs which may be associated with impotence

Drugs which may cause impotence:	*Diseases which may be associated with impotence:*
● alcohol	● diabetes
● opiates	● hepatitis
● some drugs used to treat depression	● thyroid disease
● some drugs used to treat high blood pressure (clonidine, methyldopa, reserpine)	● some forms of pituitary disease
	● severe depression
	● debilitating diseases

A number of men become impotent because of illness or because of the treatment required for an illness. Diabetes often causes impotence, and certain drug treatments for high blood pressure may produce impotence. Alcohol, taken excessively over the years, is often associated with impotence. The reason for this is not clear, but it may be because of liver damage.

A few impotent men have low circulating levels of the male sex hormone, testosterone. This may account for the increasing number of men who become impotent as they grow older. At the age of 40 about 1 per cent of men are impotent, by the age of 70 it has increased to 25 per cent. It is not clear if this increase is due to a lack of testosterone in older men, or to the prevalent belief that old people do not 'indulge' in sex.

Most impotent men have no disease and are not taking any drugs. They fail to obtain or sustain an erection for psychological reasons, which induce the brain to send messages to the spinal cord inhibiting the erection. In many cases, the impotence is due to guilt or anxiety about sex, which may have originated in a sexually repressed childhood, when the boy learnt that sex was to be equated with sin, shame, or lust. In other cases the anxiety may be due to marital disharmony. A destructive marital relationship can cause impotence, and conversely impotence can cause a destructive

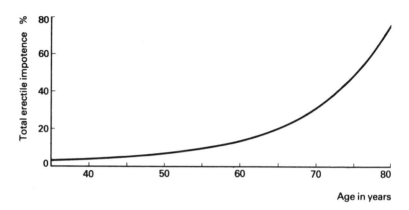

22 The increasing frequency of erectile impotence with age as determined by Kinsey in 1948

relationship. The anxiety can also turn into depression, which in turn can lead to impotence, when the man feels that nothing is worth while. Conversely, depression can be caused by impotence as, in our culture, a man who cannot get an erection loses his self-esteem, and may feel that because of his sexual failure he will lose his sexual partner.

The anxiety which leads to impotence may be due to a set-back in a job. A competitive, ambitious man may become severely insecure and depressed when an anticipated promotion does not occur. Since in American culture 'making it' has both occupational and sexual connotations, the man who fails to make it in his job may also fail to make it sexually. He may become impotent.

A new development has occurred in the past decade which is said to threaten a man's sexual self-esteem. This is the effect of women's liberation on men brought up traditionally who believe in the double standard of sexuality. They have learnt that women need sex less than men, but should always be sexually available and relatively submissive.

When a woman asks for equality in sex, when she shows that she is not sexually submissive, when she makes sexual demands on the man, he may see this as a threat to his masculinity. If the couple can talk about their sexuality, the threat recedes, but many vulnerable men cannot. The threat is magnified and the man becomes impotent, to avoid the anxiety of having to perform sexually at a woman's request.

Many men, however, whose childhood attitudes to, and experiences of, sexuality are identical with those of men who become impotent are able to perform well sexually with a liberated partner. This must mean that anxiety about a woman's sexuality only causes impotence in men who are especially sensitive or vulnerable about their sexuality.

*

There are two types of impotence. In the first, the man has never been able to obtain or maintain an erection and consequently has never been able to have sexual intercourse. This is called primary impotence. In the second type, the man has enjoyed sexual intercourse, and has had firm erections, but finds that he can no longer achieve an erection or have sex.

Primary impotence is caused, most frequently, by a strictly moralistic rearing in which sex, except for procreation, is thought evil. The story of Ron demonstrates this. Ron was a man of 24 who had married at 22 and had consistently failed to achieve an erection. He was a serious man who had been brought up by strict parents of firm, almost fundamental, religious convictions. As an adolescent boy he had had wet dreams and had been punished by his father for self-abuse. His bed was inspected each morning after the episode for further evidence of his evil sexual indulgences. He had obtained no information about sex, beyond the opinion that it was dirty, should only take place between married people and then only to procreate children. Within the family his mother had been dominant, and her influence over Ron was marked. He had had no sexual contacts before marriage and, in fact, very few dealings with girls. He had met his wife at a church social. She was as sexually inexperienced as he was. Their courtship had been austere in the extreme, and the maximum body contact between them had been to hold hands and occasionally to exchange a chaste kiss. The honeymoon was a disaster. Both partners lacked sexual knowledge, both were tense, both believed that sexual indulgence was carnal, not spiritual. After two years of futile attempts to have sexual intercourse, Ron sought help.

*

A dominant mother, who is strictly religious and believes sex to be evil, is not the only background pattern found in men who have primary impotence. Childhood experiences, and attempted coital episodes in adolescence, can lead to a personal sexual insecurity, which is equally destructive to a man's masculine self-image. Homosexual preference, in which the man has either been the passive partner, or imagines himself as the passive partner, can lead to impotence when, either to please a dominant mother, or to try to find a gender-identity, the man marries.

The end-result of these various pathways is that the man develops anxiety and tension to such a degree that his sexual performance is suppressed. He becomes impotent.

*

The background of a man who becomes secondarily impotent is rather different, although many of these men have had a strict upbringing in which sex was either not mentioned or said to be dirty.

Most men who have secondary impotence develop the disorder as a result of persistent anxiety that they fail to meet what is considered in our culture a 'normal' sexual performance. Premature ejaculation, for example, is a relatively common antecedent of secondary impotence. This is the reason why premature ejaculation is erroneously classed as impotence by many sexologists. It is not. However, the anxiety of the premature ejaculator that he is failing regularly as a lover, and that he is less virile than his fellows, can lead to a psychological retreat from sexual contact, which is typified by impotence.

Harold was in his mid-thirties when he sought help for secondary impotence, which had begun two years previously. His first sexual experience had been when he was in the army. He and twenty of his mates had visited a brothel and had queued up for the two available prostitutes. His urgency, and her desire to get to the next client, had established a rapid ejaculatory pattern which had persisted in his other pre-marital sexual experiences. Once married, his rapid ejaculation had been accepted by his wife as a transient adjustment phase. However, its persistence had nagged her and although she was occupied with their three children, she eventually sounded out her married friends about their sexual experiences. The result was destructive. Most of them enjoyed sex, and often reached orgasm.

She complained tentatively to Harold, who tried various home remedies, but without any real success. Eventually, his wife reached breaking point and in a domestic row, triggered by a trivial incident, she told Harold that 'he couldn't care less about her sexual tensions, or he wouldn't come so quickly'.

Harold tried even harder to avoid ejaculating prematurely, and failed. The tension mounted, and he sought excuses to avoid having to try and fail. He began to work late, to claim exhaustion from overwork at the office, and to say that he was not feeling well. His wife, increasingly anxious, induced him to see a doctor about his tiredness. In the interview the doctor did not enquire about Harold's sexual relations, and Harold was too embarrassed to mention that he had a sexual problem. The doctor checked him thoroughly and found him fit. He suggested a holiday, gave him some vitamin pills, and forgot him.

The tensions within the marriage increased, and finally the breaking point was reached. One night Harold's wife sought sexual intercourse with him when he was emotionally drained and deeply concerned by his sexual failure. The encounter was a disaster. Harold failed to achieve an erection. His wife tried to comfort him and to convince him it was only because he was tired, but on the next occasion he failed again. His anxiety about his sexual performance increased each time he failed to get an erection. Each failure aggravated his anxiety about failing.

*

Secondary impotence may be due to stress and fatigue, particularly if associated with a heavy use of alcohol. This is shown by the case of Tom.

Tom is an advertising executive whose job demands that he entertain a good deal. He is not averse to this for he enjoys the company, the food, and the drink. Tom is not an alcoholic, but he drinks a good deal. His wife is considered to be an asset to his career. They used to enjoy sex in the early years of their marriage. Recently, because of the frequent parties, and the alcohol, their sexual encounters have been less frequent. All too often, Tom has fallen into a deep sleep the moment his head has hit the pillow – and next morning has been hung-over.

One night after a long lunch engagement, at which his friends were in top form, and an evening party, at which he was in top form,

Tom and his wife drive home. More accurately, Tom's wife drives home, as Tom is tight. But tight or not, he decides that tonight he is going to be the male sex expert. He will fix their marriage with a good 'screw'.

When they get home he pours a beer for himself while his wife puts the car in the garage. She has been somewhat terse in the car, for Tom's 'top form' has irritated her and she has been embarrassed by it. While Tom is drinking his beer she goes to bed.

After a while Tom follows, still alcoholically intent on proving his virility. A sleepy wife sleepily submits to Tom's advances, and nothing happens. Tom fails to get an erection.

Over the next few days, he notices a coolness in his relationship with his wife, and assumes it is because of what he did at the party (he cannot remember what), although he vaguely remembers he failed in bed.

He does not talk about it with his wife, but decides he will prove to her that their marriage is in spendid order and that he is a great lover. First, he buys her some flowers, and then decides that perhaps it might be a good idea to have a couple of drinks before he goes home and perhaps a bottle of wine with dinner. The evening is a success. His wife is pleased with the flowers, has forgiven her husband, and is sexually stimulated by him, so that she is keen to have sex when they get to bed.

The result is bitter, traumatic failure. Tom, who is anxious about his sexual performance, has also had just too much alcohol, so that he is depressed, rather than stimulated, by it. He again fails to get an erection, and his anxiety is magnified.

Communication between the couple ceases. Tom wonders if his problem has happened to any of his friends, and tries to find out, with no success. He visits his doctor, convinced that his sexual failure is due to illness, only to find he is healthy. (He does not mention his erectile failure and his doctor does not enquire if he has a sexual problem.)

By now Tom is very anxious about his sexuality. He feels that the only way he can avoid the emotional trauma of failure is to avoid sex. He increases his work-load, he increases his alcohol consumption, he develops an addiction for late-night television and for early-morning jogging – anything to avoid being put in a situation of needing to get an erection. Meanwhile, his wife begins to wonder if he has a mistress, or whether she no longer attracts him because she is growing old. She becomes suspicious and irritable, and to try to prove that Tom still loves her, makes tentative demands that they have sex. But neither of them discusses their problem, each is too concerned with his or her own reaction, and besides is embarrassed to talk about sex.

Tom avoids his wife's sexual advances, finding excuses because he is afraid he will fail once again. After a period of rejection, she decides that she too will become sexually celibate. It is too traumatic to be rejected.

All communication between the couple ceases. They avoid physical contact, and avoid verbal expressions of affection. They have become isolated, unhappy, and anxious. And Tom is increasingly anxious about his impotence. It is to be hoped that at this point he will seek help.

Table 8 Mental exercises which may help an impotent man

- Learn to relax by deep breathing and muscle relaxation. Go limp, don't think.
- Stop worrying about your partner's reaction to your 'performance'. Ask her. She'll tell you she wants to help you, not to criticize you.
- Stop worrying about your own erection. Let it happen: don't wonder if you'll get an erection, or if you do, if it will be a poor, limp effort.
- Dive into fantasy! Imagine a sexual situation in which you are the hero. Have fun with your imagination – forget your penis!

*

I have stressed the psychological causes of impotence, but I must also stress that these should not be accepted until an impotent man has been checked physically to make sure that he has no disease which may cause impotence. A physical check and a careful history will exclude diabetes, high blood pressure, alcoholism, drugs, and those nervous diseases which cause impotence; and impotence resulting from extensive pelvic surgery. Tests on the blood and urine will exclude diabetes, liver damage, and low levels of testosterone, or perhaps raised levels of another hormone called prolactin. In most studies of impotent men between 10 and 20 per cent have a physical cause, but the majority of men are found to be free from disease or drugs.

Another way of differentiating between impotence due to disease and that caused by psychological problems is to find out if a man gets nocturnal erections. In men who normally get erections and men who are impotent for psychological reasons, erections occur about every ninety minutes during sleep. The erections coincide with rapid eye movements (REM sleep). Men whose impotence is due to physical disease get no or few erections during REM sleep. If an impotent man is prepared to be investigated in this way, it can be established if his impotence is due to physical disease or to psychological problems, and this knowledge makes treatment easier.

The investigation is simple and painless. The man spends a night in a room in the laboratory, and a soft band is placed around his penis. This is connected to a recording instrument. When he has an erection during sleep, the band is stretched and the erection is recorded. The next morning the results are discussed with the staff and advice is given.

Because impotence may be an early sign of disease, a man who develops this distressing sexual dysfunction should seek medical help and should not be embarrassed or ashamed to admit that he has become impotent. There is definite evidence that the earlier impotence is treated, the better the success rate. Once his doctor has excluded any serious disease, the man can then receive treatment for his sexual dysfunction.

The desire to increase sexual function, and especially to relieve impotence, is of great antiquity, as is the use of drugs. Over the centuries a variety of treatments have been advocated for impotence. The fact that there have been so many suggests that none has been successful. One drug, of particular interest in Asia, is rhinoceros horn. Powdered rhinoceros horn was used as an aphrodisiac, particularly to reverse 'waning sexual strength'. Its use is an example of sympathetic medicine, which has a long history. The horn of a rhinoceros resembles an erect penis. Therefore the failure to obtain an erection could be overcome by drinking powdered rhinoceros horn.

Throughout the centuries the desire to make money out of other people's suffering has induced smart operators to sell a wide, and apparently increasing, variety of drugs. The drugs have followed fashions. One hundred years ago in the U.S.A. the chosen remedy was snake oil (notice the sympathetic medicine). Today vitamin E is said to help.

The truth is that none of the many drugs which have been

available has any effect, except a psychological one, upon impotence.

Perhaps a more scientific treatment, but usually no more successful than other treatments, is to give an impotent man a series of injections of the male sex hormone (androgen) in the form of methyltestosterone. The argument is that a man's libido is due to the androgens which circulate in his blood and stimulate the sex centre in his brain. If his libido is reduced, as evidenced by his inability to obtain an erection, injections of androgens will stiffen him up! Large quantities of testosterone have been given by injection to impotent men with no improvement, except that due to the psychological effect of an injection. Unfortunately, few of the enthusiasts have used a scientific approach – that of the double blind trial. In a double blind trial of a drug, a series of injections (or tablets) are made up, one half containing the drug under test, and the other half containing an innocuous substance, which is indistinguishable in appearance, taste, or feel from the drug under test.

Only when the trial has been completed is the key broken and it is disclosed which patients have been given the drug and which the placebo. The purpose of a double blind trial of a drug is to reduce the bias from psychological influences, and to try objectively to evaluate the value of a drug. Psychological influences are so significant that they must be excluded. An example of their influence is shown by the experience of a group of women who were all taking the pill. A number complained of side-effects of such magnitude that they wished to change the brand of pill they were taking. They were granted their wish and given a brand of pill which was beautifully packaged. Immediately most of the unpleasant side-effects disappeared. It was obvious to the women that the new pill was better than the old one. Unfortunately, there was a flaw in their feeling. The new pill was identical in chemical composition with the old one – only the name and the package were different.

Few investigations using a double blind trial have been made in treating impotence by using male hormones, and of those which have, most have shown no significant improvement among impotent men given testosterone, unless the impotence was due to disease.

Recently it has been clear why this is so. It is now possible to measure the levels of testosterone circulating in the blood with considerable accuracy. Dr Lawrence and Dr Swyer, who conduct the endocrinology clinic in University College Hospital in London, found no difference in the circulating levels of testosterone between impotent men with normal genitals and men who were not impotent. Low testosterone levels were only found among men whose impotence was associated with a disease of the pituitary gland which prevents the normal development of the genitals at puberty. Very few impotent men have low blood testosterone levels. However, if they have, their impotence may respond to testosterone injections, or tablets of a special form of testosterone. These men tend to be old and, in their case, testosterone often works, although it is uncertain whether the hormone has a direct effect or whether the cure is due to the expectation that the drug will work.

More imaginative, if less aesthetic, has been the development of splints to treat impotence. It is the scientific equivalent of the old army gibe 'If your cock won't stand up, lash it to a toothbrush'. An original, if bizarre, suggestion was to implant the penile cartilage of a whale into the penis of a man. This experiment is said to have been attempted in Russia and has never been repeated! The disadvantages are obvious.

Penile splints of various kinds are available in sex aid shops and most are not much use. Essentially they are all similar, consisting of a metal strip covered with plastic and terminating at each end in a rubber ring – in fact, rather like a glorified toothbrush! The idea is that the penis is held erect by the appliance. It usually isn't.

Another type of appliance comes from Japan. If a man can manage some degree of erection, he slips his penis through the hole in a firm rubber ring which he then pushes down to the base of his penis where it fits tightly. The idea is that the pressure of the ring will prevent the blood draining out of his penis until the ring is released, and in this way his penis will fill with blood and become firm. It is also not very effective.

The most advanced of the penile splints was first made in England. It is called the Coitus Training Apparatus, and it is made to fit over the penis, so that the head of the penis protrudes. Some impotent men have found it helps considerably but, like all the other appliances, it is not the real answer, for the sexual disorder does not lie in the penis but in the anxious mind of the impotent man.

In the past decade, particularly in the U.S.A., surgeons have devised operations to help men whose erectile impotence is caused by disease, particularly diabetes and vascular disease. Two main surgical approaches have been made. In the first, a silastic (silicone) splint or prothesis, cut to the appropriate length, is inserted between the loose skin of the upper surface of the penis and the underlying cylinders. The penis containing the prothesis is no longer limp, and can be inserted into the vagina, but it is not a hard, erect penis and its size always remains constant. As the author of one report, Dr Pearman, says, it 'assists' but does not replace the other factors necessary for successful copulation.

The second method is to insert an implantable inflatable prothesis into the penis. The advantage of this is that the device can be inflated by squeezing a small bulb in the scrotum when the man wants to obtain a larger firmer penis. At other times the penis is small and limp.

The surgeons are enthusiastic about their results, claiming that their patients 'are the happiest people in the world'. But in very few instances have the partners of the men been asked what they think.

Sex is not just intercourse and the happiness of the treated men may be linked to the myth that it is. If the cause of the man's erectile failure is due to disease, and his sexual arousal is unaltered, penile implants have a significant place. But if the man's impotence is due to a failure to become sexually aroused, or is due to psychological disturbances, the surgery is likely to be followed by failure.

Unless the surgeon has sought information about these matters and has discussed the procedure with the man and his wife (or partner) before operation, the results are likely to be poor. The penile implant only helps a man obtain a penis which is sufficiently firm to insert into a woman's vagina. It produces neither an orgasm nor ejaculation, nor does it necessarily improve the woman's sexual pleasure – that will occur only if her man is able to respond to her sexual desires.

Microsurgery is an alternative surgical approach to help a man who has erectile impotence due to diabetes. In diabetes, narrowing of small arteries occurs, and if the arteries supplying the penis become narrow, the inflow of blood needed to fill the penile cylinders and produce an erection cannot occur. New microsurgical techniques are being developed which will, it is hoped, enable surgeons to cut out the narrow segments of the arteries supplying the penis and join the cut ends of the healthy arteries. These will then respond by dilating to sexual stimulation and the man will regain his ability to obtain an erection.

The problem in most cases of impotence is not in the man's penis but in his brain, in his perception of his sexuality. As impotence is most often due to anxiety and to the fear of failure to perform sexually, it is logical that help should be obtained from a psychiatrist or psychologist. Unfortunately, psychiatrists, like other people, are the product of their childhood and their training. Those who adhere to one school of psychiatry have contempt for those who adhere to other schools. This applies especially in the psychiatry of sexual dysfunction. Hell hath no fury like a Freudian frustrated!

Psychoanalysis, by uncovering childhood problems, frustrations, and unhappy relationships with parents, may relieve some impotent men, but the method is time consuming, expensive, and the results are not very good. The place for psychoanalysis seems to be in the treatment of problems which may arise during the course of sex therapy. Conventional psychiatry is even less successful in treating secondary impotence.

Because secondary impotence is much more a problem of adult anxiety and fear of sexual failure than of childhood trauma, two principles which underpin therapy have been stated by the behavioural psychologists, whose effectiveness in the therapy of secondary impotence seems greater than that of conventional psychiatrists and psychoanalysts.

The first axiom is that both sexual partners must be involved in the treatment of the man's sexual inadequacy.

The second axiom is that a man whose inability to achieve an erection has undermined his masculine self-image and destroyed his self-esteem must be convinced that he can get rid of his fear of failing sexually, and that sexual arousal will lead to erection. Neither sexual arousal nor erection can be willed or commanded. They occur as a spontaneous reaction to sexual desire and appropriate, effective stimulation. The impotent man has suppressed the reflex which normally produces an erection, by sending 'don't' messages from his brain sex centre. The brain sex centre in turn is receiving the 'don't' messages from the man's subconscious brain.

His fear of failing puts him in the position of a spectator of his own sexual performance, as well as being the actor. As a spectator he evaluates his own performance anxiously, while as an actor he strains to perform, he strains to get an erection – and he fails. The more he tries, the more he fails. In his spectator role, he criticizes himself subconsciously and becomes increasingly detached from involvement, because of the trauma his failure causes. Until he can become a full participant in sex, he will go on failing.

Table 9 Improving the chance of cure of impotence

Your chance of cure is greater if

- you have a helpful, co-operative, loving partner who wants to help you help yourself
- you want to be cured for your own pleasure, not just to please your partner
- you have the time to undertake the programme in a relaxed, quiet, unhurried manner
- you are not under stress or depressed because of your job or because of financial problems

It is obvious that the man who comes for treatment is far more personally insecure, and has far greater anxiety, than a man with one of the other sexual problems. His deep conviction that his manhood is suspect, and that he is a sexual failure, is augmented by his anxiety that other people will learn of his sexual inadequacy. He may fear that his wife has told her friends of his defective sexuality.

The man's partner is also frustrated. She has tried comfort, she has tried sympathy, she has tried aggression, in an effort to help her man, with no effect. She, too, becomes tense and anxious, as she thinks that his impotence is due to her lack of physical appeal, or that he is obtaining sexual relief with another woman while denying her any sexual experience. She may be worried that he is a latent homosexual.

The essence of the therapy is to restore the man's belief in his sexuality, not just to treat his symptoms of impotence. At the same time his partner's fears for her man's sexual ability need to be changed. Sex therapists seek to replace the fears by pleasure. They seek to enable the couple to re-establish that human sexual contact is pleasurable. They seek to enable the couple to re-establish (or to establish for the first time) communication with each other about sexual matters. They seek to remove inhibitions and childhood or adolescent hang-ups.

To remove the fears, to make the man an active participant, and to establish communication, the couple undergo a course of training. They learn about their problems in discussions with therapists, and they do sexual exercises. The therapist stresses that the ability to have an erection is as natural as any other physiological process – eating, breathing, or urinating – and that a man will respond by having an erection if the stimuli are the right ones and if the fear of failure is eliminated.

The exercises (which were described in Chapter 8) and the discussions with the therapist are needed for the cure of impotence. It is also essential for the man to have a medical examination to make sure there is no physical cause.

The differences between the treatment of premature ejaculators and impotent men are only minor. Obviously the squeeze technique is no longer appropriate, and equally obviously non-genital pleasuring is stressed more as, during this pleasuring, the man learns to become involved sexually, without the anxiety of having to perform well sexually.

Using these techniques more than 60 per cent of impotent men will be cured. In the future, other techniques may reinforce the ability of sexual therapists in curing a most distressing male sexual dysfunction.

11

Sexually transmitted diseases

He was the Voltaire of pelvic literature – a skeptic as to the morality of the race in general, who would have submitted Diana to treatment with his mineral specifics and ordered a course of blue pills for the Vestal Virgins.

Oliver Wendell Holmes, writing about Phillippe Record (1799–1889) a venereologist who differentiated syphilis and gonorrhoea

Curse great English dinners and military and civil clubs, all is drunkenness and pox afterwards with us.

Lord Herbert (1787)

It has pleased divine justice to give and send down upon us unknown afflictions, never seen nor recognised nor found in medical books, such as this serpentine disease . . . at the time that the Admiral don Xristoval Colon (Colombus) arrived in Spain, the Catholic sovereigns were in the city of Barcelona. And when they went to give them an account of the voyage and of what they had discovered, immediately the city began to be infected and the aforesaid disease spread as was seen later on through long experience.

Ruy Diaz de Isla, 'A Treatise on the Serpentine Disease' (syphilis), 1512

DISEASES WHICH ARE TRANSMITTED FROM PERSON TO person during sexual intercourse used to be called 'venereal diseases'. Today the preferred term is 'sexually transmitted diseases'. Venereal disease sounds dirty; and in many people's minds implies that a man has had sex with a prostitute.

Today it is known that a person is more likely to get one of the sexually transmitted diseases by having sex with a friend than by paying a prostitute.

There are at least eight diseases which are sexually transmitted and, initially, usually affect the genitals, although some of them, if not treated, can have serious effects on general health. The diseases are gonorrhoea, non-specific urethritis (NSU), syphilis, genital herpes, trichomoniasis, candidosis, genital warts, and chancroid.

Since most people have intercourse with a partner who is of the other sex, both men and women usually are infected with equal frequency. But there are some differences. NSU, for example, is a disease which infects men exclusively. Trichomoniasis and candidosis infect women much more commonly than men.

Syphilis and gonorrhoea are the most serious of the diseases as far as health is concerned. Syphilis, if untreated, can have devastating effects. Gonorrhoea, especially in women, can cause sterility, if it is not treated adequately. NSU is annoying, rather than serious, although it may cause arthritis in a few men. Trichomoniasis and candidosis, which mainly infect a woman's vagina, causing an irritating, uncomfortable discharge, are annoying, but not life-threatening. Men often do not even know that they have been infected.

The World Health Organisation has stated that the sexually transmitted diseases are now the most common group of diseases found in the world, and that gonorrhoea is the world's second most common infectious disease (only measles is more common). It has been estimated that over 200 million people are infected with gonorrhoea each year and over 50 million with syphilis. It is likely that NSU is increasing, and in some countries may now occur more frequently than gonorrhoea.

No one knows the number of people infected by trichomoniasis or by candidosis, or the number who have genital warts, but it is considerable.

Luckily, there is an effective treatment for each of the sexually transmitted diseases, which will give a complete cure – provided you follow the treatment properly.

Why has there been such an increase in the number of people infected by the sexually transmitted diseases in recent years? Why are so many young people, particularly women, becoming infected?

The first reason is that there is now an increasing sexual permissiveness. If a person only had sexual intercourse with a single partner it would be possible to eradicate the diseases. This situation has never existed. In the past there was a double standard of sexuality. Young men were expected (if not encouraged) to 'sow a few wild oats'. In other words, to have sexual experiences before they settled down. Young women, by contrast, were expected to have no experience and to be virgins at marriage. After marriage, men could continue to have sex with other women, but wives were expected to remain sexually faithful to their husbands.

In recent years, especially in Western nations, many women have rejected this double standard of sexuality. Adolescent girls, particularly, have become more active sexually, and so have adolescent males. Both sexes have more casual sex, in which there is no commitment, and they enjoy sex with a greater number of partners. The result has been an increase in the spread of sexually transmitted diseases, particularly gonorrhoea. This is because at least 50 per cent of women infected by men with gonorrhoea develop no symptoms, and consequently do not know that they have the disease. But they have and can spread it to infect their next sexual partner.

Another reason why the sexually transmitted diseases are spreading is because people are increasingly mobile. Work may take a person to a place where he (or she) has few friends. People increasingly take holidays in other countries.

In these unfamiliar places it is easy to make an acquaintance in a pub, a hotel, or a club, to have an exciting sexual experience – and to become infected with a sexually transmitted disease.

Sexually transmitted disease can infect a middle-aged business man, who got gonorrhoea when on a visit to another city, a sailor, or a long-distance truck driver, who is either denied a permanent companion, or separated from her for a long period; but the age group most likely to be infected are those aged 15 to 25.

Moralists may say that people should be chaste and avoid sexual contacts. The fact remains that people are not chaste and nine out of ten people, male or female, get gonorrhoea if they have sexual intercourse with a partner who has gonorrhoea. If they have sexual intercourse with a partner who has active syphilis they have one chance in three of being infected. And the more times they have intercourse with an infected partner the more likely they are to be infected.

Gonorrhoea

Gonorrhoea is an acute infection of the genito-urinary tract, and is almost always spread from person to person by sexual intercourse. In very rare cases it is spread by other methods. It can, for example, be spread from an infected mother to the eyes of her infant during childbirth.

The organism which causes gonorrhoea is a small bean-shaped germ called *Neisseria gonorrhoeae* (gonococcus), which is transferred from the urethra or from the entrance to the womb (the cervix) of an infected woman to the urethra of the man who is having sexual intercourse with her. If the man is homosexual it can be transferred during anal intercourse. Occasionally if the throat of the man's partner is infected with gonorrhoea, he may be infected during fellatio.

The urethra, the cervix, the rectum, and the throat are lined with a single layer of cells, which the gonococcus finds easy to penetrate, and, having established a base, it multiplies very quickly. The vagina, which is lined by several layers of cells, is not affected, as the gonococcus is unable to penetrate this wall of cells.

The gonococcus is a very fragile organism and dies very rapidly if it is not within the warm human body. Small falls in temperature kill it, and even if the infected discharge from a man's urethra contaminates clothes or other articles, those articles are rarely infectious, as drying quickly kills the gonococcus. For this reason the myth that you can get gonorrhoea from an infected towel, a lavatory seat, or infected clothing should be remembered for what it is – a myth!

You will know if you have been infected between 3 and 5 days after sexual intercourse. The first thing you notice is that you have developed discomfort or tingling in your urethra. Very quickly a discharge appears which is creamy, thick, and purulent, and which drips from your penis. You will also find that it is uncomfortable to pass urine and, when you do, you get a burning feeling in your urethra. The area around the eye of your penis is usually reddened, but you feel quite well apart from these symptoms. If you do not seek treatment, the infection spreads upwards along your urethra and, in 10 to 14 days, the part of the urethra nearest to your bladder becomes inflamed. When this happens, the burning and pain on passing urine increase, and you may feel unwell, with headaches or fever, due to absorption into your blood of toxic products from the infection.

If you do not seek treatment, the symptoms disappear in a few more days, or the disease spreads to involve organs which are adjacent to the urethra, particularly the prostate gland and the bladder, or even the testicles, where it causes an acute inflammation with a painful swelling and the chance of permanent damage which could cause sterility.

In the days before antibiotics were available, the only treatment for gonorrhoea was the use of local antiseptics. These were not very efficient and may have aggravated, rather than cured, the disease. In those days, the symptoms of chronic gonorrhoea commonly developed. The most common, the most painful one, was a narrowing, or stricture, of the posterior urethra. This led to difficulty in passing urine, or to the failure to pass urine at all. The treatment was painful, and consisted of pushing narrow metal or plastic rods along the urethra to try and stretch the narrowed portion. The operation was called dilatation of the urethral stricture, and the sufferer had to submit to this at frequent intervals.

In men, gonorrhoea is diagnosed by taking a specimen of the urethral discharge, and placing it on a slide. After appropriate staining, the slide is examined under a microscope, when clusters of bean-shaped gonococci, which seem to prefer to lie in pairs, are found inside pus cells. In women, the diagnosis is often more difficult and, when gonorrhoea is suspected, smears are usually taken from the woman's urethra, upper vagina, and cervix. These smears are placed on special glass dishes which contain a nutrient material and the dishes are heated, or incubated, for two days. In this way, any gonococci present will grow, and the growth will be seen on the material in the dish. If a specimen from this material is then examined under a microscope the typical bean-shaped germs of gonorrhoea can be identified.

With the diagnosis made, treatment can be started. If you have acquired gonorrhoea, you can help stop the disease spreading by persuading the person who infected you to be seen by a doctor so that she (or he) may be treated.

During treatment, you have to stop drinking alcohol, as this seems to lead to relapse; and, obviously, you must not have sexual intercourse, because you may infect your partner. Until the discharge ceases you should wash your hands after passing urine or defecating and should wash your genitals each day with soap and water, and dry them with a towel which nobody else uses.

You will also be given treatment. Today penicillin is the most efficient killer of gonococci, although increasing numbers are becoming relatively resistant to penicillin, so that higher and higher doses are needed to cure the disease. The reason for resistance is not clear, but it may be due to the abuse of penicillin, given in inadequate doses for inappropriate, or trivial, disorders over the past twenty years. By 1977, in many nations, between 20 and 40 per cent of all cases of gonorrhoea had become relatively resistant to normal doses of penicillin. It has also become increasingly obvious that the more simple the treatment the more effective it is. This has meant that new strategies have had to be developed.

Penicillin remains the treatment of choice for gonorrhoea, but medical research has discovered that penicillin is more effective in killing resistant gonococci if another drug is given at the same time. The usual method in the treatment of gonorrhoea is for the patient to take two tablets of this drug, called probenecid, either an hour before, or at the time of receiving the penicillin, and a further tablet 6, 12, and 18 hours later. Probenecid blocks the excretion of penicillin by the kidneys and so enables higher levels to be obtained in the blood. This gives penicillin a more lethal effect on the gonococcus. The penicillin is given as a single injection into a muscle, or else you take a number of capsules by mouth all at one go. In women who have gonorrhoea, and homosexual men who have a gonococcal infection of the rectum, a second injection of penicillin is sometimes given on the next day, and probenecid tablets are taken every 6 hours for two days. During treatment the doctor also takes a sample of blood to check for syphilis.

In most cases this treatment is curative, but since gonorrhoea may lurk in the body it is essential that you re-attend the doctor, or the hospital clinic, for follow-up. Seven days after receiving the penicillin you pass a specimen of urine, which is examined by the doctor, who also takes further smears from the urethra. In the case of homosexual men, specimens are taken from the rectum for examination. The smears are examined under a microscope and 'cultured' to make sure that no gonococci are present. Some men treated for gonorrhoea develop a urethral discharge between 5 and 25 days after receiving treatment. This is due to another sexually transmitted disease, which infected them at the same time. It is called non-specific urethritis, and is discussed below.

If the examination shows that the man is still infected with gonorrhoea, it may be that he has been infected by one of the penicillin-resistant varieties of the gonococcus, which are causing so much concern. Other antibiotics are available to combat these strains.

Whether gonococci are found or not, smears have to be taken each week for three weeks after the course of injections has been completed. If any of them show that gonorrhoea is still present, a second course of antibiotics is given. A final check is made 3 months after the disease was diagnosed. Smears are again made, and a sample of the person's blood is tested for syphilis. If no gonococci are found, and the blood test for syphilis is negative, the man is considered cured.

Non-specific urethritis (NSU)

A disturbing condition affecting men particularly, which appears to be sexually transmitted, has increased in reported numbers in the past two decades in several countries. In England and Wales, for example, 11,500 cases were reported from hospital clinics in 1952; ten years later this had risen to 25,000, by 1972 to 50,000, and by 1980 to over 110,000. In 1980, 40,000 more cases of NSU were reported than of gonorrhoea.

The condition is called non-specific urethritis, because no specific cause, such as gonorrhoea, trichomoniasis, chemical irritation, or anxiety-induced irritation, can be found.

About 10 to 30 days after sexual intercourse, usually with a casual partner, the man discovers that he has a discharge from his urethra, which may be clear or purulent. When he urinates, the passage of the urine along his urethra causes pain, although often this is only mild. Occasionally the symptoms are more severe. The man develops bladder pain and an urgent and frequent need to pass urine. If he seeks medical examination he should avoid passing

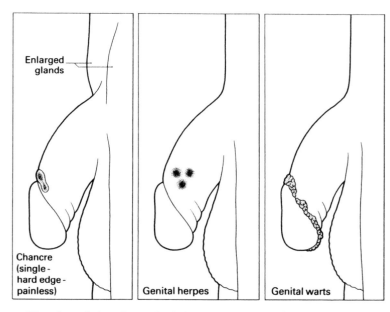

23 The primary lesion of syphilis – a chancre on the penis

24 Genital herpes

25 Genital warts

urine for at least two hours before seeing the doctor. The doctor may massage his penis along the urethra, to express a bead of pus, or it may be present without the need to do this.

The pus is placed on a slide and examined under a microscope and usually 'cultured' as I described in the diagnosis of gonorrhoea. Neither the slide, nor the culture, shows any organisms. All that is found are numerous pus cells, which are merely special white blood cells. However, recent research has shown that swabs taken from the urethra of between one-quarter and one-half of people who have NSU show a virus-like bacterium, called chlamydia.

It will be appreciated that clinically the disease is identical with gonorrhoea in its early stages, and the diagnosis can only be made by excluding gonorrhoea and other specific infections. For this reason, and also because NSU can have unpleasant complications, it is essential that a man who develops painful urination and a discharge from his penis seeks a medical opinion and has the appropriate treatment when a diagnosis has been made.

The complications follow the spread of the causative organism to the man's bladder or prostate gland. If the bladder becomes infected, the man complains of severe pain, especially when he passes urine, which he wants to do all too often, and is often unable to do because of the pain. If the organism spreads into the prostate gland, it causes discomfort deep in the pelvis. Sometimes the spread is without symptoms, but from the warm security of the prostate gland, the disease may affect distant organs. In fact, a peculiar group of symptoms seem to follow untreated NSU. These are conjunctivitis, urethritis, and painful swellings of several of the bigger joints, a form of acute arthritis. The conjunctivitis and urethritis start days, or weeks, after exposure to infection, and settle quite quickly. The arthritis starts rather more slowly and persists. There may be associated fever and a feeling of being vaguely ill. There is reason to believe that the group of symptoms – called a syndrome – are due to an allergic reaction to persistence of the organism in the body, probably in the prostate gland. The syndrome settles after a few months, and the joints usually recover, but further attacks are usual, and these may lead to permanent damage and deformities of the affected joints.

These insidious developments are largely (but not completely) avoided by adequate treatment of the initial infection. Treatment is to avoid all sexual intercourse until the symptoms have disappeared, and for four to six weeks after that. In addition antibiotics, especially 'broad-spectrum' antibiotics such as tetracycline are prescribed.

During the treatment and for six weeks after it has been completed the man has to avoid drinking alcohol as this seems to increase the resistance of the disease to cure.

Syphilis

Syphilis is a sexually transmitted disease, and since most couples have genital sex, the primary lesion of syphilis, which is called a chancre, usually develops on a man's penis or on a woman's vulva. However, in about 25 per cent of women, the primary lesion develops on her cervix and is invisible, but highly infectious should she have sexual intercourse with an uninfected partner. Without treatment, the person who has syphilis remains infectious for about two years, after which the chance of infecting another person diminishes. The organism which causes syphilis is a tiny slender corkscrew-shaped organism which is invisible to the naked eye. It measures about 20μ in length. A μ (pronounced mew) is one-thousandth of a millimetre in length, so that 500 organisms placed end to end would be needed to measure one centimetre, and 1250 to measure an inch. The organism is called *Treponema pallidum*, and it is coiled along its 20μ length. Usually there are about twelve coils. The *Treponema pallidum* can only live in the moist warm atmosphere of the human body, and dies within a very few hours outside it. But once inside the body it thrives.

When a man is infected, 1000 or more of the tiny organisms enter his body through an invisible break in the pink surface of the mucous membrane of his penis. Within 30 minutes of being infected, the organism has spread to the lymph glands in his groins, where they are held up for a short time. They then invade his bloodstream and are carried throughout his body.

The organisms multiply at a tremendous rate, doubling every 30 hours, so that by three weeks after being infected, at least 10,000 million treponemes are circulating through his body, and during this time he has few or no symptoms to show that he has been infected.

However, the organisms do not have it all their own way. The *Treponema pallidum* has a fatty shell but, inside, it contains protein. When a 'foreign' protein is injected into, or inoculated into, the body (as is the case of infection by syphilis), the body reacts. The foreign protein stimulates certain blood cells to multiply, and these cells are sensitized to the particular protein, so that should a further infection occur, they mobilize to attack the invader at its point of entry, rather in the way in which a country attacked by a foreign invader tries to immobilize the invading army on the beaches. Unfortunately, in the first, or primary, infection by syphilis the body's defences are inadequate, and the treponemes are not contained, so that they get into the bloodstream and multiply rapidly.

It takes about three weeks for the defences to be mobilized, which is why the person who has been infected with syphilis has no symptoms or signs for three weeks. Then the sensitized blood cells attack the treponemes, which are still multiplying in the tissues of the beach-head – in this case the mucous membrane of the penis. This attack causes the first sign of syphilis, a raised pimple on the penis. In the next few days many of the treponemes are killed, as are many of the white blood cells, with the result that a zone of hard tissue develops around the pimple. It also leads to a reduction in blood supply to the pimple, so that its centre dies and sloughs off leaving an ulcer. The infected person has a hard chancre. In time the ulcer heals, leaving a scar. This takes from 3 to 8 weeks. Unfortunately, in some cases, the ulcer is quite small, or is not even noticed, so that the infected person does not seek treatment.

At the same time as the white blood cells are being mobilized, the treponemes which have invaded the bloodstream cause another reaction. They induce the blood to make a chemical substance called an antibody. The formation of antibody to the treponemes is a slow process, but 4 to 8 weeks after the primary infection, it can be measured by taking a sample of blood from a vein. Once formed, the antibody to syphilis tends to persist for years, unless the syphilis is cured, when it usually disappears from the blood over a period of about a year.

Once antibody has been formed, blood tests can be made which will detect syphilis. In the U.S.A. these blood tests are necessary before marriage licences are issued. In many other countries similar tests are made in early pregnancy to make certain that the woman does not infect her unborn baby.

Unless the person is treated during the stage when the ulcer is present (called primary syphilis), the disease will continue to develop. Six to eight weeks after being infected the person feels ill, may have a sore throat or headaches, and usually develops a skin rash. The rash starts as faint pale pink spots on the person's body, but rapidly spreads to appear on the face. Some infected people develop low, grey-coloured, flat-topped growths around the anus, or in the mouth (where they look like snail tracks and are called mucous patches). These lesions can last for up to 12 months and then disappear. They are called the secondary stage of syphilis. The final stage in a person who has untreated syphilis is unpleasant. Some people with the untreated disease develop chronic painful ulcers on the skin or, worse, in a bone. In some, the disease affects the brain causing mental decay.

All the horrible outcomes can be avoided if a man who develops a painless ulcer on his penis between 10 and 90 days after sexual intercourse goes to a doctor for the cause of the ulcer to be diagnosed.

If syphilis is the cause, penicillin is the cure. The antibiotic is given daily for 10 days by injection or, using a larger dose, twice weekly for three weeks.

When the injections have been completed, the person is examined, and blood tests are taken, every month for six months and then at nine months and one year after the disease was diagnosed. If the disease is not treated until the second stage, a much longer follow-up is needed, so any man who thinks he may have syphilis should be treated as early as possible.

Syphilis is curable and preventable. If every sexual contact of an infected person could be traced and examined, and if the person who had syphilis were treated, the disease would disappear. This is why it is so important that you inform your doctor of all your sexual contacts if you contract syphilis.

Genital herpes

Recently, an increasing number of sexually active women and men have become infected with genital herpes. The condition is caused by a virus which is similar to that which causes cold sores on a person's lips. The virus, usually herpes simplex virus type 2, or HSV2, prefers to grow in moist areas, choosing especially the entrance to a woman's vagina and the shaft of a man's penis.

A few days after being infected during sexual intercourse with a partner who has the herpes blisters on her vulva or in her vagina, the man notices a localized burning feeling on the shaft of his penis. The burning is followed by a crop of small blisters which burst, forming shallow, painful ulcers. After a day or so the ulcers are covered by scabs, which separate in about four days leaving a faint scar. The whole disease lasts between 7 and 10 days.

Unfortunately, there is no treatment; and even more unfortunately, the infection tends to recur after a long or short interval. This is because the virus invades the nerves supplying the area, where it lies dormant. When something occurs, such as stress, its activity is triggered and it moves along the nerves back into the skin, where the blisters form once again. About 5 per cent of people infected with HSV2 develop recurrences.

Genital herpes has a further danger. A man who has herpes on his penis may infect his sexual partner. If the infection occurs on the cervix of her uterus, the virus may be a factor in the development of cancer, years later.

The lesson is clear. If you develop genital herpes, avoid sex until the disease has disappeared.

Genital warts

Small warts, which may be in a single cluster, but more usually are in multiple clusters covering large areas of skin around the genitals, are not uncommon. Women seem to be more affected than men, but as the disease is sexually transmitted, both sexes are affected.

The warts develop when a virus enters the skin through an invisible abrasion, which occurs during the movements of sexual intercourse. Once within the skin (or in the thinner mucous membrane of a woman's vagina), the virus lies dormant and only starts multiplying after two or three months. When it does, warts form.

They are more common in people between the ages of 18 and 25. In men they are found on the foreskin, or, in circumcised men, on the skin edge just beneath the glans of the penis. But they can grow in other moist areas, and are around the anus in people who enjoy anal intercourse.

Apart from looking unsightly and, occasionally, being itchy, they do not cause much discomfort and they can be cured using a special ointment (containing podophyllin) or by burning them with a small needle cautery.

Trichomoniasis and Candidosis

These two infections more commonly infect a woman's vagina, but can spread to her partner's penis. Both cause a vaginal discharge which is usually itchy and may smell. Trichomoniasis is the name of the infection caused by a tiny animal (a flagellate) which infests the vagina of 10 to 20 per cent of sexually active women, but only causes symptoms in a few. Candidosis (or monilia) is caused by a fungus and infects about 25 per cent of sexually active women, but only produces symptoms in about 5 per cent.

If a man's partner is diagnosed as having trichomoniasis he should take a course of tablets and should wear a condom when they have sex, until they have both been cured. One course of tablets for 7 to 10 days usually does this. The preferred drugs are metronidozole and tinidazole. Recently research has shown that a single large dose is almost as effective as the seven-day course.

If the woman has candidosis, the man may get an itchy penis. Should this happen, treatment with an ointment called nystatin, which kills the fungus, is available.

Chancroid

Chancroid should be mentioned, although this sexually transmitted disease is unusual in temperate climates. It is caused by a small organism which infects a man's penis or a woman's vulva. Within 3 to 7 days of having sexual intercourse with an infected partner, one or more small, painful pimples appear on the man's penis, usually on the skin covering the shaft of the penis. Quite quickly the pimples increase in size and then ulcerate to form small, soft-edged, ragged-shaped ulcers, with grey pus-covered centres. At the same time the glands in the man's groins become swollen and reddened. Provided the man seeks treatment, cure is certain. But the disease is painful.

12

Homosexuality –
an erotic preference

The problem of the genesis of homosexuality ceases to be
of great concern once one is prepared to accept
homosexuality as neither a sin nor a pathology but rather
one way of ordering one's sexual drive, intrinsically no
better nor worse than the heterosexual and with the same
potential for love and hate, fulfilment or disappointment.

Dennis Altman (1971)

. . . With all the money, training and effort that society
puts into heterosexual marriages, it's pretty terrible for
them to fail a third of the time. The whole society is
organised to make marriage work . . . and yet look at all of
the unhappily married people. With all the crap
homosexuality puts up with, it does pretty well; and with
all the help heterosexuality gets, it's doing pretty badly.

Dick Leitch

. . . The homosexual's life is a barren one; his sex life is
likely to be loveless one night stands, often with little or no
communication; his life, even when filled with friends, is
basically alone; and rarely is there any long-term mutual
commitment between two persons . . .

Richard H. Kuh,
'Homosexuality: Two opinions', Playboy (April 1971)

No known method of treatment or punishment offers hope
of making any substantial reduction in the vast army of
adults practising homosexuality. Rather than pretending
they don't exist, or hoping to eradicate them by sheer
weight of disapproval it would be far more realistic to find
room for them in society, so that they can live unmolested
and make their contribution to the common good.

D. J. West (1955)

TO THE MAJORITY OF PEOPLE IN ANGLO-SAXON COUNTRIES, homosexuality – which in most people's minds means male homosexuality – causes feelings of disgust or fear. This reaction is not found in many non-Judaeo-Christian non-white societies, where homosexuality is accepted, at least within certain limits.

Why homosexuality should provoke these feelings in our type of society is not entirely understood, but what is known indicates that the response is emotional rather than rational. But then the attitude of many people to heterosexuality is not entirely rational. In spite of today's more open discussion of human sexuality, many people continue to consider sex a 'delicate' matter which, in general, should not be talked about. Many people continue to lament today's sexual permissiveness, hoping for a return to a time when pre-marital chastity (for women) was a supreme virtue and sex was never mentioned. The period which is taken as the epitome of moral sexual restraint appears to be the last decades of the nineteenth century. Yet the surface respectability of those years hid a sewer of depravity. Child brothels were common, every kind of perversion was catered for, abortion was performed in dangerous circum-stances, and 'baby farming' (with a mortality of over 80 per cent in the first year of life) was used to get rid of unwanted children. Puritanism, on the surface, hid sado-masochism, exploitation, and a sexual double standard of obscene dimensions.

Even today many people are worried that women should express their desire for, and equality in, sexuality in strong terms.

Others decry the sexual manuals which explain that variety in sexual techniques is normal, and do not insist on penile-vaginal intercourse as the only proper way of sexual expression. To many people, sexual pleasuring by masturbation, fellatio, and cunni-lingus is unnatural and shameful; they would prefer human sexuality to be mainly for the purpose of procreating children.

In this cultural atmosphere it is little wonder that many people perceive homosexuality as disgusting or obscene. Homosexual relationships cannot lead to procreation and cannot include penile-vaginal union. They must, therefore, be doubly unnatural, erotically hedonistic, and a threat to the fabric of society. Those who subscribe to these opinions find support in the Judaeo-Christian religions.

The Judaeo-Christian revulsion against homosexuality requires further consideration, as the Christian Churches have been one of the strongest influences in society's condemnation of homosexuality and its persecution of overt homosexuals. The revulsion and condemnation are not based on ethical but on cultic considerations.

It began when, under Moses, the Jews escaped from Egypt and, after long wanderings, took over land in Canaan. Both the Egyptians and the Canaanites had religions in which idolatry and ritual sexual intercourse with male as well as female temple prostitutes were part of the cult. To preserve their exclusiveness as a free people in a hostile land, the Jewish leaders ordered their people to avoid all the ritual of the Canaanites, especially the idolatry and the ritual sexual intercourse. To emphasize their ruling they called such acts abominations (Lev. 18:20, 22; 20:13; Deut. 23:18). The word itself (*to' ebah*) means that the practice is to be *loathed on religious grounds*. Homosexuality was condemned because of its connection with a ritual abhorrent to the Jews, namely idolatry.

The writers of Leviticus first expressed this abhorrence when they wrote: 'If a man lies with a man as with a woman, both of them shall have committed an abomination: they shall be put to death; their blood shall be upon them.' It should be pointed out that in the same chapter, death was the penalty if you cursed your father or mother, if you committed adultery, if you fornicated with your father's wife or with your daughter-in-law.

Jesus does not mention homosexuality, either to condemn or to condone. Paul does. Writing to the Corinthians, a people notorious for their depravity, he says, 'neither adulterers, nor fornicators, nor idolators, nor homosexuals (whether active or passive), nor thieves, nor the greedy, nor drunkards, nor slanderers, nor swindlers will possess the Kingdom of God' (1 Cor. 6: 9–10). Later, writing in Rome, which was also considered a depraved city, Paul, in condemning idolatry, argued that those who persisted in worshipping idols would be abandoned by God and would, therefore, 'take up dishonourable passions' as divine retribution for their sin. Women would 'exchange natural relations for unnatural'; and men would, after 'giving up natural relations with women, burn with passion for one another'; and would commit 'shameless acts with each other . . .' Continuing, Paul says that those who return to idolatry will 'break all the rules of conduct'. They will be 'filled with every kind of injustice, mischief, rapacity and malice'; they will be

'one mass of envy, murder, rivalry, treachery and malevolence . . .'
(Rom. 1:18; 1:22–8).

It is clear that Paul condemned homosexual acts only in a list of
other evils, as an example of what would happen if people forsook
God for idols. The passages also suggest that he only condemned
heterosexual men who abandoned their heterosexual relations for
homosexual relations. He neither states, nor implies, any strictures
on men who had always been homosexual.

The early Christian Fathers condemned homosexuality frequently, relating the fate of Sodom to its acceptance of homosexuality as normal. Again, a study of the Bible does not support this
belief. Sodom was depraved; there was a lack of justice there (Isa.
1:10; 3:9), the people lied and were adulterers (Jer. 23:14); they were
proud, slothful gluttons (Ezek. 16:49). Jesus said Sodom was
wicked, but did not say why (Matt. 10:14–15; 11:23–4; Luke 10:12;
17:29). Even Jude (1:7) is only vaguely explicit, saying that Sodom
was burned because the people 'committed fornication and
followed unnatural lusts'.

There is nothing in the Bible which indicates that homosexuality,
as such, is to be condemned as evil. The references, *in context*, imply
that those condemned are heterosexuals who turn to homosexuality
for ritual reasons or for novelty, not those who have always been
homosexual.

However, Christian teaching over the centuries has emphasized
the evil, unnatural aspect of homosexuality and has encouraged, by
this, the belief that homosexuality is a sin. This has induced people
to react to homosexuality and to homosexuals with fear and disgust.

The disgust shows in the spate of stories about homosexuals in
which the stereotype is a mincing, limp-wristed, lisping figure of
fun. The fear shows in the oppression of homosexuals, from
persecution at the authoritarian end of the spectrum, through
discrimination, to tolerance – but not acceptance – at the
humanitarian end.

Some psychiatrists suggest that those who demand the harshest
penalties for homosexuals and who most fear homosexuality are
themselves repressing their own homosexual tendencies. These are
the men who are authoritarian and usually conservative. In early life
they have identified strongly with a strict father and most of their
attitudes derive from him. They uphold class distinctions and
traditions; they believe in toughness and discipline in education;

they pronounce on the sanctity of family life (although their covert behaviour often belies their pronouncements); they deplore the sexual permissiveness and the disrespect of youth, and they abhor homosexuality.

Women who have been brought up in a similarly conservative manner may be even more hostile towards homosexuality, regarding it as a sin, and are often more outspoken that homosexuals should be punished by society for their 'deviation'.

Those who would discriminate rather than harass also tend to have formed their opinion of homosexuals from parental attitudes and from peer group pressures. They often state that they have no 'objection' to homosexuals, but they know that homosexuals are 'deviants', and if a known homosexual seeks employment, they find reasons why he should not be chosen.

At the humanitarian end of the spectrum are those 'liberals' who claim to have no moral or aesthetic objection to homosexuality and who say they are tolerant of homosexuals. Donald West, whose book *Homosexuality* is one of the best available studies, suggests that society should *tolerate* homosexuals, but notes that toleration is not the same as encouragement. 'No doctor', he writes, 'should advise a young person to rest content with a homosexual orientation without first giving a grave warning about the frustration and tragedy that so often attends this mode of life.' No one would suggest that tolerance is encouragement; but is tolerance enough? Tolerance, Dennis Altman points out, is not acceptance: 'The difference between tolerance and acceptance is very considerable, for tolerance is the gift extended by the superior to the inferior.' The true humanitarian attitude to homosexuality is not tolerance but acceptance. But acceptance of homosexuality as a normal lifestyle will only occur if the accumulated myths about homosexuals are exposed . . . as myths.

One such myth is that there are very few homosexuals in society and that they are easily identifiable by their dress, their way of talking and walking, and their flamboyant behaviour.

*

Before trying to find out how many homosexuals there are in a community it is helpful to define what is meant by a homosexual. To many psychiatrists, a homosexual is a person erotically attracted to a member of the same sex, the implication being that the sexual passion is largely or entirely physical. Such a definition omits the emotional component of eroticism felt by most homosexuals. Perhaps a better definition is that a homosexual is a person who prefers the continuing company, the emotional and physical contact of persons of his or her own sex, and preferentially responds erotically to a person of the same sex. Homosexuality, in the words of Dennis Altman, himself a homosexual, is 'as much a matter of emotion as of genital manipulation'.

The idea that homosexuals can feel as much passion, and can love as deeply, as heterosexuals is threatening to many heterosexuals who have tried to debase homosexual love to mere genital contact; but the evidence is that the definition just given is closer to reality.

Even this definition may be inadequate. Christopher Isherwood perceptively wrote: 'You first know you are a homosexual when you discover you can fall in love with another man'; and this neatly brings an abstract definition into a human context.

There is some evidence that human beings are essentially bisexual, but that conditioning in childhood and role models of parents turn them into unisexual, usually heterosexual, beings. This suggests that there is a continuum between exclusive heterosexuality at one end and exclusive homosexuality at the other end. Most people are exclusively heterosexual, some are bisexual, some are exclusively homosexual.

In such a continuum, how many people in society are exclusively homosexual? Is the number small or large? Most reported investigations are of little value because they are based on selected groups, or are anecdotal.

One investigation stands out as likely to provide a reasonable estimate of the prevalence of homosexuality in a community. This is Alfred Kinsey's very carefully organized and meticulously conducted survey of over 4000 American men carried out in the late 1940s. The men represented as far as was possible a true sample of American society. Kinsey took great care to check his information in many ways, so that he could avoid the charge (which, as he had anticipated, occurred) that his findings were biased, because of his evasions or exaggerations. What he found surprised, horrified, and was denied by most Americans, but despite the attacks, his findings have not been disproved. In fact, they have been validated by subsequent surveys in the U.S.A. and in Britain.

Dr Kinsey and his colleagues found that 4 per cent of the men were exclusively homosexual; that 10 per cent had been more or less exclusively homosexual for a period of three consecutive years; and that one man in four had had some homosexual activity, although this was usually physical. The physical contact implied that the man had reached orgasm by the tactile or oral stimulation of his penis by another man.

It seems that one man in twenty-five in Australia, Britain, and the U.S.A., and probably in other Western countries, is exclusively homosexual; and one man in ten has had a homosexual relationship of some duration.

The number of exclusively male homosexuals in the U.S.A. is not less than 5 million, in Britain more than 1 million, and in Australia more than 300,000. The prevalence of female homosexuality has been investigated less fully, but it appears that exclusive homosexuality among women may be less common. This may be because female sexuality has been ignored until recently, and in our society men are expected to have, and to need, sex more than women. As well, men are more likely to talk about their sexual exploits than women. Because of these facts, the difference in the proportion of male and female homosexuals may be less than has been reported.

If female homosexuality is half as common as male homosexuality, then, by addition, in the U.S.A. 8 million, in Britain 1.5 million, and in Australia half a million people are homosexuals. This large number of people cannot be treated with contempt. They should not be persecuted because of the fear of, and disgust for, homosexuality showed by many heterosexual people.

In addition to the people who are exclusively homosexual, a much larger number are homosexual (or bisexual) for a period and in certain circumstances, but become heterosexual in their erotic relationships when the circumstances change. When men and women are forced to live together in conditions where there is an absence of heterosexual contacts, homosexuality as a means of emotional contact, or for the relief of physical tension, is not uncommon.

If so many people are exclusively homosexual, it would suggest that the stereotype of a homosexual – the mincing, lisping, flamboyant, limp-wristed man, or the 'butch' woman – is inaccurate. In fact, only a tiny minority of homosexuals – probably less than one in twenty – fit the popular stereotype. This minority may be compensating for social rejection, or perhaps 'advertising' for a partner, or may be so disgusted with the attitudes of 'straight' society that they act out a flamboyant homosexual role, or may enjoy behaving in this way.

Over 95 per cent of homosexuals are unidentifiable in the community. They are invisible, because they have no distinguishing characteristics, no brand, no stigmata. They are your neighbours. They are found equally in all social classes and in all occupations. They have no peculiarities of manner which identify their erotic preference. Some maintain an image of heterosexuality to the extent of being married; some have 'come out' and openly admit their homosexual preferences. No greater number have soft skin, a smooth face, poor musculature, 'feminine' hands and gestures, or a feminine body fat distribution than are found among heterosexuals. They are not more 'neurotic' than heterosexuals, nor more aggressive.

In fact, apart from their erotic preference, homosexuals maintain masculine or feminine interests and attitudes to the same degree and with the same variety as do heterosexuals.

A male homosexual could be, and is as likely to be, a rugby forward as a window dresser, a lawyer or doctor as an actor, a business executive as a hair-stylist, an academic as a chorus boy, a metal worker as a shop assistant.

Table 10 Homosexual and heterosexual behaviours compared

Homosexuals are not more likely than heterosexuals to

- commit violent, especially sexual, crimes
- be sadistic
- molest children
- suffer from severe mental illness
- be neurotic
- become alcoholic
- relate less adequately to another person

*

Why do between 3 and 5 per cent of the population become exclusively homosexual when they reach an age to make a choice of sexual preference? Is homosexuality due to a genetic or a hormonal defect?

In a society which shows hostility and contempt towards homosexuals, many heterosexuals and some homosexuals would like to believe that homosexuality is inherited, due to defective genes. Some heterosexuals who fear homosexuality would like this as evidence of a defect which leads to a perversion or makes a deviant. Some homosexuals, who are frightened by society's hostility to them, would like to believe that they are homosexual through no fault of their own. However, only one study has suggested an inherited origin of homosexuality. It lacked objectivity and was based on a selected group, most of whom were 'criminals or severely abnormal'. There is no reason to believe that homosexuality occurs because of the inheritance of defective genes.

There is also no evidence in humans that homosexuality is due to an abnormal hormonal balance which occurred pre-natally. This is in contrast to lower animals (and birds) whose sexual 'preferences' and attitudes can be reversed if sufficient doses of the inappropriate sex hormone is injected into the mother at a precise time during her pregnancy.

Nor is there any evidence that once adult, people with a homosexual erotic preference have lower blood levels of the male hormone, testosterone, although one investigation suggested this. Recent, more accurate measurements of blood levels of testosterone show that there is no difference between those of heterosexuals and those of homosexuals.

A homosexual preference is neither inherited nor due to hormonal imbalance, but it may be due, to some extent at least, to conditioning during infancy and childhood. In several studies of homosexuality by psychoanalysts, one or more of the following relationships or behaviours were said to lead to a homosexual erotic preference.

● Too intense or possessive mothering

● A weak, affectionless, or absent father

● A combination of an intense relationship with the mother and a distant or weak relationship with the father

● Strict, unbending, moralistic, uncommunicative, sexually repressed parents

The problem of accepting this psychoanalytic research is that many heterosexuals have similar unsatisfactory relationships with their parents, and most homosexuals come from happy, well-adjusted homes.

Perhaps the explanation is that an unsatisfactory childhood, operating in one or more of the ways I have described, may prepare the way for homosexuality and the preference is facilitated or inhibited by emotional experiences occurring in adolescence, or later. These experiences do not include 'mutual masturbation' or 'ejaculation competitions' which occur quite normally in the development of adolescent sexuality.

If the reasons for homosexuality are unknown, is there any information about how a homosexual identity develops? Obviously such information can only be obtained from a homosexual who has 'come out', who is articulate and not fearful. One such person is Dennis Altman and I am grateful to him for permission to quote his experiences, which he relates in his book *Homosexual*. He writes:

The development of a homosexual identity is a long process that usually begins during adolescence, though sometimes considerably later. Because of the fears and ignorance that surround our views of sex, children discover sexual feelings and behaviour incompletely, and often with great pangs of guilt. This is true even for the heterosexual, as a whole literary tradition, whose recent variations include Philip Roth's *Portnoy's Complaint* and Dan Wakefield's *Going All The Way* makes clear. How much greater, then, is the guilt of the teenager who discovers himself attracted to others of his or her own sex. Dave McReynolds, the pacifist and political activist who first wrote openly of his homosexuality in 1969, has described how he waited for each birthday hoping he would become 'normal' and his guilt on realizing he was irredeemably 'queer'. Others, like myself, manage to enter into our twenties without a full realization that we are not like others – that we are, in fact, one of 'them'.

Elsewhere in the book he writes:

Entry into the homosexual world was in some ways a great relief, for I discovered that I could attract others sexually and came to understand how far sexual attraction is a matter of a person's ability to accept and project his or her own sexuality.

He questioned whether childhood experiences had influenced his homosexuality:

Most homosexuals I know had unhappy adolescences, though who can say if their homosexuality produced the unhappiness or the unhappiness their homosexuality. In my case I was aware of not belonging, of being excluded through some perception by my peers that I was apart from them. I had no idea why exactly that was: I put it down, as do others in similar situations, to excessive bookishness or timidity or artistic bent, anything other than the real cause.

These passages suggest that a homosexual identity is established at or after puberty. They confound the common belief that seduction of a young boy or adolescent by a homosexual plays any part in causing homosexuality in the child.

This myth is still assiduously propagated by those who have an immoderate fear of homosexuality. It is completely untrue. Cases of child, or youth, molestation by older homosexuals are uncommon. Far more cases of 'interference' with little girls, including their rape, by heterosexual men are reported. Homosexual child molestation is essentially non-violent, in contrast to heterosexual assaults on children. Father Michael Ingram, a Roman Catholic priest and a trained psychologist, has investigated the problem. He studied 91 cases, in which boys under the age of 14 had had sex with a male adult. None of the men had been violent towards the boys, none was disturbed mentally. He found that most of the children, many of whom came from broken homes, had behaved seductively, had 'regularly come back for more', had 'worshipped' the man, and had been fully willing, co-operative participants. He could find no evidence that any of the boys was hurt in any way; and none that the boy would become homosexual as a result of the experience. In all cases the relationship between the man and the boy had been characterized by gentleness and concern.

This confirms that the fears of those who are disgusted by homosexuality are groundless – a young boy who is seduced by (or seduces) a homosexual adult is not likely to become a homosexual or to be harmed by the experience.

Of course, some homosexuals are psychopaths and paedophiles, just as some heterosexuals are. In neither case is the erotic preference a relevant factor in their mental pathology, which has a deeper origin and is related to insecurity, a defective self-image, or mental disturbance.

Psychopathic paedophiles are frequently sadistic and society is rightly offended, whether the victim is a boy or a girl. But because of society's attitude towards homosexuality, the disgust is greater if the victim is a boy. Psychopathic individuals also seem to be the main target (but by no means the only target) for much of the child pornography which is being produced in increasing quantities.

In many Western cities child prostitution is increasing. The young people are usually rootless, having been rejected by their parents, and have drifted to the supposed excitement of the city. Any employment they have is transient and many are hooked on drugs, the two most usual being heroin and barbiturates. They engage in prostitution (and in pornography) to pay for their drugs and to permit them to live what they perceive as 'the good life'. With this background they are preyed upon by pimps and pornographers and are available to satisfy the sexual needs, to reduce the loneliness and insecurity, and to satisfy the desire of the men – homosexual and heterosexual – for the dominance and subjugation of another human being.

*

Homosexuality is neither a sin nor a pathology, it is an alternative life-style; yet in many Western societies homosexuals continue to be harassed, discriminated against, or, at best, barely tolerated. The fear of persecution, the guilt engendered within a homosexual by societal attitudes, and (as Dr West writes) 'the intense and irrationally motivated hostility of Anglo-American culture to homosexuals, is to blame for many of the attendant social evils' which beset homosexuals, shape their identity and distort their lives.

Societal attitudes towards homosexuality, whether overt or covert, although modified in recent years, are still strongly hostile. To be a homosexual is to risk oppression. The oppression may take the form of persecution or harassment by the authorities. It may take the form of discrimination in employment, as employers are reluctant to employ a known homosexual and often sack a homosexual employee who 'comes out' and acknowledges his homosexuality. This is especially the case in the teaching profession, although the seduction of children by homosexuals is unusual, as I have mentioned. Even those people who say they are tolerant of homosexuality add to the oppression of homosexuals, as they fail to distinguish between tolerance and acceptance. Homosexuals are victims of the oppression which results from a minority group being treated as figures of fun, to be mocked or derided (as in most films, plays, and 'fag-stories'). While a homosexual may realize that the gibes of heterosexuals hide deep fears and an irrational hatred of homosexuality, the effect may be to make him insecure or flamboyant.

It can be argued, on good evidence, that the effect of societal oppression makes a homosexual wary. It makes him (and to a lesser extent her, as female homosexuality is less subject to sanctions) defensive, emotionally insecure, over-sensitive to real or imagined slights, so that defensive mechanisms are created which may make the individual seem paranoid to the heterosexual majority. The oppression has an even deeper, more sinister, effect in that it may become internalized and damage the self-image of the oppressed. If you tell a person often enough that he is psychologically ill, inferior, and/or a sinner, and if by your hostile attitude he realizes you mean what you say, in time the victim may come to believe the insults, and either become indrawn, tense, and anxious, unable to relate deeply to others, or adopt those characteristics which he is expected to have.

The internalization could account for the blatant way in which some homosexuals demonstrate feminine traits when they 'come out' and are prepared to be identified as homosexual. It could also account for the transient relationships of some homosexuals, although there is evidence that most form lasting, emotionally satisfying relationships. Those who are less able to adapt to the hostility of society and are inflicted with self-doubt are often tense and show apparently irrational anger, even when among friends. They are scared of forming lasting relationships. Instead, they make frequent casual sexual contacts, because one-night stands are easier to handle emotionally than a lasting relationship. (The reader may note that promiscuity is also common among heterosexuals, and that it has been quantified in neither group.) A further factor in the transience of many homosexual relationships may be the life-style which society insists they adopt. Since 'open marriage' is nearly impossible, since many relationships have to be maintained in a furtive way, and since children can neither be conceived nor adopted, the legal and moral ties which hold together many heterosexual relationships are less binding, and separation easier to effect.

To what extent do homosexuals see themselves as oppressed by society? An American study by Dr Weinberg and Dr Williams of the Institute for Sex Research is revealing. They surveyed over 1000 male homosexuals in the U.S.A., over 1000 in the Netherlands, and over 300 in Denmark. The American men were more fearful about being known as homosexual than were the Europeans, because of the greater acceptance of homosexuality in Europe. When asked what would result if their erotic preference were known by heterosexuals, over 60 per cent of American men believed it would lead to problems at work, and nearly 50 per cent believed some of their heterosexual friends would break off the friendship.

This perception of what heterosexuals would think of them made them less happy than heterosexuals and reduced their faith in others; it also led, in a proportion of the homosexual men, to anxiety and shame. This is because a person's feelings about himself are influenced by how he imagines other people perceive him, regardless of whether those perceptions are accurate or not.

The survey showed that those men who accepted their homosexuality, and who were least concerned about society's reaction to them, were least likely to have psychological problems such as depression, alienation, loneliness, and guilt. By contrast those few homosexual men who believed homosexuality was a 'mental disease' had the most problems.

However, contrary to the current medical belief, the majority of homosexual men were as normal psychologically as the majority of heterosexual men. Psychiatrists have noted the high degree of psychological disturbance in the homosexual men they see, either because the man has consulted them, or because the police have sought an opinion about a homosexual they have arrested. Dr Weinberg's study rejected this psychiatric view, pointing out that most of the homosexual men surveyed were well adjusted. This statement applied particularly to those men who had a stable relationship or who had 'come out' and openly admitted their homosexuality.

The degree to which homosexuals are affected by the hostile attitudes of society should not be exaggerated. Even though newspapers and magazines constantly allude to homosexuals as demoralized, deviant, degenerate, or perverted, and are happy to report sensational cases of child molestation or sex murders, which in turn help to maintain an adverse climate of opinion towards homosexuality, the majority of homosexuals live quiet, unobtrusive, 'normal' lives, hoping to be invisible in society; or else form into protective groups against a generally hostile world.

Even when living these quiet lives, fear of discovery or fear of oppression lurks constantly, and the internalization of social hostility may make a loving relationship more difficult. These observations are reminders that homosexuals are an oppressed group.

The ignorance of most of society towards homosexuality extends to their sexual behaviour. It is believed by some, for example, that anal intercourse is the only way a homosexual man obtains sexual enjoyment. Many sexual contacts between homosexual men are not anal. Most homosexual men enjoy mutual pleasuring and oral-penile stimulation, each partner in turn sucking the other's penis so that each reaches orgasm. If anal intercourse takes place, in most relationships the partners alternate in passive and active roles.

Recent studies by Masters and Johnson in their clinical laboratory have shown that most physiological sexual arousal patterns and responses of homosexual men are identical to those of heterosexual men. There is one important psychological difference which favours homosexual men. This is that homosexual men have a greater concern than heterosexual men that each partner is sexually pleasured. Homosexual couples also have a greater degree of verbal and non-verbal communication during love-making than do heterosexual couples. In other words, more homosexual men find out what their partner's sexual desires and responses are than do heterosexual men, and by acting on those responses help their partner to greater sexual pleasure.

Although many homosexual relationships are fulfilling, problems may arise, as they may in heterosexual relationships. The first of these problems is that of sexually transmitted disease, the second is the effect of age.

Although most homosexuals live with a relatively permanent partner, a number of homosexual men have transient, 'one-night stand' relationships. As the number of sexual partners increases, so does the chance of acquiring a sexually transmitted disease. Reports from England and the U.S.A. indicate that both gonorrhoea and syphilis are increasing among homosexuals and heterosexuals. Over 50 per cent of heterosexual women infected with gonorrhoea have no signs or symptoms, and the women constitute a 'hidden reservoir' of infection so that the disease is spreading among heterosexual men. It is now evident that among homosexual men, gonorrhoea of the throat (following fellatio with an infected partner) or of the anal canal is often symptomless and, because of the transience of some homosexual relationships, the spread of gonorrhoea is increasing.

Syphilis is also increasing, although to a much lesser extent than gonorrhoea. What is disturbing, according to reports from the U.S.A., is that a homosexual man with syphilis names, on average, ten contacts, while a heterosexual man or woman with syphilis names four. This makes control of the disease much more difficult.

Viral hepatitis is also more common among homosexual men, and may cause permanent liver disease. Viral hepatitis occurs in two forms, type A and type B. The disease may be associated with jaundice or may be almost symptomless, but men who have been infected can be detected by blood tests. A study in the U.S.A. showed that homosexual men were twice as likely as heterosexual men to have had viral hepatitis type A; and the acquisition of the disease was associated with frequent oral-anal contact. A study in Britain showed that about 5 per cent of homosexual men attending a genito-urinary clinic had been infected some time previously with viral hepatitis type B, and the prevalence was fifty times greater than among heterosexual blood donors.

The second problem, that of age, affects homosexuals more than heterosexuals. Among heterosexuals a lasting relationship is usual although, of course, separation or death may terminate it, and one or other partner may have transient relationships with others. Among homosexual men permanent relationships seem less common, and many homosexuals place a premium on youth. As a man grows older his body becomes less attractive and he has to work harder to find a partner, becoming more at risk of punitive action by the police, when he frequents known homosexual cafés or lavatories.

This view of the older homosexual may not be correct. Dr Weinberg's study, to which I referred earlier, indicates that most older homosexuals are well adjusted, and have a lower sexual drive than when younger. He found there was no truth that, with age, homosexual men became more unhappy, more lonely, more depressed or had more psychological problems than when they were younger. Most had adapted to growing old.

*

The punitive action of society against homosexuals who transgress the existing laws, or against whom laws are officiously applied, can do more damage to the individual than committing magistrates imagine.

The laws against homosexual acts are enforced by the police, usually by the vice squad. In some places, the vice squads act in an excessively punitive manner towards homosexuals; in others, they act with restraint, unless pressured by civic leaders, clergymen hostile to homosexuality, or aspiring politicians wishing to remove the 'permissiveness and degeneration threatening our values'. The legal penalty of most homosexual acts which are not 'in private between consenting adults' (which in England and Wales means that no more than two people may be in the room, or by extension the house) may be a prison sentence, although increasingly such punishment is not being given.

Yet there can be few institutions better suited to damage a homosexual's self-esteem and more likely to subject him to physical degradation than prison. Most prisoners are young and fit men who, of necessity, have to suppress heterosexual urges and can find relief from sexual tension only by masturbation or a temporary homosexual relationship. When a known homosexual is put into this environment he is at physical and mental risk, and the experience may permanently injure him both mentally and physically. Even if injury is avoided, the experience can do nothing to diminish the individual's homosexuality – and presumably the purpose of imprisonment is treatment rather than to 'teach the poofter a hard lesson'.

To send a homosexual to prison is, in the words of Dr Stanley Jones, 'as futile from the point of view of treatment as to hope to rehabilitate an alcoholic by giving him occupational therapy in a brewery'.

The question must arise: is homosexuality a pathological condition which needs treatment? And if it is, does treatment do any good?

The answer to the first question is a matter of belief obscured by emotion, rather than a rational decision made upon unequivocal evidence. It will be clear by now that I do not believe homosexuality to be either a sin or a pathology. But many people do and, true to their belief, contend that homosexuals must be treated. Even if 'cure' – that is, a turn to a heterosexual erotic attachment – is uncertain, they believe that the treatment may help those tortured by neurotic reactions of guilt, depression, and anxiety, or at least may make the man a better-adjusted homosexual. With this latter view there can be no argument, although it seems that a homosexual's maladjustment is as much due to societal attitudes to homosexuality as to his own psychological disturbance.

Treatment to 'cure' homosexuality is ineffectual, whether prolonged deep psychoanalysis or aversion therapy is used. Aversion therapy is particularly offensive. In this form of behavioural modification, the homosexual is attached to a machine which gives him an electric shock. He is then exposed to erotic pictures; when a male is shown, the shock is given, when the picture shows a female, the shock is withheld. The theory is that the 'patient' will learn to associate male erotic pictures with pain and will change his erotic preference as a consequence. Treatment rarely produces a complete conversion of an adult from exclusive homosexuality to satisfactory heterosexuality. Although enthusiastic psychoanalytic and aversion therapists report high percentages of success, most report soon after treatment, on selected patients, who are usually under the age of 25 and often bisexual. The committed homosexual rarely changes permanently, and the longer the follow-up, the less effective is treatment shown to be.

This confirms Professor Curran's opinion that attempts to convert a homosexual to heterosexuality should only be made rarely, and then only when careful evaluation of the homosexual's attitudes convinces the therapist that he is sincere in his desire to change. If the homosexual is only trying to change to reduce his guilt, or diminish the fear society has engendered in him, treatment will fail.

A homosexual who has emotional problems is in the same situation as a heterosexual who has emotional problems – both may need skilled counselling or psychiatric help to resolve those problems and to adjust better to their environment.

It is true that a homosexual is likely to be more anxious and insecure and to have a larger amount of 'self-hatred' than a heterosexual. This is largely or completely induced by the hostility, insensitivity, and ill-feeling of the society in which he lives and by the stupidity and ignorance of the authorities he may have to face if apprehended by the law.

These attitudes and actions are indefensible when one man in twenty-five is homosexual.

13 Middle age and its problems

It wasn't just a sexual thing – that soon no woman will want to make love with me. It was everything in my life. It all seemed pointless. I had no hope. I'd been overlooked for promotion, I wasn't going to get to the top. I felt a sense of failure – I'm not a failure but I'm not a success. It all seems futile.

Australian man (1979)

MOST MEN, IN THEIR MIDDLE YEARS, HAVE MARRIED, HAVE had children, have established themselves in a job, and have purchased (or largely purchased) a house, a car, and the other household mechanical contrivances which modern society believes are necessities. Established in these ways, they might be expected to have reached an equilibrium in their emotional, sexual, and social lives, and be able to look forward to some years of enjoyable activity before the inevitability of old age slows them down.

Yet in our society many men in their middle years, between the ages of 40 and 65, are not in emotional balance. For many, some part of the middle years are years of emotional stress, anxiety, and instability. For others, the diseases of affluence, coronary heart disease, high blood pressure, obesity, and lung cancer may strike, often unexpectedly, and either kill the man or reduce his capacity for activity and enjoyment.

Of the many hazards in these years, four conditions seem to be the most common and the most important. All seem to be influenced by our way of life, as all are less common in developing countries, with different cultural values. They are the crisis of adjusting to middle age, coronary heart disease, high blood pressure (hypertension), and increasing obesity.

As so many men are affected by one or more of these conditions, they require discussion. In this chapter I shall discuss the adjustment to middle age, obesity, and high blood pressure. Coronary heart disease, which is common and disabling, is discussed in the next chapter.

The crisis of middle age

> Donald would never admit it, of course, but he is searching for something that will take him back. He's using her younger face to hide behind so that he doesn't have to see his own.
>
> Respondent in *The Male Menopause* (1976)

Middle age, especially during the years between 40 and 55, is often a period of stress.

In a society which emphasizes achievement, particularly financial success, and which worships the work ethic, middle age signifies a time when most men have reached their peak in terms of promotion and decision-making. To the man who has dreamt of high achievement, the reality of his lower status may be a cause of anxiety. He has not achieved what he hoped he would, and his remaining working years stretch dully, routinely, towards retirement, which itself holds no real attraction.

Traditionally, in most cultures, middle age brought a man respect. He was perceived by others as having wider experience, more skills, and greater wisdom than younger men. He was consulted by others, and was relieved of many routine duties. As his strength decreased, his position and influence in society increased. He kept his self-esteem. Today, the brilliance of youth is stressed and increasing age is discounted – you become an 'oldie' by 30 and a 'wrinkly' by 50. Advertisements on television and in magazines equate youth with success in sex and work; middle age is equated with declining powers. It is seen as a period when a man needs medicaments, when his teeth are false, and when he should be arranging affairs for his nearing death. In middle age, he is not even given the tentative respect that youth gives to old age.

In a society which emphasizes youth, the changing body contours of the middle-aged man, his receding hairline, his sagging chin, and his enlarging belly make him aware that he is no longer young.

In a society which stresses health and vitality, middle age is a time when health becomes of increasing concern, and when physical disabilities become more common. A middle-aged man becomes more conscious of the diseases which may attack him or his friends.

In a society which stresses sex, the sexual relations of a man with his permanent partner may have become routine, unimaginative, and dull over the years. The shock of the realization that they are both middle-aged may lead to a reduction in his sexual activity, or to a relationship with a younger woman.

In a society which accentuates competition, the middle-aged man may be less able to compete in his job, in sport, or in appearance, with younger men. This may make him feel that he has not been as successful as he had hoped he would be. He may think that he is being superseded by younger people. He may feel that he will not have fulfilled himself before he dies or becomes senile.

These feelings of anxiety affect many middle-aged men. They induce doubts about the man's own significance, and, as important, about his significance to others. He may wonder what has gone wrong. He may ask himself whether it is due to his own failure or to the conspiracy of others. He may wonder if his youthful dreams were just fantasies. He may lose his self-esteem and become depressed and uncommunicative.

In other words, he is in a period of emotional instability, and undergoing a crisis of identity. This is the crisis of middle age.

*

The period of instability in middle age has been termed the male menopause. The term is based on the fact that women, between the ages of 45 and 55, reach the menopause – which means that their menstrual periods cease. But the menopause has come to describe far more than that. It is used to define the period of hormonal and physical turbulence which precedes and follows the actual cessation of menstruation, for which the more correct term is the climacteric.

During the climacteric in women, certain physiological changes occur. The most important one is the disappearance from a woman's ovaries of all the remaining egg cells. With their disappearance the ovaries are unable to produce the female sex hormone, oestrogen. This, in turn, leads to the over-production of the pituitary hormones (the gonadotrophins) which regulate the function of the ovaries.

The hormonal turbulence either may lead to, or be accompanied by, emotional disturbances – by feelings of rejection, by depression, and by emotional caprice. The emotional instability is aggravated by society's stress on youth, by the woman's belief that with the menopause she is no longer feminine, and by her fear of ageing. Not all women are affected, and of those who are, few are affected to the same degree, or for the same length of time. Most women need to talk about their feelings to a sympathetic listener. Many need more help than this. For example, women who have 'hot flushes' are helped considerably by oestrogen hormone tablets. Other women who become severely depressed at this time benefit by being counselled and by being prescribed drugs. Nearly all women re-establish their emotional and hormonal stability after a period of time which varies from six months to several years. They have passed through their menopause.

It is wrong to call the emotional instability of a man's middle years the 'male menopause'. There are two reasons: he does not menstruate, and no changes occur in the production of his gonadotrophin hormones, his testosterone levels do not decrease, nor does he produce fewer sperms. But many middle-aged men do go through a period of emotional anxiety, of depression, and of stress. To call this the 'male menopause', because it occurs during the same years that a woman inevitably ceases to menstruate, is catchy and comforting. It is comforting because it implies that the 'crisis of middle age' is not due to a man's actions or inactions, but to his altered hormones and, consequently, is inevitable. This is not true: our faults are not in our hormones, but in ourselves.

The emotional problems of middle age may be due to a man's actions – or to his lack of action. They will only be solved if he alters his way of life. He does not lack hormones, he does not need hormone injections and they do not help!

*

Why a man should become emotionally unstable in his middle years is not clear. The physical changes in his body may provoke nostalgia for a lost youth. He may attempt to come to grips with the nostalgia by wearing youthful fashions, by having his hair cut in a youthful way, or by behaving 'inappropriately'. (This presupposes that there is a conventional way in which each age group should behave.) The crisis may be provoked by his feeling that he is not being treated by others important to him in a way which flatters him. His children argue with or disregard him. His superiors seem not to appreciate what he believes is his real worth. His job no longer gives him satisfaction. He may feel he is unattractive sexually. He may fear that he is becoming old.

To varying degrees, these emotional stresses may produce a physical reaction. The man may undergo a personality change. He may become moody, impatient, or intolerant. He may have periods of lassitude, when nothing matters and everything is too much of an effort. He may sleep long or be unable to sleep. He may be unable to concentrate, or may over-concentrate on things which he perceives as important, simultaneously appearing to be losing his memory for recent events. Some men react to their emotional frustrations by over-eating, as compensation; others escape from the stressful, ugly reality into a haze of alcoholism.

In most marriages, the age of each partner is within five years of the other, so that the period of the man's emotional instability may coincide with his wife's menopause. This period of her life is often one of emotional turbulence, when she questions her role as a housewife and mother.

If both partners are affected by the emotional stresses of middle age, minor conflicts and misunderstandings may be magnified and become major causes of hostility or frustration, so that the couple become irritated with each other. This in turn aggravates the emotional instability. In this situation, some men lose their zest for sex, because their emotional instability leads to depression. Depression is a major factor in reducing a person's sexual desire and capacity. Some men may even become impotent. The impotence may last for a few months, or may persist for years, damaging further the relationship with the man's partner and destroying his self-esteem. In other cases, a man may lose his sexual zest because he perceives his sexual relationship as monotonous or boring. His partner no longer excites him. He has become too familiar with the way she responds, with her expressions, with her behaviour. He knows in advance what she will do. Sex has become a routine duty, not a time of mutual enjoyment and sharing. How the man reacts depends on how he has perceived sex when he was young. If he was brought up to believe in the double standard of sexuality and that women have a relative lack of sexual passion, he may perceive that sex with a familiar partner is boring. He sees sex as something special for him, not as a mutual enjoyment. He expects the woman to stimulate him, but feels no need to stimulate her. Because he is not stimulated, he blames his wife for their sexual problems, rather than putting some of the blame on himself. If neither partner has been able to tell the other, over the years, about his or her sexual desires and needs, and if there has been little communication using body language, by middle age their sexual relationship may have deteriorated. It is easier to blame your partner than to look for faults in yourself.

In this situation the man may seek an extramarital relationship, often with a younger woman, whom he perceives as having the qualities his wife lacks. (Why younger women should agree to, or encourage, sexual relationships with an older man is not clear: it may be because of a Freudian father-fixation, or because the older man is more experienced, or because older men are fair game and the relationship will bring financial and perhaps social rewards.) As the relationship evolves, it reassures the man that he is still sexually attractive, that he is not becoming impotent, and that someone demonstrably believes him to be important. The new relationship gives him an exciting sexual experience, but this is not the main reason for it. More importantly, the relationship increases the man's self-esteem. He feels wanted and important.

This feeling, together with the firm, warm body of his lover, may cause the man to make comparisons between her and his wife. He may perceive his wife to be sexually unattractive, despite the fact that in reality she may be a better, more skilful lover.

Although obsessed with his new partner, he may feel guilty particularly if he retains affection for his wife, as he sees the damage the new relationship is causing. Even so, the obsession may be so strong that he is prepared to sacrifice everything – the years of marriage, his wife's needs, his position, and his possessions, to be with his new love. It may work out well; but for many, the passion passes, the fantasy fades, and reality returns in a year or two, when it may be too late to repair the broken bridges. It is of little help for the man to be told that he is making a fool of himself – he may be, but he will not recognize it, and in his emotional instability, the charge diminishes his self-esteem even more. It may also be unhelpful if his wife reacts fiercely, as Doris Odlum writes in *The Male Predicament*.

A great deal will depend on the attitude that the wife adopts to the situation. The man is completely unreasonable and in many cases prepared to sacrifice his wife, his job and all his future security. If she is in an unstable state herself and going through the menopause, or if the marriage has previously been unsatisfactory, she is likely to react with hysterical outbursts, nagging and jealousy. She may discuss her husband with her friends or even inform his employer. In some cases she demands a separation or starts proceedings for a divorce. On the other hand if she is stable and mature she may treat the situation with understanding or forbearance and if his infatuation diminishes and he begins to see reason the marriage may even be strengthened and their mutual affection and understanding increased.

Doris Odlum's views suggest that women should accept the man's affair, at whatever cost to their own emotional health. Some women have been conditioned by their upbringing to do this, and accept the double standard of sexuality. Others are as 'mature' as the hypothetical woman in the quotation, but see no reason why they should be the victim. They fail to see why the *man* should not be sufficiently 'mature' to appreciate that his wife may also be in an emotionally unstable state, and that his actions may be aggravating her distress. Most men in this type of relationship would be horrified if the wife had a lover, but see no contradiction that they have a lover themselves.

In these circumstances, the woman should show her distress and anger, not only because she feels angry and humiliated, but to avoid repressing the anger which may damage her own emotional well-being. But she must also be aware that by over-reacting, she may put herself in a position from which she cannot withdraw. If the couple want to continue living together, to rediscover the depth of their relationship, they have to be able to talk with each other. The first conversations may be heated and destructive, but if they persist they may well find that they have not been communicating for years, and may be able to become reacquainted.

Perhaps this is what Doris Odlum meant by 'understanding and forbearance', although her words imply a passive, submissive woman. If she meant that the couple should try to talk with each other, so that the hidden resentments, the anger, the anxieties, the fears, and the misunderstandings can be ventilated and exposed, the couple have a stronger chance of renewing their regard for each other and strengthening their relationship.

Sometimes the loss of a man's sexual interest may be due to the competing demands of his occupation, or his male-directed interests. The latter vary from playing golf, drinking with his mates, or watching sport. The competitive world may become all-consuming to him, and, if he believes that he has to work hard and long to provide financially for his old age and for the security of his family, he may be so exhausted by his job that he avoids sex. This is encouraged if he believes the myth that sexual intercourse is weakening. As mental, rather than physical, fatigue is the greater deterrent to sexual responsiveness, and as he may be under some mental stress from the responsibilities of his job, his sexual drive suffers. Physical fatigue may also be a factor, as few middle-aged men are physically fit. Most men are overweight, over-indulge in food and alcohol, and take little exercise.

Over-indulgence in alcohol is particularly depressing to a man's sexuality. Alcohol is a sedative. In small quantities it may reduce his sexual inhibitions but in larger amounts it reduces his performance, so that he either fails to obtain an erection or to reach orgasm. This may lead to the fear that he is becoming impotent. He may hide his fear by becoming angry with his wife, or showing his contempt for her, in the hope that she will not expect him to be sexually active.

His fear of sexual failure may be intensified because he has noticed changes in his sexual responses and has interpreted these as evidence of a declining sexual capacity. In our society, many men equate sexual success with worldly success, and the diminished ability to perform well sexually is taken as an indication of a decline in general efficiency.

As a man grows older his sexual response changes. In his early twenties, a man responds to sexual excitement by rapidly obtaining an erection. During sexual intercourse, he reaches orgasm quickly, ejaculates powerfully, and is able to repeat the sequence after a short time.

By his middle forties, a man takes longer to get an erection, he takes longer to reach orgasm, his ejaculation is less powerful, and he needs a longer time before he can start the sequence again.

Unfortunately, if a man's upbringing has stressed male dominance in sexuality and has equated sexual prowess with the frequency and force of his orgasm, the inevitable changes of middle age may make him feel that he is less sexually potent than when younger, and he may fear a rapid decline, the end of which is impotence. This, in turn, may deter him from sexual activity.

His concern may be increased by the fact that his wife has a greater desire and capacity for sex. Many women in their climacteric years, and after, experience enhanced sexuality.

A middle-aged man should be aware that there is a wide variation in the sexual changes which occur. Some, perhaps most, middle-aged men function sexually as well as, or better than, they did when young. In middle age, the delay in obtaining an erection is well compensated for by the fact that a man can maintain his erection for longer without ejaculating, and so is better able to pleasure his partner. As well as this, his diminished ability to have frequent orgasms is compensated for by the deeper intensity of his total sexual response.

*

What can be done to help a man adjust to the crisis of middle age? The first step is for him to be aware that he has to adapt to middle age. He has to recognize that he is no longer in his twenties, full of the aspirations of youth. He has to recognize that many of his hopes have not been achieved. He may have to accept that his status is not as high as he had hoped it would be. He may have to accept that his work is monotonous. The days stretch greyly on towards retirement, the challenge has gone. He has to accept that his body is ageing and is less responsive than it was. The years of over-eating, too much alcohol, too little exercise, and stress have had their effect. His chin is less firm, his belly is more flabby, his waist is thicker, his hair is thinner, and his face is beginning to show the marks of ageing. He has to recognize that he is being challenged by his children who may reject his conventional views, repudiate his values, ignore his advice, and behave in a way he regards as bizarre. He has to recognize that his wife may also be going through a period of readjustment and needs help just as much as he does. Both may have to accept that their relationship may have lost the excitement it once had. The man may have to recognize that neither his wife nor his children talk to him, or he to them – they talk *at* each other, but are unable to communicate *with* each other.

If he is able to recognize these problems and is flexible enough to adjust to them, he will emerge from the crisis of middle age with greater insight. He will be able to create new dreams and visions, he will become curious about life and about living. He will become more of an individual and less of a stereotype.

Escape from the crisis of middle age begins when the man begins to realize that status and possessions are less important than warm, giving relationships. In many cases it may mean that he and his wife (or his permanent partner) will have to recognize each other as individuals, not as stereotypes who fit into conventional sex-roles and never stray from them. It may mean that he will have to renegotiate his relationships. This may not be easy as, over the years, his wife may have had much of her self-esteem taken from her. She may have become depressed and have let herself go physically because her husband has failed to see her as an individual. Alternatively, she may have realized that her man is petulant, boorish, and selfish, perhaps an alcoholic or a workaholic, and she has had to work hard to keep the relationship going.

Escape from the crisis of middle age is well advanced when the man accepts that he needs help. With help, he can escape from the dull routine of work, he can widen the range of his activities, he can change direction, and he can have a stimulating sex life. He needs to see that he must talk about his problem. He needs to see that co-operation and sharing are more important than acquisitiveness and competition. He needs help to build up his self-esteem. He needs to see through his dissembling, his fantasies, his deceptions (about himself and about others), and his delusions. He needs to learn about his strengths and to accept his weaknesses.

If he is overweight, he will feel better if he loses some weight. If he drinks heavily, he will feel more awake if he drinks less. If he is slothful, he will become healthier if he takes more exercise – not competitive exercise to 'beat' someone, or 'duty' exercise to keep himself fit for work, but an active pursuit he enjoys.

If his problem is sexual, particularly if he is concerned that he is, or will become, impotent, and sees this as a loss of his masculinity, he needs help. He does not need hormones, but he does need counselling, together with his partner. The aphorism that 'in a sexual problem there is no uninvolved partner' is as true in this condition as in others.

If he is depressed, irritable, and unable to see any light at the end of his dark tunnel, he may need help from health professionals: his family doctor, a psychiatrist, or a psychologist. He may be prescribed drugs, but he should be made aware that they are only temporary crutches, until he can 'find himself again', able to appreciate and adjust to his middle years.

The process of adjusting to middle age and of overcoming the crisis is neither quick nor painless. Adjustment to reality rarely is. But it is worth while. A middle-aged man may perceive that much of what he once thought of as important is trivial and ridiculous. With this insight he can discover what is important to him. It may mean that he will have to learn new skills. This may cause him anxiety because of the myth that middle-aged people cannot learn easily. It is untrue. Given the motivation, middle-aged people can learn as easily (if rather more slowly) than young people.

Adjusting to middle age means that a man has to redefine his own sense of identity and know what he is – warts and all. It means that he has to give as well as to take. One way in which he can give is to help his partner adjust to *her* crisis of middle age.

*

In a study in Britain, it was found that over one-quarter of men were unaware of the nature or the extent of their wife's progress through the climacteric. Most did not even know what the climacteric was, what changes it caused, and that the emotional turmoil experienced by the woman would pass. Many men were unaware that a woman in her climacteric, who is adjusting to her crisis of middle age, needs much more love, understanding, encouragement, and contact than when she was young. For many women this is a time when children have finally left home to form their own relationships and are no longer dependent upon their mother, who may be left with an emptiness in her life, which is not helped by an apparently insensitive man. The couple, for the first time for many years, have to reappraise and understand each other. They have to rediscover the companionship which characterized their early years of marriage and which has vanished.

It is also important for the couple to look at their sex life. A British scientist, Dr Ballinger, has found that women who were dissatisfied with the sexual aspects of their marriage were more likely to have greater problems (and particularly depression) during the climacteric.

If the marriage has ceased to be one of total commitment (or, at least, one which has a number of vital, exciting aspects) and if this has been replaced by passivity, or by hidden conflicts, the menopausal woman may feel unwanted and rejected, and become emotionally brittle.

Many men are unaware that their behaviour, or their reaction to the woman's behaviour, may aggravate the emotional upset. Many men are unaware that the woman may have hostile feelings towards them, because of lack of sensitivity, or apparent disinterest in what she is doing. It may be helpful, rather than destructive, if these feelings are shown openly.

They can start readjusting to each other by doing together things that they both enjoy, such as gardening or going out for a meal, or visiting the cinema or theatre.

It is important that they re-examine their sexual relationship, and talk with each other so that they become more sensitive lovers.

If their relationship becomes strong enough to survive the turbulent middle years, they can look forward to an even closer relationship as they grow older. It also seems that the more outside interests each partner has, provided that these do not take precedence over the relationship, the stronger is the bond between the couple. Of course, a balance has to be obtained, and this can only be achieved if the couple talk to each other.

The alternative is increased hostility between the partners, increased depression, and the possibility of breakdown of the marriage.

Obesity

> Over-eating in an abundant culture requires neither courage, skill, learning, or guile. Gluttony demands less energy than lust, less effort than avarice.
>
> G. V. Mann (1971)

A man may escape the emotional instability, the anxiety of middle age because of his curiosity about life, because of his creativity, or because of acceptance of himself as he is, but he may still become a victim of the dangers of over-indulgence in food and drink and the hazards of high blood pressure.

An individual is said to be overweight, or fat, if his weight is 10 per cent more than it should be for his height, weight, and age. If his weight is 20 per cent or more than his desirable weight, he is obese. In our society 10 per cent of 40-year-old men are obese; and 15 per cent are obese by the age of 50.

The main reason why people become fat is because, over the years, they have eaten more energy (in the form of food or drink) than they have expended for the basic energy needs of their body (breathing, heart beating, digestion, tissue repair) and for activity. This excess supply of energy is converted into fat and stored in the adipose, or fatty, tissues. Adipose tissue covers the body beneath the skin, but fat seems to be laid down particularly on the neck, across the shoulders and upper arms, over the abdomen, and on the thighs.

It is true that some people can eat all they wish and, to the annoyance of their weight-conscious, dieting friends, remain thin. The reason is thought to be that they are more efficient in the way they handle the extra energy and are able to disperse it into their surroundings, in the form of heat. Also, these people are often more active.

It seems, too, that the tendency to fatness may start very early in life. Investigators have found that if a baby is obese it has an 80 per cent chance of becoming a fat adult. If a mother, through misguided kindness, overfeeds her baby, by giving it extra semi-solid cereal baby foods too early in life, she may be laying the foundations for obesity later in life. In the first year of life, babies form fat cells to help store the extra energy the body receives from overfeeding. These fat cells differ from fat cells formed after the age of 1 which are designed to meet a need and once that need has gone disappear. In contrast, the fat cells formed before the age of 1 persist. If a fat adult, who was a fat baby, tries to lose weight, the cells simply become emptier and smaller, and in some strange way, these 'hungry' cells send out messages which stimulate the person's appetite, so that dieting becomes difficult.

Of course, not all fat adults were fat when they were babies. Excess food and excess drink taken for social reasons or because they are enjoyed, rather than because of hunger, supply more energy than is needed for daily activities and this is turned into fat.

As a man (or a woman) grows older, the energy needed for the basal body functions decreases, so that even if he keeps to the same diet, he is likely to put on weight. This is recognized in tables of ideal weight.

By referring to Figure 26 you can calculate if your weight is within the normal range for your age, if you are overweight, or if you are obese.

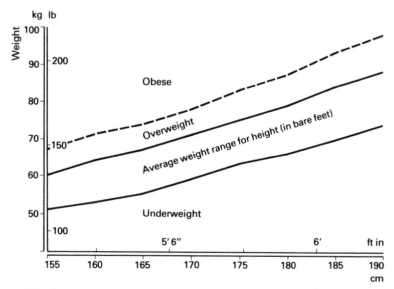

26 'Ideal' weight range for men by age, showing the ranges considered overweight and obese

If a man is obese does it matter? It does. Obesity is a health hazard! Obese people are more likely to develop gall-bladder disease and arthritis. Obese people are more likely to become diabetics. Obese people are more likely to develop high blood pressure. And obesity adds indirectly to the risk of having a heart attack.

In our society, a large proportion of the population is overweight and an important minority is obese. Investigations in the U.S.A. and Britain show that nearly 30 per cent of men are overweight and about 12 per cent are obese. (An even larger proportion of women is overweight and obese, but that is not really relevant to our present discussion.)

As men grow older, an increasing proportion become fat, and this coincides with the danger period for heart disease, diabetes, and hypertension.

*

Obesity is a factor in many lethal or disabling diseases which affect our affluent civilization. If you are fat, and especially if you are obese, you will have to make a decision. Are you prepared to reduce your weight, so that you reduce the dangers of diabetes, hypertension, arthritis, and perhaps coronary heart disease? If you want to reduce your weight until it lies within the normal range for your age, your height, and your physique, you can do it. But you will need self-discipline and persistence.

A diet sheet alone will not enable you to lose weight. You have to be motivated to keep to the diet. Your motivation will be helped if you accept the following propositions:

● The only person who can beat your obesity is you! But you can be encouraged in your determination to lose weight if you are helped by advice from a nutritionist, your doctor, or one of the organizations like Weight Watchers International.

● You have to keep to your chosen diet and not cheat, so that you eat less energy than you use up.

● There is no quick way to lose weight permanently. Permanent weight loss is a slow process. Although with some so-called miracle diets you can lose a lot of weight quickly, you put it on just as quickly. 'Crash diets' may be dangerous.

• Don't gorge, eating only one large meal a day – eat the same amount of food in several small meals, and try to eat each meal at the same time each day.

• Before you start eating decide what you are going to put on your plate and don't add more. And eat your meal slowly.

• Try and take some exercise most days – provided you enjoy exercising! It need not be dull exercise, you can swim, walk briskly, garden actively, or even play golf, as long as you play it energetically. Spend at least half an hour taking exercise. This will help you lose weight and will make you feel fitter.

If you are able to accept all, or most, of these propositions you are ready to try the diet. Here it is. You can see that it enables you to eat nearly the same foods as the other members of your family and lets you lead a reasonable social life.

These are the basic principles of the diet:

• *You can eat as much of the following foods as you like – provided you are sensible:*

Meat	Green leafy vegetables
Fish	Cheese
Eggs	Butter

But always grill your meat or fish instead of frying it.

• *You can eat the following foods with some limitation:*

Milk	Up to 600 ml (1 pint) a day
Fresh fruit	Not more than 3 of the following in any one day: apples, grapefruit, oranges, peaches, pears.
	When in season, you can replace one of the above with 120 g (4 oz) – an average serving – of cherries, blackberries, gooseberries, grapes, plums, strawberries, or raspberries.

• *You must restrict the following foods because they contain carbohydrate but you can substitute one for another:*

Using bread as the measure you can have up to 3 slices a day (60 g) or the equivalent.

Bread (preferably wholemeal)	
Oatmeal	Nuts
Cornflakes	Biscuit (not sweet)
Potato	Baked beans

In doing your calculation, it helps to remember that in energy supplied, $1\frac{1}{2}$ slices of bread = 1 average-sized potato = 1 average serving of oatmeal porridge, cornflakes, and baked beans = 3 small sweet biscuits.

● *You have to avoid the following foods:*

Sugar (whether raw or refined)
Sweets and chocolates
Jams and honey
Pastries and puddings
Cakes and buns
Canned fruits
Soft drinks (except soda water)

● *You should avoid alcoholic drinks.* But if you cannot, limit yourself each day to:

Beer	250 ml (10 fluid oz)
or whisky	30 ml (1 fluid oz)
or wine	125 ml (5 fluid oz)

This diet is easy to follow. It lets you have a reasonably normal social life and will enable you to lose weight, although you will only lose it slowly. On this diet you can expect to lose about half to one kilogram a week, which is about the best weight loss to achieve.

High blood pressure

> A number of populations have now been identified in which hypertension is rare or uncommon and in which there is little or no tendency for blood pressure to rise with age. Most of such populations live in peasant-type communities. When people of the same racial group are studied in 'urban' or 'westernized' environments, their blood pressures tend to resemble those of Western man. The environmental determinants of hypertension are the subject of speculation; possibilities include dietary factors such as salt, potassium and carbohydrate intake, and environmental factors, especially those linked with crowding.
>
> R. R. H. Lovell (1973)

In recent years, medical researchers have become aware that high blood pressure (hypertension) exerts a sinister effect on a person's health, and may lead to premature death. For example, an investigation of men who worked for the People's Gas Company in Chicago showed that the higher the man's initial blood pressure, the greater was his chance of having a heart attack, a stroke, or some other disease of the heart or arteries within twelve years. The effect of a stroke on a man's entire life can be even more devastating. At a World Health Organisation Seminar in 1971, the medical experts concluded that there was no single measure which would make such a contribution to the quality of life in old age as the prevention of stroke.

To understand why this is so, you need to know something about your blood pressure.

Table 11 The direct complications of high blood pressure

● Stroke
● Haemorrhage into the retina of the eye
● Heart failure
● Kidney damage

All these can be prevented if hypertension is diagnosed and adequately treated.

Your heart is a pump which beats 70 times a minute, 4200 times an hour, 100,000 times a day, and 365, 000 times a year, forcing blood through all your arteries. The blood carries vitally needed oxygen to your tissues and removes waste products for discharge from your body through your lungs or your kidneys. To keep the blood flowing against the resistance of the elastic-like walls of the arteries the heart has to exert a pressure.

In 1905, a Russian physician, Korotkoff, discovered that if a pressure cuff was applied to the upper arm, the blood pressure could be measured by listening to the sounds with a stethoscope over the artery in the fold of the elbow. With each heart beat, the blood pressure rises to a peak. This is the systolic pressure. Between heart beats, the pressure falls to a lower level. This is the diastolic pressure. By pumping up the cuff so that no blood flows through the artery and then releasing the air slowly, the blood flows in squirts and 'thumps' loudly on the artery wall which the doctor can hear through his stethoscope. This is the systolic pressure. As the cuff empties, the character of the thumps changes; the sounds become soft and then disappear. The disappearance of the sound identifies the diastolic pressure. Your blood pressure varies throughout the day and responds to all kinds of stress or emotion, when it tends to rise. During sleep it is at its lowest. The temporary rises are normal and natural, but the doctor or nurse tries to take a resting pressure.

If your resting pressure is normal, you have no further worries, but if it is raised the doctor usually takes the blood pressure again after a two-week interval (and preferably after a further two weeks) before he diagnoses that you have high blood pressure, as it is known that transient rises in blood pressure can occur. If you have a raised blood pressure at both or at all three of these examinations, you have hypertension.

The problem which arises is what should be considered a high blood pressure. We know from studies in many Western nations that a person's blood pressure rises as he or she grows older. We also know that rises in blood pressure with increasing age are more frequent among people in developed countries and only occur rarely in the developing countries, except among those who have adopted a 'Western' way of life.

This suggests that high blood pressure may be due to our way of life, or to our diet, rather than because we have inherited a tendency to hypertension. Some investigators suggest that the stress of modern life is a factor, others suggest that we eat too much salt, or too many refined carbohydrates.

What is a high blood pressure? Different authorities give different levels, which means that any decision is arbitrary. By observing the frequency of stroke, heart attacks, and other cardio-vascular

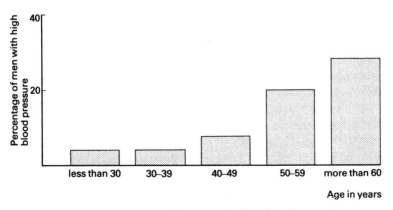

27 The relationship between age and hypertension (high blood pressure)

accidents and relating these to the level of the person's blood
pressure, an expert committee of the WHO has recommended that
if your systolic blood pressure exceeds 160, or if your diastolic blood
pressure exceeds 95 (especially if both are above those levels), and if
these results are found at three examinations at least two weeks
apart, you have high blood pressure.

In a community, about 7 per cent of men and 9 per cent of women
aged 40 to 49 have high blood pressure; and in older age groups the
proportion increases. The more overweight you are the more likely
you are to have high blood pressure.

In most cases, you feel perfectly well and you are unaware that
you have high blood pressure. But unless you take action in middle
age, by changing your life-style and, perhaps, by taking prescribed
drugs, you have five times the chance of having a heart attack or a
stroke before you reach the age of 65, and an even greater chance of
one of these disasters occurring after that age.

The higher the blood pressure, the harder the heart has to work to

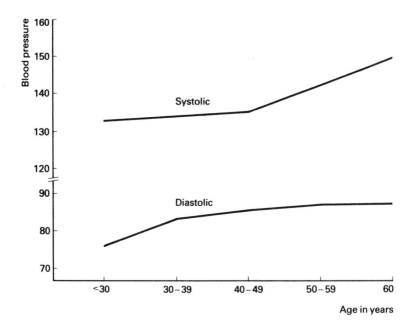

28 The 'normal' levels of blood pressure related to age

overcome the increased resistance of the arteries to the flow of blood through them. Over the years, unless you are treated, the muscle wall of the heart thickens and the coronary blood-vessels cannot supply sufficient blood to it. If this happens, you may develop heart failure. The high blood pressure may affect the smaller arteries of your body as the blood pounds along their inner surface, day in, day out. It may hasten the onset of atherosclerosis, the hardening and thickening of the arteries which, if it affects your coronary arteries, may cause a heart attack, or if this occurs in the brain, may lead to a stroke.

Many people believe that a 'stroke' is only a problem of old age. It is not. In an investigation in Victoria, Australia, it was found that one out of every five people who had a stroke was under the age of 65 and that at least one-third of victims of stroke had untreated (or inadequately treated) high blood pressure.

What should you do to avoid this disastrous event?

This, for a start!

Whenever you visit your doctor for whatever reason, insist on having your blood pressure checked, particularly if you are aged 35 or over, unless it has been checked and found to be normal in the previous year.

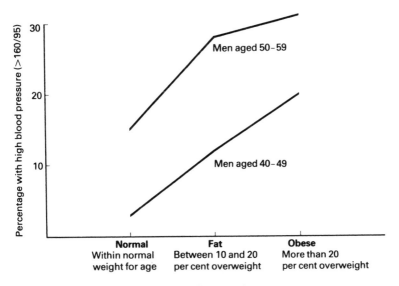

29 The relationship between weight and hypertension

As I have mentioned, a single high blood pressure reading does not mean you have high blood pressure, because anxiety, fear, and stress can raise your blood pressure. But if the readings remain high, that is above 160/95, on three measurements taken at least two weeks apart, you have high blood pressure.

If your doctor finds that you have hypertension, he will want to do some tests to try and find if there is an underlying cause, and to try to estimate more accurately the state of your heart and arteries. He will listen to your heart with a stethoscope and will examine the back of your eyes with a small instrument. He will take an X-ray of your chest and do an electrocardiogram. He will also order some laboratory tests. In these ways he will be better able to advise you what to do.

At present the answer is not as clear cut as most doctors would wish. All would agree that if you are under the age of 70, and your systolic blood pressure is consistently above 180 or, more importantly, if your diastolic blood pressure is consistently above 110, you need treatment. You will have to alter your life-style and you will be prescribed drugs. But if your systolic blood pressure lies between 160 and 180, and if your diastolic blood pressure is persistently between 95 and 110 – in the so-called grey area – no firm decision about the need for treatment has been reached by medical scientists. For example, drug treatment would be appropriate if you were a 45-year-old man whose systolic blood pressure was 160 after three checks, who smoked more than 30 cigarettes a day (and refused to give up), and who had evidence of heart strain on an electrocardiogram. Equally, a 45-year-old man who took exercise, smoked sparingly, but who had the same degree of hypertension might not need treatment.

Table 12 The relationship between raised blood pressure, stroke, and coronary heart disease: the higher the blood pressure, the greater the risk

	Risk of	
Diastolic blood pressure	*Stroke*	*Heart Attack*
less than 80	1	1
80–110	1.5	2
more than 110	9.0	3.5

The problem of drug treatment is that, although it is very

effective in reducing your high blood pressure, there are some side-effects of the medication, and the drugs have to be taken for life. Because of this, many doctors want to be sure that people whose blood pressure is permanently in the 'grey area' will benefit more (by having fewer strokes and fewer heart attacks) than they will be disadvantaged by having to take drugs for life.

In the past five years research has taken place in Australia, Britain, and the U.S.A. to resolve this problem. During the same period new drugs have been developed which have fewer side-effects. The consensus which is beginning to appear is that the majority of people under the age of 70 whose blood pressure lies in the grey area will benefit by taking anti-hypertensive drugs, although it is just as important for them to change their life-style so that they help control their own blood pressure and reduce their dependence on the drugs.

There are a number of simple measures which a man should adopt to avoid the problems of high blood pressure.

● If you are overweight, get your weight down. If you do, you may find that your blood pressure comes down too.

● Cut down the quantity of salt you have in your food, or add to your food, so that you take no more than 2 g (one-third of a level teaspoonful) a day. You can do this by avoiding salty foods, such as bacon and salted peanuts, and by not adding salt to the food on your plate.

● You should stop smoking! Smoking increases the tone of the branches of small arteries so that they become narrow. This change aggravates high blood pressure and increases the risk of a stroke.

● Take more exercise, but only take exercise you enjoy and after talking it over with your doctor.

● Try to reduce the emotional tension and strain in your life. Your blood pressure level is determined by your autonomic nerve system and by chemicals secreted by various organs in your body. The impulses from your nervous system and the release of the chemicals are influenced by your emotions. If you can relax more at work and at home, if you can stop worrying about trivial matters, if you can put things to one side for a while, you will reduce your emotional tension, and this will help to reduce your high blood pressure.

• If you can do all these things you may find that you do not need drugs, as your blood pressure has fallen to normal. But if you do need drugs, several are available. The first, and most frequently prescribed, drug is called a diuretic, because it increases your urine flow. It also reduces your blood pressure to some extent. None of the diuretics available is more effective than any other (whatever the twenty-five manufacturers say). There are a few minor side-effects from the medication but most people can take them without any disturbance. Nearly 65 per cent of people with mild hypertension only need to take diuretics, but for the remaining 35 per cent of people with hypertension, the effect of diuretics is not sufficient, and other drugs have to be taken as well.

At the present time an increasing number of physicians choose a group of drugs called 'beta-blockers' because they have fewer side-effects than previously available drugs.

The dose of beta-blocker drugs which most effectively reduces a person's high blood pressure will differ because each person seems to respond differently to a fixed dose. It takes a few weeks for your doctor to find the dose most appropriate for you, but once he has found it, you can continue on that dose for a long time, and you will only need to have check-ups every three or six months. Unfortunately, the beta-blockers have some side-effects. These are not disabling but may be disturbing. They include a feeling of lassitude, occasional light-headedness, and sometimes episodes of insomnia or of weird disturbing dreams, but they usually only occur with large doses of the drug. Some people are unable to take the beta-blocker drugs. They include people with asthma, diabetes, and heart failure. Other drugs are available to help them.

Unfortunately, in surveys it has been found that:

• Half of the people with high blood pressure in a community have not been detected. They have hypertension and do not know it, because they have not had their blood pressure checked.

• Half of those people who are known to have high blood pressure are not taking any medication.

• Half of those people who are being treated are inadequately treated, namely, they are taking too small a dose or using an inappropriate drug.

If the level of hypertension is such that you need drugs and want to prevent the complications of high blood pressure you must receive and continue to take your treatment in the appropriate dose. Yet only half the known people who have a high blood pressure are taking medication. In an investigation in the U.S.A. it was found that even though the people with hypertension visited their doctor every three months, they still failed to take the prescribed drugs. When the men were asked why, they answered that they did not realize that they had to take the drugs permanently. When they felt better, they stopped! And, of course, their blood pressure rose, so that they ran a greater risk of having a stroke or some other cardio-vascular complication.

It appears from this story that the doctors were not communicating adequately with their patients and were not educating hypertensive people properly. In an attempt to overcome this unsatisfactory situation, a community effort was made in Baldwin County, Georgia. Specially trained nurses visited hypertensive people in their homes, they took blood pressures and helped the people understand why the drugs were needed. Within a few months 86 per cent of people known to have hypertension were taking their medication, and, in nearly all, good control of their blood pressure had been achieved. Unfortunately, the effort was a pilot scheme, and once it had proved its efficiency it was abandoned. However, it showed what could be done to reduce the serious effects of untreated hypertension in the community.

It is important that action is taken by the community, and by individual people, to detect and to treat high blood pressure. If hypertension is controlled, fewer people – especially men – will have a stroke or a heart attack, and the misery consequent upon these disasters will be reduced.

The time to take action is now. The method of taking action is not difficult, but it does need community involvement.

Each community may wish to devise its own strategies, and the following suggestions may help in starting a programme to reduce hypertension and its consequences.

● In offices, management should make it possible for all staff, or at least those aged over 35, to have annual blood pressure checks, if they wish. Anyone found to have a high blood pressure should have it checked again at least twice. These checks can be made by nurses, more cheaply and as efficiently as by doctors.

• In factories, unions should expect, and management should encourage, similar programmes to be started.

• The community can help by arranging for free blood pressure checks, carried out by trained volunteers, in supermarkets, factories, and offices in the district.

• The individual can help by mobilizing community organizations to persuade people to have their blood pressure checked annually.

• You can help by insisting that when you visit your doctor, for whatever reason, he takes your blood pressure, if it has not been taken in the previous year.

• People who have hypertension can help by forming community-based associations or clubs, to arrange counselling programmes, and to encourage other people with hypertension to continue medication and have periodic check-ups.

14

The heart is the matter

A coronary heart disease is a chronic, often symptomless disease with acute manifestations in the late stages. Therein lies the dilemma.

Lancet (April 1976)

There is considerable evidence that the causes of coronary heart disease are largely environmental and are rooted in the modern, affluent way of life. Coronary heart disease risk factors such as cigarette smoking, physical inactivity, obesity and plasma lipid (blood fat) concentrations reflect aspects of our social behaviour.

Report of a Joint Working Party of the Royal College of Physicians of London and the British Cardiac Society (1976)

... It is further reasonable and sound to designate 'rich' diet as a primary, essential, necessary cause of the current epidemic of premature atherosclerotic disease (coronary heart disease) raging in western industrialized countries. Cigarette smoking and hypertension are important secondary or complementary causes.

Jeremiah Stamler (1978)

WHEN MEN AGED 45 TO 64 CONGRATULATE THEMSELVES, IN a sexist way, that they avoid the discomforts that affect pre-menopausal and menopausal women, they should reflect that their life and health, during this period, are at greater risk than the life and health of women.

Statistics from Britain confirm this. Dr Clayton and his colleagues examined the death rates from heart disease between 1950 and 1973 among men aged 35 to 64. They found that the death rate had risen by 80 per cent in younger men and by 30 per cent in older men.

Since 1968, the death rate from coronary heart disease of men aged 35 to 64 has fallen by about 20 per cent in the U.S.A. and in Australia, while that in Britain has not altered significantly. In the three nations the mortality rate for men of this age group is about 225 per 100,000 men, aged 30 to 64.

In our type of society, in any year, a large number of men in the prime of life will have a heart attack. One-third of men aged 35 to 64 who have an acute heart attack will die as a result within a few days, most of them dying within a few minutes or hours. Only six men in every ten who have had a heart attack will be alive one year later. While a heart attack is the most common form of death in old age, the tragedy of a heart attack at a time when a man has just reached the peak of his achievement is obvious. After years of initiative, diligence, and hard work he has acquired the possessions he feels he needs; he has a wife and a growing family; he is reasonably secure financially, he looks forward to a satisfying life, and then suddenly, unexpectedly, usually without warning, he has a heart attack.

A man's heart attack affects not only him, but also his wife and family. Only recently has the extent of the wife's emotional and social disturbance been recognized. The period of greatest stress and anxiety is when the man is in hospital, but stress continues long after his return home. Many women whose husband has had a heart attack initially are anxious, depressed, unable to sleep or to concentrate. The stress is reduced if the medical staff keep the woman fully informed and involve her in her husband's rehabilitation.

The involvement of the woman not only benefits her psycholog-ical state, but helps the man to make a more rapid recovery, if she encourages him to keep to his diet, to exercise properly, and to stop smoking, all of which are beneficial to his health.

The effects of a heart attack on the marriage are considerable, and can cause great stress unless clear advice is given. Many victims of heart attacks continue to be alternately depressed or irritable for some months. Not all couples understand, or are given sufficient information, about sexual activity after one of them has had a heart attack. Others are misinformed. In a study in Britain, Dr Richard Mayou found that one-quarter of the couples had less frequent intercourse and one-quarter avoided sex almost completely.

Statistics from England and Wales show that one man in twelve will die of a heart attack before he retires. The sudden death of a man in middle age has many consequences. Not only has he missed at least twenty-five years of life, but his death leaves his wife with the sadness and loneliness of bereavement, the problems of probate, and perhaps the responsibility of growing children to cope with alone.

In the past twenty years, large numbers of coronary intensive care units have been established, at very considerable expense, which help to reduce deaths among some of those people who survive long enough to reach the unit. But as only about 75 per cent of men who suffer a heart attack reach a coronary unit alive, cardiac units do not really solve the problem. It is like putting the ambulance at the bottom of the cliff to retrieve the victim who has fallen.

The principal way in which premature death from heart attacks will be reduced to any large extent and in which any real impact can be made on this disease of civilization is to prevent an attack.

*

There has been a vast amount of research into the 'epidemic of heart attacks' and at least 100,000 scientific articles have been published in the past twenty years.

Although the research has been unable to identify the cause of coronary heart disease, it has established that an important feature is a narrowing of the artery by a raised, thickened patch, which has a rough surface. As the blood pounds through the artery, it becomes turbulent as it passes the patch, and this may begin the process of a blood clot forming on the patch. If the patch is in a coronary artery, and if a clot forms, the artery may be blocked by the clot. That part of the heart muscle which is supplied by the artery no longer receives oxygen or nourishment, and some of the muscle fibres die. The reduction in blood to the area of muscle sets up a sequence of events which cause pain and the other effects which make the diagnosis of a heart attack possible. If a large number of muscle fibres of the heart are affected, the heart ceases to beat properly, then it stops beating and the person dies. If fewer heart muscle fibres are damaged, recovery is likely.

The account describes how heart attacks occur. It does not explain why they occur when they do. But, by investigating the histories of men who have suffered heart attacks, scientists have identified certain factors which increase the risk of developing coronary heart disease.

The most important risk factors, apart from age and sex, are high levels of cholesterol in the blood serum, high levels of triglycerides in the blood, raised blood pressure or hypertension, and cigarette smoking.

High serum cholesterol

A high serum cholesterol is a measure of a person's intake, from his diet, of lipids or, more accurately, of the two chemical substances which make up the lipids, fatty acids and cholesterol. Our diet is rich in both.

People who live in the developing nations eat a diet which consists mainly of cereals (wheat, maize, or rice), vegetables, with eggs and milk eaten infrequently and meat eaten only on feast days. But for us who live in the rich developed nations every day is a feast day, and over 40 per cent of our calories are provided by the fat we eat. Most people in rich nations eat a good deal of red meat. Red meat is good for you as it is composed mainly of protein. But, in addition, red meat is also rich in fatty acids, particularly if it is 'marbled' meat, and if we cook it by frying it in animal fat.

Fat occurs in natural foods in two forms, saturated fat and polyunsaturated fat. In the meat we eat, most of the fatty acids are saturated, in the vegetables the fats are usually polyunsaturated. We also enjoy gravies, cakes, biscuits, ice cream, and puddings; all of these contain 'hidden' saturated fat.

As well, many of us enjoy eating eggs and kidneys, which are rich in cholesterol. Although everyone needs to eat some cholesterol, we eat excessive amounts, and the quantity we absorb from our food is increased, because our diet contains a lot of saturated fatty acids, and only a small amount of fibre.

In animal experiments and in trials of diets in humans it has been found that the more saturated fatty acids and cholesterol the diet contains, the higher is the level of cholesterol in the blood.

For the past twenty years the people of the city of Framingham in Massachusetts in the U.S.A. have agreed to be examined by medical scientists. From their studies it has been found that the higher the level of blood lipids – and especially cholesterol – the greater the risk of having a heart attack. For example, if you are aged 40, do not smoke, and have a normal blood pressure and your blood cholesterol is less than 5.44 mmol/l you have one chance in a hundred of having a heart attack in the next six years. But if your blood cholesterol is over 7.38 mmol/l your risk of having a heart attack in the next six years rises to 6 per cent.

In the past few years, it has been discovered that cholesterol is carried in our blood in two forms. In the first, the cholesterol is attached to substances called high-density lipids. In the second, it is attached to lower-density lipids. What is interesting is that if you have a high level of high-density lipid-cholesterol, you seem to be *protected* against coronary heart disease, but if you have a high level of lower-density lipid-cholesterol you are at higher risk of developing a coronary heart disease. In fact, Dr William Castelli, Director of Laboratories at Framingham, says:

The high-density cholesterol level is the most powerful single lipid predictor of coronary artery disease. It may not be as powerful in younger age groups . . . but it is clear that in persons over 50 years of age, knowledge of the high-density lipoprotein cholesterol levels is more important than knowledge of total serum cholesterol levels. And the test can be performed simply and cheaply by any laboratory that does cholesterol estimations.

If the laboratory tests show that you have a low level of high-density lipid-cholesterol (that is, a level below 0.9 mmol/l) it is a cause for concern, as you have fourteen times the risk of developing heart disease.

It is thought that the high-density lipids actually aid in removing cholesterol from the tissues, and especially from the lining of the coronary arteries.

If it is good for you to have a high level of high-density lipids, how can you raise your levels of the substance and at the same time reduce your high blood cholesterol? Exercise is one way – athletes have higher levels of high-density lipids than sedentary people. Change in diet is another – cut out 'junk foods' like hot dogs, meat pies, hamburgers, ice cream, and potato chips, and eat less marbled meat; instead, eat wholemeal bread and cereals, fish, lean meat, vegetables, and fruit.

Unfortunately, drugs to reduce the blood cholesterol level are rather ineffective, and are no substitute for changes in your life-style and in your diet.

High triglyceride levels

Some scientists, but by no means all, believe that a high triglyceride blood level is an important risk factor in coronary heart disease. Your blood triglyceride level is increased if you eat a good deal of 'refined' carbohydrate and drink a good deal of alcohol. Refined carbohydrate is the white flour from which we make our bread, cakes, and sauces. It is also the sugar which we are increasingly eating. In fact, our sugar consumption has risen by 100 per cent in the past hundred years. And like the fats we eat, at least half of the sugar we eat is 'hidden' in ice cream, cakes, biscuits, soft drinks, and sauces.

Professor John Yudkin is the spokesman of those who believe that the amount of refined carbohydrate we eat is important in producing heart disease. He has examined the relationship between sugar intake and the deaths from coronary heart disease in many countries and has found that the higher the sugar intake the greater the risk of death from heart disease. His group have also shown that a high sugar intake from the diet is associated with a greater chance of having a high blood sugar (or more accurately glucose intolerance), a higher level of blood triglycerides, and a higher level of blood cholesterol. He has also noticed that a raised serum triglyceride level is found in men who develop heart attacks.

Professor Yudkin's belief receives support from a recent study of coronary heart disease in Edinburgh and Stockholm. The investigators, led by Dr Oliver, found that deaths from the disease were two and a half times as common in Edinburgh as in Stockholm among men under the age of 60, although the mean serum cholesterol values were the same in the two cities. However, the Scotsmen had higher serum triglyceride levels, smoked more, and had higher blood pressures.

Our diet contains a high amount of refined carbohydrates, especially sugar, and of fats, and often the two are found together in our food, particularly in ice cream, rich sauces, and pastry.

Again the question has to be asked whether drugs or diet will reduce the serum triglyceride level. As in the case of serum cholesterol levels, drugs are relatively ineffective in reducing the serum triglycerides, but diet is fairly effective. If you cut down your sugar intake and eat less food made from white flour, your serum triglycerides will fall.

Dieting is particularly important if you are overweight and have diabetes, as both of these factors add to the risk of developing coronary heart disease.

High blood pressure (hypertension)

Evidence from many countries shows that a high blood pressure accelerates the appearance of coronary heart disease. For example, Professor Morris of London has recorded that among a group of middle-aged London bus drivers, who were examined at intervals for at least ten years, the higher their blood pressure was, the greater the chance that they would develop coronary heart disease. And, as Professor Morris writes: 'moderate and severe hypertension can be lowered by today's potent and fairly well tolerated medicines'.

How do you know if you have a raised blood pressure? It is quite simple: have your blood pressure taken.

Cigarette smoking

In an investigation in the U.S.A. of over one million men and women, two scientists, Dr Hammond and Dr Garfinkle, have found that men aged 40 to 49 who smoke 40 or more cigarettes a day have a 70 per cent greater chance of developing coronary heart disease than non-smokers. In England, Sir Richard Doll and Dr Hill found that moderate cigarette smoking trebled the risk of dying from coronary heart disease among those aged 45 to 54.

Doctors are becoming increasingly aware of the dangers of cigarette smoking. Dr Wilhelmsen of Göteborg in Sweden has found that smoking increases a middle-aged man's chance of having a heart attack considerably, and the risk increases dramatically if he has hypertension or a high blood cholesterol. In Australia, the National Heart Foundation calculate that over 4000 premature deaths were caused by smoking in 1975. If you are aged between 45

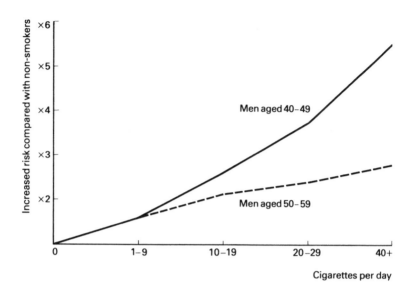

30 The increased risk of coronary heart disease among cigarette smokers

and 54 and you smoke 10 to 19 cigarettes a day your risk of having a heart attack doubles, while if you smoke more than 20 cigarettes a day, it trebles.

Cigarette smoking is as great a risk factor in coronary heart disease as high blood pressure and high blood cholesterol.

There can be no doubt, in spite of protestation and propaganda from sections of the tobacco industry, that smoking is a health hazard.

But there is good news! When you give up smoking your risk of dying from a heart attack falls steadily. After about four years it is the same as for a person who has never smoked.

Exercise

Exercise seems to protect people against coronary heart disease. A group of doctors in Stanford University, California, have studied 41 men who ran more than 25 kilometres (15 miles) a week and compared them with men who took no exercise. They found that the blood levels of triglycerides, cholesterol, and high-density lipoproteins were significantly lower in the blood of the men who exercised. Another American physician, Dr Froelicher, checked

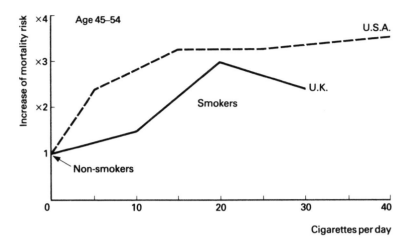

31 The relationship between death from coronary heart disease and the number of cigarettes smoked

over fifty papers about exercise and heart disease up to February 1976 and concluded that there was suggestive (but not conclusive) evidence that exercise protected men against heart disease.

*

All scientists now agree that risk factors have been identified which increase your risk of having a heart attack, and if you have more than one risk factor your risk of a heart attack increases spectacularly.

The risk factors probably start early in your life and, over the years, their effect is cumulative.

The sequence may go like this.

A person who eats too much refined carbohydrate, particularly sugar and fats (especially saturated animal fats), from early childhood is at greater risk of having a heart attack than an individual in a less sophisticated, and less overfed, society. Fats, in susceptible people, may lead to high levels of cholesterol in the blood, which over the years may be an important factor in heart disease. The excessive consumption of sugar (and other refined carbohydrates) has several consequences. It raises the blood triglyceride levels, and increases the stickiness of blood platelets, which is a factor in blood clotting and so may be involved in heart disease. If you habitually eat more carbohydrate (especially sugar) and fat than you need for the things you do, you accumulate the excess as body fat, which results in obesity. Fat people are more likely to develop diabetes, as are people who eat excessive quantities of sugar and refined carbohydrates over the years.

Diabetes in association with obesity increases the risk of coronary heart disease. Obesity also predisposes an individual to high blood pressure, which in turn is a major factor in heart disease. In both men and women, under the age of 40, cigarette smoking seems to play a more important role than high blood pressure. But after that age, the role of cigarette smoking diminishes, and high blood pressure increases the risk of heart disease more than cigarette smoking. The place of exercise in the prevention of heart disease is unclear; it is probably beneficial, it certainly helps to reduce obesity, but in sudden, unaccustomed bursts it may be lethal. After a heart attack, regular, sensible exercise becomes increasingly important.

If you are tense, competitive, anxious, and cannot relax, you are likely to eat (or drink) empty calories to excess; you are likely to exercise fiercely or not at all, and you are likely to smoke heavily. Unless you can, in the words of St Matthew, 'change your foolish ways', you are asking for a heart attack.

Studies have been made, in the U.S.A. particularly, to see what the combined effect is of the major risk factors. In two large studies involving over 10,000 men aged 40 to 59 who, when first examined, had no evidence of coronary heart disease, the factors of high serum cholesterol (which the researchers took as 6.47 mmol/l or more), high blood pressure, and smoking more than 10 cigarettes a day were examined. The men were examined at intervals for nearly fifteen years and every heart attack was recorded. This is what the research showed.

If none of the three risk factors was present at the beginning of the study, only 20 in every 1000 men had a heart attack; if one risk factor was present, the risk of a heart attack doubled; if two were present, it doubled again; and if all three were present, the risk was eight times higher than that of the men who had none of the risk factors.

There can be no doubt that the risk factors of cigarette smoking, diets rich in fat and refined carbohydrate, high blood pressure, and, perhaps, obesity add to your chances of having a heart attack. It is possible for you to reduce your risk of developing coronary heart disease if you are prepared to alter your life-style and to modify your eating habits. It is never too late to start. It is not easy to get people to change their life-style, although there are hopeful developments. The best approach is for us to stop smoking and to alter the character of our diet, so that we avoid the excessive consumption of sugar and saturated fat which are so much a part of our present dietary habits.

Nutritionists interested in heart disease are convinced that if the dietary habits of people were changed, preferably from early childhood, the risk of heart disease would diminish. Unfortunately, food habits are formed very early in childhood. Once these habits have been imprinted on the brain, they are difficult to change and any attempt to do so is considered a threat to the individual's personal freedom.

Yet it is clear to the unbiased observer that changes in our food habits have occurred over the years, and are occurring with increasing frequency since radio, and particularly television, became so popular. The advertisers and the persuaders in the media manipulate our minds and alter our food habits, usually adversely. We no longer consume, or wish to consume, 'peasant' foods – cereals, breads made from unrefined flour, fruits, and vegetables, with only occasional feasts of fatty meat.

Our minds have been bent to believe that fatty meat is the best, the most nutritious, the most 'savoury'. Pastry cooks and biscuit manufacturers have persuaded us that our desire for sweet, sugary, fat-based foods is inborn. To convince us further, advertisers equate cake-making with home-making, and the manufacturers provide packaged cake-mixes so that a cake can be made with little effort. Confectionery makers convince our children that sucrose-based sweets are beneficial and that chocolates, made from saturated fats and sucrose, are the right of every child. Soft-drink manufacturers, who add sugar and synthetic agents, convince us that a child who does not drink Coke or one of the other sugar-loaded drinks has harsh parents, and is unloved.

Habitually, we eat too much food based on sugar and refined carbohydrate and too much fatty meat. By doing so, over the years, we have contributed to our risk of having a heart attack.

*

The heart *is* the matter. Coronary heart disease is killing large numbers of men when they are in the prime of life. Even if a man does not die from the first attack he has an increased chance of having another one within five years.

It seems a terrible waste of human life. The answer is not to call for more, bigger, better-equipped coronary care units in more hospitals to treat heart attacks (although some are needed) but to start measures which will prevent heart disease. And to start now!

What should be done? This has been studied by expert committees in most developed nations, who have issued carefully worded reports signed by eminent physicians. The most recent is a report by a Working Party of the Royal College of Physicians of London and the British Cardiac Society. It supplements earlier reports from the U.S.A., Sweden, New Zealand, and Australia.

Essentially, the reports recommend that if you want to prevent coronary heart disease you will have to alter your life-style and your eating habits.

First, your diet

● *If you are obese* – which means that you have eaten, over the years, more energy than you have expended each day – get your weight down to what is normal for your height and age.

● *You should reduce the amount of saturated fat in your diet*, because a high intake of saturated fats increases your blood lipid level, especially your blood cholesterol level. At present many of our favourite 'national' foods are rich in saturated fats. In England, these are sausages and mash, or roast beef and Yorkshire pudding; in America, 'marbled' steak and apple pie; and in Australia, the meat pie.

This is what you should do:

● eat grilled foods instead of fried foods

● eat lean meat instead of fatty, 'marbled' meat

● alternate fish or chicken with beef or lamb

● cut down the amount of butter you eat – or if you prefer, replace butter (made from saturated fat) with soft margarine (made from polyunsaturated fat)

● *You should cut down the amount of sugar and unrefined carbohydrate (white flour products) which you eat.*

This is how you can do it:

- eat less ice cream (this is made, at present, largely from mutton or coconut fat)

- eat fewer cakes and pastries (both contain 'hidden' sugar and 'hidden' fat)

- eat less 'rich' gravies (made of fat) and sauces

- eat less, or no, sugar in your tea and coffee. Sugar in drinks is an acquired taste – almost an addiction – you can lose your addiction if you cut down the number of spoonfuls of sugar you put into your drinks – and you will lose weight too!

- re-educate your palate to eat wholemeal bread in preference to white 'pappy' bread. You do not have to eat wholemeal bread all the time – sometimes white bread is to be preferred – but eat it most of the time.

- cut down, or omit, soft drinks, except soda water, and drinks made by you from *fresh* fruit. Commercial soft drinks, including so-called bitter drinks, like tonic water, contain sugar. If you like 'mixers' with your alcohol, use soda water.

- *Several reports recommend that you eat fewer eggs because egg yolk is rich in saturated fats and cholesterol.* You do not have to be a fanatic: if you do not eat more than 6 eggs a week the difference to your fat intake will be minimal, and your cholesterol levels will not be raised.

Second, your habits

- Cigarette smoking is a major risk factor in the development of coronary heart disease. Cut out cigarettes if you can. If you cannot, only smoke after meals. And do not inhale.

Third, your life-style

- Take more exercise. You can choose the type of exercise which appeals to you most – gardening or golf; walking or cycling; swimming or jogging. It does not matter so long as you exercise.

- Have your blood pressure checked by your doctor once a year. There is now evidence that a raised blood pressure is a major risk factor in the development of coronary heart disease, and it aggravates the other risk factors. So, if your blood pressure is raised, it is even more important that you should take action, particularly if you are also overweight, if you smoke, and if you are physically inactive. If your blood pressure is raised and you use a lot of salt on your food – cut it down – preferably cut it out. Just eat the salt used in cooking.

If you make these changes to your diet and to your life-style – and stop smoking – you will reduce your chance of having a heart attack very considerably. You will do it without missing most of the things you enjoy. What is more, you will live longer to go on enjoying them. Enjoy them prudently; not wantonly!

*

Unfortunately, only a few men are prepared to take measures to prevent a heart attack and, even with preventive measures, heart attacks may occur.

If you are unfortunate enough to be the victim of a heart attack, or if you fear you may become a victim, you may want to know the answers to three questions:
1. 'What is my chance of surviving a heart attack?'
2. 'How soon can I lead a normal life after recovering from a heart attack?'
3. 'When can I lead a normal sexual life?'

What is my chance of surviving a heart attack?

The answer to this question is both discouraging and encouraging!

Careful investigation of men who have survived a heart attack in Edinburgh, in Teesside, in Belfast, and in Bristol show that most heart attacks occur at home. In the first half hour after the attack (usually before any help can be obtained) about 10 per cent of men aged 45 to 64 and 25 per cent of men over that age will die. By two hours after the attack a further 20 per cent of men aged 45 to 64 and 30 per cent of those over 64 will die. There is some evidence that if emergency 'cardiac' ambulances are available, whose crews have been trained to treat heart arrest and a very rapidly beating (although inefficient) heart, about 10 per cent of those presently dying will be saved. As this number is disappointingly small it is obvious that prevention of heart attacks is crucial.

But if you do survive those first two critical hours your chances of surviving the heart attack are good, and they are probably increased, at least if you are under 65, if you can be admitted to an intensive coronary care unit in a hospital. In recent years, intensive coronary care units have been established in many hospitals. In these units your heart is monitored electronically, and should it start beating irregularly you can immediately be given drugs which will restore its rhythm, and save your life. If it suddenly stops beating, it can be restarted by giving it an electric shock. As well as these life-saving emergency measures, the trained staff make sure that your fluids are properly balanced and that you neither become dehydrated, nor do your blood electrolytes become disordered, and they may prescribe drugs called beta-blockers, which appear to limit the degree of heart muscle damage. With this expert care, a heart attack victim usually remains in the coronary care unit for about four days, and after this goes to an ordinary hospital room or ward.

Not all physicians agree that every person who has had a heart attack need be admitted to a coronary care unit: many treated at home do as well or better. Sir George Pickering, an eminent British physician, has written recently:

Knowing what I do now, I shall opt to be treated at home without anticoagulants, should I have a myocardial infarction when I am home or within easy reach of it. An arrhythmia, cardiac failure or other complications may make it easier for my physician or my wife if I go to hospital. In that case I shall go, but think the routine of sending all patients with myocardial infarctions to coronary care units is probably dangerous; it is certainly hideously expensive.

How soon can I lead a normal life after recovering from a heart attack?

The time from your return to a general hospital ward from an intensive coronary care unit, until you are leading a normal life, is called the period of rehabilitation. In recent years, the duration of rehabilitation and the methods used have undergone critical scrutiny. The purpose of rehabilitation is to enable the person to live as full a life as possible.

It has now been realized that most heart attack victims were kept in hospital for too long and for little reason. Today, the aim is to get you back into your home environment as soon as is medically possible and to help you learn how to recover from the heart attack. The learning process may include changes in your diet, so that your weight is reduced or kept down, a reduction (or elimination) of your smoking, and a return to a programme of increasing physical activity. The programmes of increasing exercise help you to do exercises which you enjoy and which are 'normal' for you, rather than the apparently purposeless exercises used in the past. If you enjoy walking in the country, or swimming, or cycling, or golf, that is what you should do, and you will be encouraged to increase the amount you do.

Many heart physicians believe that rehabilitation is quicker and easier if you join in weekly sessions of group therapy with other people who have had a heart attack; others believe that the programme should be much more casual. But most physicians know that your co-operation and enthusiasm are needed for the quickest rehabilitation.

When can I lead a normal sexual life?

In recent years, research has shown that a man who has survived the immediate days after a coronary can become active much earlier than was believed previously.

Many men have believed, quite wrongly, that the excitement of sex may lead to a second, more severe, possibly fatal heart attack. Some even fear that this may happen during sexual intercourse. To the fear of dying during sex is added the anxiety of how such a death would affect the man's wife.

These fears have led many men who have coronary heart disease to avoid sex and, unfortunately, only a few doctors have the knowledge and the interest to advise their cardiac patients. However, you can be reassured! A heart attack occurring during sexual intercourse is very uncommon.

Apart from such reassurance, most cardiac patients want to know when they can resume sexual intercourse, how often is safe, what position should be used, and what are the dangers.

The answer to these questions depends on the severity of the heart attack, on the man's previous sexual activity, and on the co-operation of his partner. As a generalization, it can be said that if you have been given permission to walk up one or two flights of stairs, or to drive your car, you can resume sex, as it will put no more strain on the heart than these non-sexual activities.

After a heart attack, many men find it helpful as a method of rehabilitation to masturbate. This should be encouraged, as the strain on the man's heart is minimal and the reassurance that the heart attack has not damaged his masculinity is vital. Masturbation also prevents the development of impotence – due to fear that sexual intercourse will cause a heart attack – which affects a number of cardiac patients. Following a heart attack a man can start masturbating whenever he wants to do so. This can be in hospital or soon after his return home. At home, with the co-operation of his partner, he can have his penis stimulated by her, either with her fingers or with her mouth, and his orgasm confirms in his mind that his sexuality has suffered no damage.

Those men who find masturbation distasteful can resume sexual intercourse once they are fit to undertake mild exertion. When the man and his partner resume sex, he may prefer to use the female-superior or side-to-side position, rather than the traditional male-superior position. There is some slight evidence that the last position adds to the strain on the heart, but the matter is not settled, and the advice should be to use the position the couple enjoys most.

A few men who have severe cardiac rhythm irregularities, or have congestive heart failure, should avoid sexual intercourse until they have fully recovered, but they can still enjoy masturbation or fellatio.

A heart attack is usually a considerable shock but, provided you survive the first hours, you will find that, with help, you will be able to lead a full, active, and enjoyable life.

15
Those golden years — growing old

I will never be an old man. To me, old age is always fifteen
years older than I am.

Bernard Baruch

No reason can be seen to perpetuate the division based on
age alone between the acute care of general medical and
geriatric patients. Disease does not undergo any change at
65 years, though the older the patient the greater is the
likelihood of multiple pathology, mental confusion, slow
recovery and aggravating social circumstances.

Working Party of the Royal College of Physicians of
London, *Medical Care of the Elderly* (1977)

The average American who is 65 or older, takes 13
different drugs in a single year. This often means that
symptoms attributed to senility are actually due to
pharmacological cross-reactions. In addition to this, many
elderly people become alcoholic, partly as a result of a
reaction to pain, grief or despondence.

Report: American Psychiatric Association. Annual Meeting
(1978)

INEVITABLY, IF WE ESCAPE DEATH ON THE WAY, WE GROW old. Growing old is a mysterious biological process, during which many of the body's functions slow down. It is a process of maturing and of degeneration.

Physical ageing is inevitable. Everybody's hearing and sight diminish in sharpness as the years pass; hair becomes grey and thins; muscle strength diminishes; the kidneys function less efficiently; and illness is less easily combated. Psychological ageing is not inevitable; it depends on the person's attitude to old age.

To grow old is inevitable, to feel old is not.

We feel old because, over the years, we have lived unwisely and because we have been conditioned by society to believe that old people are inferior, dissolute, often dirty, possibly degenerate, sometimes dejected, and usually cut off from 'real' life, that is a life based on work. Old people believe this myth, because when they were younger that is how they saw old people to be. Once you believe in a myth, you become part of it; you play the role expected of you. In this way, old people play the role society expects of them – they feel old.

Many of the physical and mental disabilities attributed to old age are due more to society's perception of ageing and to our institutions, which classify people as old, than to the biology of ageing.

In our society, old age begins at 65 – the usual retirement age. You may not feel old at 65, but you are classified as old, and it takes a good deal of mental fortitude to escape the belief that you are old. This is not helped by the ambivalent attitudes that many people – young, middle aged, and old – have to old age. Because of 'conditioning' during their formative years many people think of old age as a shameful period of life. They treat old people as if they belong to a sub-human species.

Along with children, blacks, and women, old people are alternately patronized and mocked. If old people show the same sort of feelings, needs, and desires as younger people, society regards them with disgust. In our youth-oriented society, young people are expected to enjoy sex, but the idea of old people caressing, copulating, and enjoying their sexuality is considered obscene and repugnant. An older man is accused of being 'lecherous', an older woman of being 'shameless'. Younger people may properly feel the pangs of jealousy, in older people such feelings are considered to be absurd. Young people fall in and out of love; sexual love in the old is considered revolting. Young people are expected to show passion and be violent, in old people such acts are seen as ludicrous.

We rationalize why we treat old people differently. We say it is because they are less able to cope, their minds have become degenerate, their bodies weak, and their emotions unstable. We may treat our own older relatives with some respect, but we merely tolerate old people as a class.

In these various ways we diminish the humanity of older people, alternately mocking, patronizing, and being sentimental about them. We say 'he is a remarkable old man', meaning that he looks, acts, and behaves as if he were 10 years younger than his chronological age. To some extent, our ambivalent attitude to old age is due to the development of the technological society, to our increased mobility, and to our habit of living in 'nuclear' families.

In primitive, traditional, unchanging societies, old people were respected because they were repositories of the wisdom of the group and they carried, and transmitted, the group's experience to the next generation. In this type of society, only old people were able to transmit the skills needed for survival, and only they knew the rites required to keep the gods benevolent. Living in an extended family, most old people had a defined place and an identifiable role, which enabled them to keep their self-esteem and proved to them that they were respected.

Today, in our rapidly changing society, old people tend to be discarded as unproductive, unable to adapt to change, often sick, a liability both to society and to their family.

It is ironic, too, that middle-aged people have a much greater ambivalence to old people than do young people, and their relationship to the old is much less understanding. A middle-aged man has been taught to treat the old with respect, and he fulfils what he sees as a duty. At the same time, he considers the older person physically and mentally inferior, a person whom he expects to conform to society's image of age. If the old person shows that he will not, he is condemned as an 'extraordinary' old man, an old 'duffer' or a 'dirty' old man.

It is important, today, to ask ourselves why we treat the old in this way; why the old are so alienated; why so many old people are condemned by society to relative poverty, to exploitation, to loneliness, and to inferior living conditions. Goethe wrote, 'Age takes hold of us by surprise'. Today, because of better nutrition, better sanitation, and better health care, an increasing proportion of the population is surviving to become old. In many Western countries, 12 per cent of the population is over the age of 65, and by the year 2000 one person in six will be over that age. Many of us will be among them, so it is to our own advantage to think about growing old. We must avoid age taking hold of us by surprise.

*

Growing old affects different people in different ways, at different times, and with different degrees of severity. Old people are no longer as physically efficient as when they were younger. An old person's senses are less acute: for example, his hearing decreases, and he can hear high-pitched notes less easily. The disability increases with age so that some degree of deafness affects 5 per cent of men aged 50, and 25 per cent of men aged 70. The diminished ability to hear can be embarrassing, but hearing-aids help considerably. Alex Comfort has pointed out in his splendid book *A Good Age* that the cheapest hearing-aid is a piece of string, one end of which is put in your ear, the other in your breast pocket! If you wear this, people talk more slowly and clearly!

Your sight changes as you grow older, and your ability to focus easily decreases. These changes can be compensated by wearing spectacles. It is wise to have your sight checked periodically to detect the onset of glaucoma, or of incipient cataract, which occur increasingly with age and which are easily treated. As you grow older, your sense of smell diminishes, and your teeth tend to be less firmly fixed. Your hair becomes grey and, at a later age, white, due to a loss of the pigment cells. The time when this change occurs is genetically determined, as is baldness.

With age, the immune response to infection decreases, so that old people become more susceptible to infections, and minor illnesses may be more severe and lead to longer periods of restricted activity. It is possible that this change may be reduced if a nutritious balanced diet is eaten.

After the age of 70, your temperature control mechanisms become less efficient, and you feel the cold more easily. From this time on, too, your muscles begin to lose their power, and your manual dexterity decreases.

In spite of these changes, there is no truth in the belief that the mental capacity of most older people diminishes. A healthy man of 67, unless he has hypertension or arteriosclerosis, can learn a new subject as easily as a 17-year-old, although he takes longer to learn it. This is because the speed of acquisition of knowledge declines with age. In an experiment in Australia, a group of 70-year-old students learned German, using the same books and classes, as successfully as a group of 15-year-olds, at least as judged by examination results. Older people are disadvantaged as they have been conditioned to believe that they are less able to learn and that they are less competent mentally. Because of this, they may refuse to test themselves for fear of failure. Although older people learn more slowly, their greater experience in arranging their thought processes may compensate for this. Older people's speed of recall is also diminished, but 'tricks' may help them to overcome the defect.

Some evidence indicates that with increasing age a person's emotional response is altered, and his curiosity fades. The extent varies considerably between people, and in some, emotional 'instability' is evident. This means that an old person weeps easily, and becomes sentimental. In a way, many old people have escaped the convention of our culture, which is that men do not show emotion, and the change may be viewed as beneficial, rather than a disability.

Not all people adjust successfully to growing old, and the longer one lives, the more emotional problems arise. Many old people find it difficult to adapt to new concepts and, consequently, become more rigidly outmoded in their ideas and unable to accept other people's opinions. Some old people become increasingly ego-centric, increasingly demanding, increasingly indifferent to the opinions, the needs, and the relationships of others. They seem to shut themselves off from reality, protecting themselves against having to accept new values. This can lead to distrust of others who are seen to be manipulative and insensitive to the old person's real needs. Some old people become openly hostile to other people but, in most, the resentment smoulders inside, occasionally emerging to criticize, to tyrannize, and to persecute.

In this way, conflicts arise between old people and their children, already middle aged and often enmeshed in their own problems.

The old person believes he is being neglected, when filial duty should ensure that he is supported. The middle-aged son resents the demands his father places on him, but at the same time respects him and feels he has a duty to help him. This ambivalence may cause antagonism and misunderstanding, particularly in what are considered to be sensitive areas of behaviour, such as sexuality.

*

It is astonishing that, until recently, old people were neither expected to 'indulge' in sex, nor to enjoy their sexuality. Many undoubtedly did but, fearful of being condemned by a censorious society, they kept quiet about it. Kinsey and his successors brushed away these absurd attitudes and it is now known that many people over 65 enjoy sexual activity. In a careful study, Dr Pfieffer and his colleagues in Duke University, North Carolina, found that 70 per cent of men over the age of 65 were having regular and enjoyable intercourse, and by the age of 80, 15 per cent were still active sexually. Those men who had enjoyed frequent sex when younger were more likely to continue enjoying sex in old age, while those people who, in youth, had been inhibited about their sexuality were more likely to avoid sex as they grew older. Age eliminates neither the need, the capacity, nor the enjoyment of sex, unless illness intervenes. Age itself does not cause impotence, but anxiety about one's performance, conditioned by the myth that age will affect one's ability to perform, can inhibit an erection. Abstinence from sex is also a factor in impotence. This has been called the 'use it or lose it syndrome'! Sex is healthy, and whatever your age, you hardly ever need to avoid sex – unless you want to.

It is true that the changes in a man's sexual response, which may first have become apparent in middle age, continue, but not all of these are disadvantageous. In common with other physical functions (sight, hearing, physical strength, and so on), your sexual response alters as you grow old. Just as there are wide variations between men in the reduction of their physical functions, so too there is a very wide variation in the changes in their sexual response. As you grow older, you may notice that you get an erection less frequently when you fantasize about sexual situations or when you see an erotic picture or object. You may find that it takes longer for you to obtain an erection when making love and that your penis needs a few minutes of direct stimulation by masturbation or by your partner's hand or mouth before it becomes erect. You may find that for short periods, which usually last for less than a week, you fail to get an erection. Men who are obsessed with their 'performance' may see this as the end of their sexuality, but they should know that this is not true. You have not become permanently impotent: you will start getting erections once again.

None of these changes should cause you anxiety, because your capacity for erection is never lost by age, although it may be lost because you are anxious about your performance, because you drink too much, because you have been given certain medications, or because of certain illnesses, such as diabetes.

You may also notice that your penis is no longer so erect; now it angles slightly down. Again you need have no anxiety, it is just as efficient and you will enjoy sex just as much! Occasionally you will find, during the time when you and your partner are pleasuring each other, before actual intercourse, that you lose your erection and your penis becomes soft and flaccid. This is again normal, and all that is needed is to stimulate your penis again, when it will become erect once more.

Once your partner is ready, and you begin thrusting in her vagina, you will find that you last longer than you did when you were younger.

This is an advantage, you both obtain pleasure for longer, and the energy you expend will not harm you. You may find that you do not have an orgasm although you have enjoyed the sensual, erotic pleasures of intercourse. You must not be anxious that your virility and sexual ability are diminishing, the response is normal, and another time you will find you can ejaculate. The main thing is that you both enjoyed sex. And if you are still aroused, ask your partner to stimulate your penis or, if you prefer, masturbate.

Many older men find that they ejaculate less forcibly, the premonition that they are about to reach orgasm is less strong, and it takes longer for them to become sexually aroused again. These changes are normal consequences of growing old and should not cause concern.

Of course, sexual problems can arise in old age, as they can at any other age. The problems are least when you and your partner both enjoy sex and both have the same interest in sex. The problems may become marked if your partner dies and you are left alone and lonely. Society (and family) is censorious of older people who form new relationships, particularly if there is a disparity between the ages of the partners, and especially if a man wishes to remarry. The obstruction by middle-aged children may be praiseworthy, as your partner may be unsuitable, or may be due to their own selfishness as they fear you will change your will, or you (and they) will be mocked by friends and neighbours.

Discuss your relationship with them, but in the end make up your own mind; they do not own you, and your happiness is important.

*

Two situations need more aggressive action. The first is if you decide, for whatever reason, that you will live with your partner. Families tend to view this with contempt (although they accept that younger people do this quite often). Government authorities also tend to be censorious, even demanding access to your joint home to see if you share the same bed and, if you do, to reduce both your pensions. Older people should rebel against this invasion of their privacy. Neither your family, nor the state, nor the neighbours have any right to insist that you marry. It is your life, enjoy it – and ignore them!

The second problem is even more damaging. Many old people need to live in institutions because of increasing disability or because of poverty. Institutions and their managements are particularly censorious about sexuality. Not only are men and women segregated but, in some, husbands and wives are separated. This is inhumane. Any couple, whether married or not, who wish to share their lives and their bed should be encouraged to do so rather than being obstructed. By sharing their lives fully, they will enhance their sexuality, and increase the sense of their own value and their value to others. There is medical evidence that in institutions which allow their guests to live in this way, there is less depression, less need for drugs, less disability, and more happiness than in repressive, segregated homes. Although you may have to live in an institution, this does not make you less human, you have the same human rights as others outside. You have the same right to establish a relationship. You have the same right to privacy. You have the same right to dignity. You have the same right to be treated as a responsible adult.

One problem which becomes increasingly common in old age involves a sex organ, the prostate gland. As you grow older, especially after the age of 50, your prostate gland commonly enlarges. The prostate gland surrounds the urethra, the tube which carries your urine from your bladder to the eye of your penis. If the gland enlarges, you may find that you have to pass urine more often, and when you do, you only make a poor stream. Later, if the prostate grows even larger it may press on the urethra and make it difficult, or impossible, for you to pass urine.

If this should happen you need surgery, so that the enlarged prostate can be removed (prostatectomy). This can be done either through your bladder or by operating through your urethra with a special instrument. Either method is safe and successful, provided your health is good.

Many men worry that if they have to have a prostatectomy they will become impotent. Prostatectomy by today's surgical techniques does not affect a man's potency. In some cases, he no longer ejaculates any sperms, instead they go into his bladder, but he still has orgasms. If you need surgery, get your surgeon to explain what he is going to do, and make sure that he knows that you enjoy sex and want to go on enjoying it.

*

It would be ridiculous to suggest that old people do not have physical disabilities. Many more old people have osteoarthritis, a degenerate disease of the joints, than young people, and consequently find movement difficult or painful or both. Today, medicine can offer you help in coping with this uncomfortable disease but you need to start coping in middle age if you find that you have persisting pain in your joints or marked stiffness. If you are overweight, eat less and reduce your weight. Adjust your lifestyle to minimize the disability. See your doctor, who may prescribe drugs, the most useful and cheapest of which is aspirin. Unfortunately, osteoarthritis is slowly progressive, so that in old age your disability may increase. If your hip or knee joints are affected, modern surgery can make you mobile and without pain by replacing your damaged joints with plastic covers, or by fixing the joint in the most comfortable and useful position.

One bone condition becomes increasingly common as a person grows older. This is the thinning of the bone substance, so that the bone becomes more brittle and fractures more easily. The disease is called osteoporosis (or thinning bone). It is more common among women than men and it occurs earlier in life in women. You may break your forearm or, more seriously, fracture the neck of your thigh bone. Most of these fractures occur because you tripped over something in your home, or because you turned too suddenly and lost your balance. The disease can be checked by keeping active (which prevents the bones losing calcium) and by taking extra calcium, especially at night (as this is the time the calcified substance of the bone is lost). As well as these measures, avoid tripping! Make sure that your house has no loose carpets, that stairs are well lit and have hand-rails, and that you do not have little stools or tables scattered round. Make *sure* that you can get into and out of your shower or bath easily and safely, because more old people seem to fracture their hip in bathrooms than in other rooms.

A sudden stroke which paralyses a man is even more distressing than arthritis, both to the victim and to his family. Most strokes occur in people who have high blood pressure, and most can be avoided by appropriate medications. So, too, can the increasing risk of heart attacks by attention to exercise and diet. But you have to be realistic. As you grow older, your arteries become less flexible and more rigid, and a heart attack or a stroke can result.

Another condition, probably due to changes in your arteries, may also affect you, especially if you are aged 75 or older. This is a sudden unexpected black-out. One moment you are standing or walking, the next your legs give way and you collapse on the ground. You do not faint but have a clear memory of falling. In a moment or two your legs become useful again, and you are able to resume what you were doing, but you may feel anxious or worried. These attacks occur because the blood supplied to parts of your brain is reduced momentarily, and the brain cells cease to operate. The condition, often called a 'drop attack', is not dangerous, it is not a warning of an impending stroke. It just happens, and the worst thing you can do is to worry about the next one.

Rapacious, insensitive people find the elderly, who are suffering from the degenerative diseases and who have a negative attitude to ageing, easy victims. Quacks and tricksters have battened on to the old, relieving them of their money, but not of their complaints, for centuries. They still do. Beware of them and their nostrums. There is no drug, compound, or nostrum which will prevent the ageing process; but each decade or so, a new prophet arises who claims, quite erroneously, that his method will prevent you growing old.

The most recent method has been injections of live sheep embryo cells, popularized by Dr Niehans. The sheep embryo cells are supposed to transfer their nuclear material, DNA, into your cells where, by recombination, it converts them into young cells. There is no scientific truth in the claim: cellular therapy only works by convincing you that you are as young as you feel, not as old as you look. It is an expensive way to learn this truth. Nor is there any value in the vitamin compound provided by worker bees to keep the queen healthy and long-lived. Royal jelly may help in the hive but it does nothing to the human. It does not remove wrinkles from the face, nor does it tighten slack skin, but it does remove the money from your wallet. That is all! Nor does Gerovital, or KH3, which is basically the local anaesthetic, procaine, help much, except perhaps psychologically – as it may reduce depression.

Many elderly people are prescribed and take too many drugs. Because older people suffer from degenerative diseases, often of different systems, they are seen and treated by different specialists, who forget to find out what treatment other doctors have given. The result is that many elderly people are walking pharmacies. This can cause symptoms of mental decay, which are thought to be due to old age, not to doctors' errors. An example was given in the *British Medical Journal* in July 1977:

Mrs. A.B., aged 68, moved here three weeks ago to live with her daughter. She has been asthmatic for many years and has been receiving prednisone (10 mg. daily) for the past 15 years. She has also had osteoarthritis of her knees and hips for nine years and has been taking ibuprofen (800 mg. thrice daily) for three years. Two months ago she consulted her GP because of a slight tremor of her hands, and because of insomnia. He started her on benzhexol (5 mg. thrice daily) and nitrazepam (10 mg. nightly) and also gave her a supply of pentazocine to take as necessary for her osteoarthrosis. Since then, she has become increasingly incapable of looking after herself; she has become confused, disorientated, and sometimes hallucinated. Her family felt that she could no longer look after herself, and she has come to live with her daughter. We would like advice on two matters; are her drugs responsible for her recent deterioration; can we rationalise her drug treatment?

The advice from an expert was to stop most of the drugs – benzhexol, nitrazepam, and pentazocine; to re-evaluate the need for the pain-reliever she was prescribed for arthritis; and to question the need for the steroid (prednisone) she was taking for her asthma.

He wrote:

Some elderly patients respond very adversely to drugs, probably for two reasons. Firstly, certain routes of drug elimination decline with age – particularly renal excretion and hepatic drug-oxidation. Secondly, the sensitivity of some target organs increase with age – for example, the control of blood pressure and temperature deteriorate and this type of change might account for some of the enhanced sensitivity.

The real moral is that drug treatment must be instituted with extreme care, using small doses to start, and increasing in the light of the clinical response.

What happened is illuminating:

Within 48 hours of stopping benzhexol, nitrazepam, and pentazocine, Mrs. A.B.'s psychiatric state had improved dramatically. After a week she had recovered almost completely. She is now planning to return to an independent existence.

The lesson is clear. If you are over 65, check up to discover if you need all the drugs you have been prescribed, only take those you really need, and make sure you recheck, each time you visit a doctor. If you do not, you may become mentally and physically disturbed, and you will be diagnosed as being senile.

Senile dementia affects about one old person in every seven, and is severe in one-third of them. It is characterized by loss of initiative, loss of memory, decreased judgement, inability to select appropriate words or to perform calculations, disorientation, and personality disturbances. It is less common than depression, which occurs among old people because of the accumulation of stresses due to loss of status, loss of friends, loneliness, and poverty; but the two conditions are often confused by doctors.

Increasingly, gerontologists and psychiatrists are becoming aware that senility, including apparent senile dementia, is often not due to brain decay but to the inappropriate use of many medications, or to small strokes which occur in people who have high blood pressure.

Although, with age, increasing disabilities occur, and some illnesses are more common, you can minimize the effects of ageing and reduce the disabilities if you take action yourself.

● Have periodic checks from a doctor who is interested in the problems of ageing

- Eat sensibly

- Exercise moderately and regularly

- Continue to keep your mind occupied

- Remain curious about life and passionate about causes

Eating sensibly is not difficult if you have the motivation, and will help to reduce your weight, if you are fat, and control your blood pressure. As you grow older, you body needs less energy to keep it in good shape, and older people tend to be less active. For these two reasons you should take in less energy – less calories – as you need less. If you do not you will become fat. In Chapter 13 the dangers of obesity are described. A sensible diet will help you avoid this danger, and will enable you to be more healthy.

Your diet should provide you with sufficient protein to keep your tissues in good repair, sufficient calories to give you all the energy you need (which is about 9210 k-joules (2200 kcal) each day), but which avoids too much cholesterol, too much animal fat, and too much sugar. You should also eat fresh vegetables and try and buy fresh fruit, rather than buying expensive vitamin tablets which you probably do not need, unless you have been ill. You should eat wholemeal bread in preference to 'plastic', pappy, white bread, because the fibre in bread (and in vegetables too) will help you avoid becoming constipated, a condition which seems to affect many old people. You should eat cheese or drink milk (which can be mixed in foods or other drinks – you do not have to drink it 'raw' unless you want to) to provide extra calcium which is needed to prevent osteoporosis.

You can do all these things quite easily without making much change to your eating habits, unless you are so poor that you cannot afford the foods, or so ill, or incapacitated, that you cannot go out and shop for them. If this happens, there are community-based helping agencies, such as Meals-on-Wheels, who will make life easier for you.

*

Most of the problems of ageing are due to the attitude of society to the old, which 'conditions' old people to have an unreal opinion of themselves and their value. The myths can be quite insidious, sapping away old people's belief in themselves and undermining their confidence in their ability to contribute to the community. It may help all of us, in our perceptions of ageing, if we can see the myths for what they are – false.

Myth	Fact
After about 65, all old people get progressively less fit mentally and physically.	False: evidence from the U.S.A. showed that nearly 60 per cent of older people showed no physical or mental deterioration.
Old people should retire as they are incapable of meeting the demands of work.	It is true that hard physical work may prove too much; but old people are fully able to do less heavy physical work and all mental work. In occupations where there is no fixed retiring age and where people can work part time if they wish, the individuals are healthier both physically and mentally than when they are forced to retire at a fixed age. Older people have less absenteeism, less injuries, and are more helpful than younger workers.
After 65, your mind degenerates and you will inevitably become senile.	You may respond slightly more slowly, and some of this is due to the way society patronizes old people – you learn to behave as it expects an old person to behave. Fewer than one person in every hundred develops senile dementia: in other words, goes mad.
Most old people live in the past, and forget the present.	Some do, many do not. 'How much of the actual failure of old people is due to society's expectation that old people are going to be forgetful, repetitious and living in the past?' asked Dr Soddy in a study of middle age.
Most old people neither want, need, nor enjoy sex.	Rubbish!
Most old people need to live in institutions, they cannot cope with living outside.	Only 5 to 10 per cent of people over 70 live in hospitals or homes: and given a proper degree of financial and social support many of them need not and would prefer not to.
Most old people are bed-ridden.	This is false. It is true that more old people are chronically ill, but fewer are acutely ill than younger people. And, given help, many bed-ridden people can get up, get out, and do things. As a person grows older bed continues to be a

	splendid place for sleep and sex, ideal for short illness but lethal for chronic illness if the person can be induced to be mobile. An older person should not stay in bed for more than four days unless ordered to do so by a doctor.
Old people really want to opt out of having to participate in everyday matters.	They are not asked, we tell them when they get old that they need to opt out. We make them disposable objects – 'non-people'. And unhappily we forget that soon we will be old and that unless we change societal attitudes we will be eased out and made 'non-people' too.
Old people spend their time sitting, dreaming, reminiscing, and watching television – they do not want to *do* anything.	We have created a situation in which old people are prevented from working and are regarded as mentally and physically ineffective. We have made them feel unwanted and despised. To protect their self-respect many old people sit, dream, and watch television. If we treated them differently, they would do different things.
Old people need less food and only eat slops.	It is true that *inactive* old people need fewer calories, and if they have poor teeth cannot chew as easily. It is also true that, because of poverty and ignorance, many old people (and many younger people) eat the wrong kinds of foods.
Old people are usually serene, content with their lot, and grateful for what society provides.	Often old age is not a time of serenity, except in novels. Many old people are full of anxiety about their future and concern about their health. Much of this concern and anxiety is occasioned by the way younger people treat the old, some is due to the person's own perception of how old people are expected to behave.
The older a person is, the more helpless he is.	You are as old as you feel, not as old as your birth certificate states.

*

The barrier between middle and old age is not only chronological but institutional. You become chronologically old after your sixty-fifth birthday, and, in most nations, this is also the age when you retire. In our work-oriented society, retirement can cause a considerable psychological disturbance. By those engaged in monotonous work, retirement is viewed as a desired goal and is perceived as an idyllic period of perpetual holiday, when a man can do what he has always wanted to do, at his own speed and in his own way. But many people who have already retired view retirement rather differently. It is not quite so idyllic. The glamour has gone and, rather than being on holiday, a man feels that society has thrown him on to the scrap-heap. Work, which before retirement was perceived as monotonous drudgery, is now perceived as having been a source of interest, and the workplace an area where a man could meet, talk, and work with his mates.

A retired man usually suffers a loss of income, he becomes poorer, and is less able to do the things he imagined he could do. His status is lower, and because he is no longer earning his living, he may even feel he has lost his significance as a person. His fantasies of what his retirement would be like (the country cottage, the fishing, the happy hours of doing nothing, the long lie-in in the morning, the pottering about the house or garden) are often found to be fantasies, when the reality of retirement is reached.

The retired man suffers from two psychological blows: he is classified as old – which in a youth- and work-oriented society is demeaning – and as no longer being a 'useful' person in society. He loses caste, he loses income, he loses a reason for living, unless he has prepared for retirement. Retirement makes a radical break in his life, and many men feel cut off from their past, and have to readjust to their new, diminished, status. Many retired people feel useless and fill their hours with trivia, which is a quick way of distancing themselves psychologically from other humans and of welcoming death.

The arbitrary determination that at the age of 65 a man ceases to be an economically 'useful' citizen and becomes a 'useless' pensioner, living off others, is strange. The evidence that a man ceases to be able to perform most tasks when he is categorized as old is insubstantial. Nearly forty years ago, with the pressures of war, the Nuffield Foundation in Britain found that although older workers had less physical strength and suppleness, reduced hearing and less precise sight, they were able to carry on their earlier occupations just as efficiently after the age of 65 as before. They compensated for their defects by being more reliable, more punctual, and more conscientious. They worked to a better rhythm and had greater self-discipline. Although they were slower in production line jobs, their output was not much reduced and the quality of their work was higher than that of younger workers.

The effect of the decision by society to make nearly all people retire at a specific age, whether they want to or not and without considering if they are competent to continue working, has created a sub-class of society which is exploited, discriminated against, and partially dehumanized. The retired person rapidly learns to play the role of being old.

He need not and should not. Retirement should be a time for doing something different, and for pursuing ends which continue to give existence a meaning. In this way, being old will be replaced by growing old.

It is essential to decide what you are going to do long before you retire and to prepare yourself to do it. If you do not do this, it is all too easy to fall into listlessness and habit, which can cause depression and increase the chance of disease. This confirms the opinion of society that old people are bored and boring, apathetic and pathetic. Most gerontologists agree that if a person is physically fit, he will be damaged psychologically and socially if he has no useful activity to follow.

One possible solution is to make the age of retirement flexible, and to make retirement a gradual process, not a sudden blow. In the last few years before retirement, a worker should have the opportunity to work reduced hours, using the extra time to prepare for eventual retirement.

*

You can cope with many of the problems of old age if you try, perhaps with some help from your friends and other old people. The major barrier to coping is society's attitude to old people, because old people begin to believe that they should behave in the way old people are expected to behave. If society believes that old people are white-haired, toothless, wrinkled, bent, asexual, inactive, unemployable, incompetent, deficient in intellect, docile, whinging, and prejudiced, old people will have problems because they are being made into non-persons. If society believes that the only occupations of old people are grumbling, sitting, eating, watching TV, reminiscing, and sleeping, old people will have problems, particularly if they want to prove that this stereotype is a myth or, worse, if they believe in the myth. If society believes that most old people need to be in hospital or in institutions, old people will have problems because they may acquiesce and enter an institution long before they need to. And once inside, they lose their independence, their dignity, and their will to live fully.

Since society diminishes the humanity of old people by its attitudes and by its actions, elderly people may have to become militant to regain the respect they once had. Old people may have to stand up, speak up, and never shut up, until they have obtained an adequate pension, good health care, and proper housing. If that makes it sound that old people form a suppressed minority – they are! Old people should not be forced to accept crumbs from society's table, nor should they be made to believe that they should be grateful for society's charity, in the form of welfare. What they receive, they have earned. They helped to make life more comfortable for others during their working days, they paid their taxes, they fought the wars, they have earned their retirement, and they have to make society recognize this. You are as much a person at 70 as you were at 20; you have different – but no less important – needs and you have obligations – different, but no less important.

Once society puts you into the category of 'old', it makes you a non-person. You are not: you are just a different person. You need what most people need. You need your dignity as a human being. You need sufficient money, as a right not as charity, so that you can live comfortably, rather than existing in poverty. You need access to courteous, non-exploitive, appropriate health care. You need to feel that you are of use to others. Simone de Beauvoir has written about this last need:

There is only one solution if old age is not to be an absurd parody of our former life, and that is to go on pursuing ends that give our existence a meaning – devotion to individuals, to groups or to causes, social, political, intellectual or creative work. In spite of the moralists' opinion to the contrary, in old age we should wish to have passions strong enough to prevent us turning in upon ourselves. One's life has value so long as one attributes value to the life of others, by means of love, friendship, indignation, compassion. When this is so, then there are still valid reasons for activity or speech.

Old people have to plan to keep this passionate involvement with life, so that they may continue to enjoy living.

Some do, but unfortunately many do not. Once you cease to be curious about what the future holds – however short or long that future may be – you cease to enjoy living. You become listless, apathetic, and often depressed. You become the stereotype of an old person and prove society right. You also become liable to be treated with drugs, which may make you more listless and more apathetic. While it is true that if you have always chosen a mediocre life it will be hard for you to be different in old age, you can escape if you really try. You do not need to withdraw into the twilight life of ageing. You can accept that you are growing old, and know that there is still much excitement to look forward to. You can strengthen your resolve if you remember that you are still the person you have always been, but that now you are living in an ageing body, which may force you to do things more slowly, but you can do them just as well.

Just as you need to start preparing for retirement long before you retire, so you need to prepare for growing old long before you are old. If you do that, you will find that old age is, in Alex Comfort's words, 'a good age'. If you have the right attitude to growing old, you will remain far younger than you may look; and you can get a great deal of help from old people's organizations, groups, and clubs. Not only do they mitigate the loneliness of old age, but they encourage their members to keep active, physically and mentally, within the limitations of an ageing body.

It is true that many old people are difficult. They are demanding, they are self-centred, they have fixed habits which make life difficult for their family and friends. For many old people, habit is a refuge, a security blanket against an indifferent world. For those old people who have no consuming interest, a daily routine gives life a meaning. A man can look forward to his daily walk, his daily read of the newspaper, his daily bench in the park, his routine way of preparing and eating food, his fixed habit of only listening to certain radio or television programmes, his fixed time of going to bed. Habits become important because they enable the old person to merge his past recollections with his present experiences and with his uncertainty about the future. Some old people become obsessed with their possessions, and continually adjust and readjust their wills. A possible reason for this is that, in a way, possessions are solidified habits. They give the old person a reason for existing and a purpose to life. If the old person is rich, the ability to manipulate his possessions may enable him to manipulate those of his family who hope to benefit after his death. They give him a feeling of power and so a purpose for living.

These attitudes are not peculiar to old people, many middle-aged and young people seek power and status, often by devious and cruel means. Why should we expect old people to be different? In old age, people most often behave as they did when they were younger. Societal attitudes which emphasize ownership, greed, selfishness, and deceit can hardly be expected to produce old saints out of middle-aged ruthless, grasping entrepreneurs. If you were a middle-aged delinquent, you may grow into a senile delinquent.

It is also true that some old people become disabled or ill and have to be in hospital, although it is a myth that the majority of old people live in hospitals, nursing homes, or old folks' homes. As far as hospitals are concerned, studies in Britain have shown that, in 1973, about half of the hospital beds available were occupied by people over the age of 65. However, three-quarters of them were in 'acute' medical or surgical beds and most would be discharged from hospital after a short time. A quarter were occupying 'chronic' beds, but even in this case many of the people could be cared for at home if there were appropriate community services and, more importantly, help from other elderly people. Most of them would be happier and more independent at home.

Those elderly people who are not forced to live in institutions because of illness or destitution have, at some stage, to make a decision about where they will spend their remaining years of life. Should they choose to live in the house or flat they have occupied for years, or move to a smaller house within the community? Should they seek to live in a 'retirement village' or complex? Should the concept of 'almshouses' be revived?

Whatever decision is made, it is important that the old person makes the choice and that it is not dictated by others. If the choice is to continue to live in the general community, in the person's own home, or in a flat, the community needs to be pressured to provide appropriate facilities, such as social clubs, access to shops, and community helping organizations, and efforts need to be made to provide the old person with an occupation. A retirement village is usually expensive and only the well-to-do can afford it. The advantage of such places is that services are readily available; illness is not as great a problem, because of the facilities provided; and the environment encourages group activity, giving a much-needed sense of purpose to life. A disadvantage of many retirement villages is that they are relatively isolated and the inhabitants may find it difficult to go into the town centre or to visit friends, without seeking the charity of someone to take them. This can promote a feeling of being cut off from real life and create an artificial, unhealthy way of living. The old idea of almshouses, situated in the town itself, has attractions as these can provide independence for the old person and, at the same time, the facilities and services needed for the person to enjoy his independence without fear of accident, illness, or incapacity.

Nursing homes and other institutions are rarely a choice, but in most cases a necessity. Unfortunately, many are entirely unsatisfactory and, like other institutions, tend to dehumanize the inmates. Many seem geared for the profit of the proprietor and the convenience of the staff rather than for the benefit of the inhabitants. In some, rigid rules control the conduct of the inmates, there is no privacy, and the person has no area he can call his own. In some, the 'patients' are kept in bed because it is easier, tidier, and less demanding on the time of the staff. In most, sexual segregation is demanded, and rules against sexuality are enforced although, as I have written earlier, sexuality in old age should be encouraged rather than denied. Changes are occurring slowly, but more are needed, and the voice of the old must be heard by apathetic politicians and unconcerned middle-aged and young people. The welfare of old people should matter to all of us, for we will be old one day.

*

The older we grow, the closer we come to our own death, or that of a loved one. Often we do not know how to cope. This is partly because of the perception of death in our culture. In Australia and in Britain, death is ignored: people consider it unpleasant to talk about, and follow the ritual of death reluctantly. In the U.S.A., it is commercialized, made a gaudy, plastic event, where people do not die but 'pass on' or are 'called'. In other cultures, death is accepted, from childhood on, as a natural event to be celebrated or affirmed.

After the death of a loved one, the survivor has a need to grieve. Bereavement is normal, but because of our distaste for death, which we ignore or commercialize, we are uncomfortable when we greet a bereaved person. We do not know how to handle the problems and try to ignore the person during the time he is confused, indrawn, and mourning. We blame him for needing help because it makes us uncomfortable to give help. If he seems lonely, we attribute this to his age, not to his grief.

For the bereaved person, there is no right way to handle mourning. The right way is the way which suits the person. Victor Hugo had been consistently unfaithful to his mistress of many years, Juliette Drouet, but when she died he wrote, 'There is so much mourning in my life that there are no feast days any more'. Some people, bereaved and sad, remove all traces of the dead person from their house, and never speak of him. Others keep the house exactly as it was when the loved one died. Others appear callously indifferent; they seek as many experiences, sexual or other, as they can achieve, during the bereavement period. None of the ways of coping is wrong; the one you have chosen is the way that suits you.

Bereavement in old age may well be deeper in its impact than in younger people, because of the unspoken, unacknowledged support which existed between two old people. Its severity can be reduced if the couple have talked about the possibility and have arranged their affairs, so that the formalities are reduced to the minimum. The distress will be reduced further if they have made arrangements to limit the burdens of day-to-day living, by preparing for the event.

The bereaved also need help from other people, but often are too shy, embarrassed, or proud to ask for it. They want to be able to talk to someone who is prepared to listen, and is not embarrassed if they show their sorrow openly. They want to know that someone is available to be near them if they become lonely or depressed, and when they want help.

We will all die one day.

Death is rarely painful, although the events which precede it may be. In the end, most of us 'go gentle into that good night': our end is as gentle as our beginning.

GLOSSARY

This glossary is to help the reader find the definition of a new term easily. If a word is not found here it will be found in the Index, and the reader can refer to the appropriate page in the book.

Adrenal gland: this small gland, which lies like a triangular cap over the upper part of the kidney, has an outer part, called the cortex, which secretes hormones including corticosteroids and sex hormones.

Androgens: the male sex hormones. They are produced mainly by the testes but also by the adrenal cortex and the ovaries. Testosterone is the principal potent androgen.

Arteriosclerosis: the thickening and narrowing of an artery caused by swellings in its lining which narrows its lumen. Also called atherosclerosis, when the swellings are nodular and contain fat deposits in the nodes.

Climacteric: the period in a woman's life between the reproductive years and the onset of old age. It is marked by the cessation of menstruation – the menopause.

Clitoris: the small pea-sized organ at the top of the cleft of the female genitals. It is the counterpart the penis, and has a hood, which is the counterpart of the foreskin.

Cloaca: the pit at the rear end of the embryo which will eventually develop into the external sex organs and the anus.

Cortisone, cortisol: a hormone secreted by the adrenal cortex. It is essential to life.

Cunnilingus: the erotic stimulation of a woman's genitals, usually the clitoral area, with lips or tongue. It is a normal part of love-play. Also termed oral sex.

Embryo: the developing individual in the first fifty days of life. During this time all the body organs are formed.

Fellatio: the erotic stimulation of a man's penis by sucking or licking it, usually deep in the partner's mouth. It is a normal part of love-play. Also termed oral sex.

Foetus: the developing baby within the uterus, between the embryonic stage and its birth whenever this may occur.

Follicle stimulating hormone (FSH): the hormone produced by the pituitary gland in response to messages from the hypothalamus. It stimulates the growth of follicles in the ovary and the production of the female sex hormone, oestrogen.

Foreplay: see **Sexual Pleasuring**

Gender-identity: the self-awareness, and the persistence of this awareness, that a person is male or female (or ambivalent).

Gender-role: everything a person does or says to indicate to others (and to himself or herself) the degree to which he or she is male or female or ambivalent. It includes sexuality, but is not restricted to this.

Gene: one of a series of units arranged in linear order on a chromosome, which carry inherited characteristics.

Gestagen: a synthetic form of progesterone. Also called progestogens and progestins.

Glaucoma: a term indicating that the pressure inside the eyeball is raised. If the high intraocular pressure persists blindness may result.

Gonadotrophins: hormones released by the pituitary gland which programme the activity of the ovaries in females or the testes in males.

Gonads: a term given to the testes or to the ovaries.

Hermaphrodite (intersex): a congenital condition of ambiguity of the sex organs, so that the sex of the individual is not clearly defined as exclusively male or female. Usually the appearance of the external genitals is discordant with the chromosomal sex of the person.

Hypothalamus: the portion of the brain adjacent to the pituitary gland which regulates its function.

Impotence (erectile failure): the impairment or inability of a man to achieve or maintain an erection of his penis.

Libido: the term first used by Freud to describe sexual energy. Nowadays used to describe sexual desire, which leads to sexual arousal.

Lipids: the biochemical term for fats. Lipids can be separated into four main groups: fatty acids, phospholipids, triglycerides, and sterols, of which the most important is cholesterol.

Menopause: precisely, the word means the cessation of menstruation, but the term is often used to describe the climacteric.

Oestrogen: the group of similar sex hormones produced by the ovaries, which act on the various body tissues to produce a feminine body shape and aid in reproduction.

Oral sex: see **Cunnilingus** and **Fellatio**

Orgasm: the series of reflex, involuntary rhythmic muscle responses which occur in the pelvis at the peak of sexual stimulation. It is also the psychological feeling of warmth, well-being, and pleasure.

Oviduct: the tube which stretches from the uterus to a woman's ovaries. Fertilization of the egg takes place in the oviduct. Also called Fallopian tube.

Paedophilia: sexual desire, with children as its object. The child may be male or female.

Pheromones: substances (aliphatic acids) secreted by the vagina of a female animal when in heat, which attract the males.

Progesterone: the second female sex hormone produced by a woman's ovaries.

Scrotum: the bag of skin containing the testes.

Sexual pleasuring: mutual erotic stimulation so that both partners become sexually aroused. Also called foreplay.

Testes (testicles): the male sex organs which produce spermatozoa and testosterone. Also called balls.

Testosterone: the main male sex hormone.

Transsexual: a person who appears in every sense to belong to one sex but feels psychologically he or she should belong to the other sex.

Urethra: the tube which connects the bladder with the outside. In males this passes through the penis, emerging at the eye of the penis. It carries urine and seminal fluid.

Vulva: the external genital organs of a female.

BIBLIOGRAPHY

1 How you become a male

The differentiation of gender-identity from the time of conception is discussed in *Man & Woman, Boy & Girl* (Johns Hopkins University Press, Baltimore, 1972) by John Money and Anke A. Ehrhardt. The authors go into considerable detail and the book has an extensive bibliography. The work of A. Jost on sexual differentiation of the embryo and foetus is mentioned, but he writes more extensively in *Johns Hopkins Medical Journal* (130. 38, 1972).

The concept that the sex of the child can be chosen by timing intercourse, or by using particular vaginal douches, was proposed by L. B. Shettles in the *International Journal of Obstetrics and Gynaecology* (8. 643, 1970). His opinions have been critically evaluated by R. Guerro in the *New England Journal of Medicine* (291. 1056, 1974) and by R. H. Glass in *Obstetrics and Gynaecology* (49. 122, 1977 and 51. 513, 1978). R. J. Ericsson's work on sperm migration is reported in *Nature* (246. 421, 1973).

2 What makes a man a man?

The conventional Western stereotypes of men and women are discussed by J. M. Bardwick and E. Douvain in *Women in a Sexist Society* (Basic Books, New York, 1971). The older view of the innate inferiority of women was strongly supported by Helene Deutsch in *The Psychology of Women* (Grune & Stratton, New York, 1944). The psychological differences between males and females are considered at length by E. E. Maccoby and C. J. Jacklin in their book *The Psychology of Sex Differences* (Oxford University Press, New York, 1974) and by P. C. Lee and R. S. Stewart (eds.) in *Sex Differences* (Urizen, New York, 1976). John Money and Patricia Tucker deal with the same subject in a more 'popular' book called *Sexual Signatures* (Abacus, London, 1977). Margaret Mead's book *Male and Female* is available in paperback, published by Penguin Books.

The relative importance of pre-natal hormonal influences on brain circuitry and learned sex behaviour on gender-identity is discussed by John Money and Anke A. Ehrhardt in *Man & Woman, Boy & Girl* (Johns Hopkins University Press, Baltimore, 1972). The intersex Dominican individuals are described by Julianne Imperato-McGinley and her colleagues in the *New England Journal of Medicine* (300. 1233, 1979) and in an editorial in the same journal (300. 1269, 1979) by Jean Wilson.

The theories of psychosexual development are discussed by S. Freud in *Three Essays on Sexuality* (6th edn., vol. 7, Hogarth Press). A more recent work is *Psychosexual Development in Children* (Holt, Rinehart & Winston Ltd., New York, 1967). The hypothesis that lack of body pleasure in childhood is linked with an increased amount of violence in adult life is advanced by J. Prescott in the *Futurist* (64, Apr. 1975). Prescott's view that male aggression is not innate receives support from R. Leakey and R. Lewin in *Origins* (Macdonald and Jane's, London, 1977). The self-perpetuating subordinate position of women is considered by G. I. Peterson in *Journal of Personal and Social Psychology* (19. 114, 1971).

3 *Growing up*

The physical growth of children is graphically described by D. C. Sinclair, *Human Growth After Birth* (Oxford University Press, Oxford, 1973), and J. M. Tanner, *Growth at Adolescence* (Oxford University Press, Oxford, 1962). A specific problem, that of testicular growth, is discussed by R. G. Mitchell in the *Lancet* (1. 1344, 1978). The psychology of maturing is considered by J. J. Conger in *Adolescence and Youth: Psychological Development in a Changing World* (Harper & Row, New York, 1973).

One theory of the development of sexual arousal is that advanced by R. J. Stoller in *Archives General Psychiatry* (33. 199, 1976).

Sexuality in adolescence has received considerable attention, but methodologically valid surveys are few. This is understandable because most people prefer to keep their sexual behaviour private. Michael Schofield's two books are helpful about adolescent sexuality in Britain: *The Sexual Behaviour of Young People* (Longman, London, 1975) and *The Sexual Behaviour of Young Adults* (Allen Lane, London, 1973). Another important British study is that by Christine Farrell in her book *My Mother Said* (Routledge & Kegan Paul, London, 1978). Ira Reiss discussed the sexual behaviour of young Americans in *The Family System in America* (Holt, Rinehart & Winston Ltd., New York, 1971). R. C. Sorensen's survey, *Adolescent Sexuality in Contemporary America*, was published by World Publishing, New York, 1971. J. F. Kantner and M. Zelnik's two surveys appear in *Family Planning Perspectives* (4. 5, 1972 and 9. 55, 1977). F. S. Jaffe's statistics of teenage sexuality appeared in *International Family Planning* (2. 3, 1976).

The double standard of sexual behaviour in England in the last years of the nineteenth century is described by K. Chesney in *The Victorian Underworld* (Maurice Temple Smith, London, 1970) and S. Marcus in *The Other Victorians* (Weidenfeld & Nicolson, London, 1966).

The effect of 'baby farming' (sending infants to wet-nurses) on infant mortality is described in Lawrence Stone's *The Family, Sex and Marriage* (Harper & Row, London, 1977).

4 The human sexual response

The pioneering work in describing the physiology of the human sexual response was reported in *Human Sexual Response* (Little, Brown and Co., Boston, 1966) by W. H. Masters and V. E. Johnson. A popular interpretation of this work, which is easy to read, is *An Analysis of the Human Sexual Response* (Signet, New York, 1966) by R. and E. Brecher.

Masters and Johnson's original studies are supplemented by H. S. Kaplan in *The New Sex Therapy* (Baillière Tindall, London, 1974). How penile erection occurs is discussed by H. D. Weiss in 'The Physiology of Human Penile Erection' in *Annals of Internal Medicine* (76. 793, 1972).

5 How to become a better lover

General overviews of sexual behaviour can be found in Alex Comfort's *The Joy of Sex* (Penguin, London, 1975) and in *The Visual Dictionary of Sex* (Macmillan, London, 1977), edited by E. Trimmer. Both books are illustrated and are most informative. The sexual behaviours and concerns of American women are reported by S. Hite in *The Hite Report* (Macmillan, New York, 1976), and the complaints of married women are analysed by E. Frank in the *New England Journal of Medicine* (299. 111, 1978). The concept of sex as work is advanced by L. Lewis and D. Brisset in *Medical Aspects of Human Sexuality* (October 1968).

Bernie Zilbergeld's book *Male Sexuality: A Guide to Sexual Fulfillment* Bantam Books, New York, 1978) – called in some countries *Men and Sex* – is an excellent work, written with insight and compassion, about the myths men have about their sexuality and their sexual problems. The book makes commonsense suggestions about how men and their partners can enjoy their sexuality more. To non-American eyes it is perhaps overwritten, but it is well worth reading.

6 The choice of children

A large number of books, reports, and papers appear annually. Constantly updated information about birth control appears in *People* published by The International Planned Parenthood Association (London). Medical textbooks also give information, e.g. *Fundamentals of Obstetrics and Gynaecology*, 2nd edn., vol. 2 (Faber & Faber, London, 1978) by Derek Llewellyn-Jones. Books on birth control written for the general public are also available, for example *The Pill* by John Guillebaud (Oxford University Press, Oxford, 1980).

7 *The expectant father*

The participation of the father in pregnancy and childbirth has not received much consideration until recently. Additional information can be obtained from *The Rights of the Pregnant Parent* by V. H. Elkins (Visa, Camberwell, Victoria, 1978) and from *Everywoman* by Derek Llewellyn-Jones (Faber & Faber, London, 2nd edn., 1978). Sexuality during pregnancy and childbirth is discussed by J. C. Butler and N. N. Wagner in *Human Sexuality* edited by R. Green (Williams & Wilkins, Baltimore, 1975). *Pregnancy & Parenthood*, edited by Anne Loader for the National Childbirth Trust (Oxford University Press, Oxford, 1980), gives useful advice and information.

8–10 *Sexual problems*

An overview of sexual problems can be found in *Understanding Human Sexual Inadequacy* (Bantam Books, New York, 1970) by F. Belliveau and L. Richter. Sexual problems are considered in detail in a book written for health professionals: H. S. Kaplan's *The New Sex Therapy* (Baillière Tindall, London, 1974). *Forum* magazine, published in Britain and Australia, is a monthly periodical which discusses interpersonal relationships and sexuality.

Another book which discusses sexual attitudes and problems is *Contemporary Sexual Behaviour: Critical Issues of the 1970's*, edited by J. Zubin and J. Money (Johns Hopkins University Press, Baltimore, 1974). Rosenzweig's comment, in Chapter 8, is from this book.

The problem of erectile impotence is discussed in the books already mentioned, and is analysed by H. Burger and D. M. de Kretser in the *Australian Prescriber* (1 (6). 115, 1977).

11 *Sexually transmitted diseases*

More information can be obtained in a book written for non-medical people, *Sex and V.D.* (Faber & Faber, London, 1974) by Derek Llewellyn-Jones. A standard medical textbook is R. S. Morton and J. R. Harris, *Recent Advances in Sexually Transmitted Diseases* (Longman, London, 1978).

12 *Homosexuality – an erotic preference*

Of the many books available, most show a marked bias against homosexuals. Two of the more balanced books, easily obtainable, are D. J. West's *Homosexuality* (2nd edn., Penguin, London, 1968) and C. A. Tripp's *The Homosexual Matrix* (Signet, New York, 1976). I. Bieber edits *Homosexuality – a Psychoanalytical View* (Basic Books, New York, 1963). Many of the opinions expressed are now superseded. Michael Schofield's book, *Sociological Aspects of Homosexuality* (Longman, London, 1965), is an interesting account of interviews with three groups of homosexual men (in society, in prison, undergoing psychiatric treatment), a group of paedophiliacs, and two groups of heterosexual men (one under psychiatric care, the other a control group). From this he develops a theory of homosexuality which, in 1965, was in advance of public opinion.

Dennis Altman discusses the prejudices and misunderstandings which surround homosexuality in *Homosexual* (Penguin, London, 1973).

The opinion that homosexuality is not condemned in the Bible is supported in a careful study by a number of theologians, in A. Kosnik's *Human Sexuality* (Paulist Press, Chicago, 1977). This analysis is most valuable, and should be studied by Christians who fear homosexuality.

The opinions which male homosexuals have about themselves are examined by M. S. Weisberg and C. J. Williams in *Male Homosexuals* (Oxford University Press, New York, 1974) and by A. Hodges and D. Hunter in *With Down Cast Eyes* (Pomegranate Press, London, 1974).

In 1973, the American Psychiatric Association, by a 60/40 vote, declared that homosexuality could no longer be considered a mental illness. The Association was unable to go as far as to say that homosexuality was a normal sexual preference. They implied that it is not an 'optimal' mental condition, but provided no evidence for their views. The Association's statement meant that ill-conceived attempts to convert a homosexual to heterosexuality were ill advised; which is what Desmond Curran had said thirty years earlier in *Psychological Medicine* (Livingstone, Edinburgh, 1943).

13 Middle age and its problems

Adjustment to middle age is considered in several books, notably K. Soddy and M. Kidson's *Men in Middle Age* (Tavistock, London, 1967). A book written on a more emotional level, containing long anecdotal passages, gives insight into the expectations of middle-aged men; this is D. Brownskill and A. Linacre's *The Male Menopause* (Miller, London, 1977). Marital problems receive attention in J. Dominian's *Marital Breakdown* (Penguin, London, 1968); and sexual problems are discussed in E. Pfeiffer's article 'Sexual Behaviour in Middle Age' in the *American Journal of Psychiatry* (128. 82, 1972).

The problems of obesity are discussed by Derek Llewellyn-Jones in *Every Body – a Nutritional Guide to Life* (Oxford University Press, Oxford, 1980) which contains a bibliography.

The prevalence of hypertension (high blood pressure) among American men is examined by J. Stamler in the *Journal of the American Association* (235. 2299, 1976). An assessment of the problems of hypertension can be found in the *World Health Organisation's Technical Report,* 469 (WHO, Geneva, 1971). The value of treatment of hypertension is documented in a series of papers relating to the Veteran Administration's Co-operative

Study in the U.S.A. (*Journal of the American Medical Association*, 202. 1028, 1967; 213. 1143, 1970; and *Circulation*, 45. 991, 1972.) This subject is also discussed by J. C. Petrie in the *British Medical Journal* (2. 289, 1976).

The effect on blood pressure of salt added to food is discussed by E. D. Fries in *Circulation* (53. 589, 1976).

14   *The heart* is *the matter*

The association of risk factors in the development of coronary heart disease and strategies for prevention are lucidly explained in two recent publications: *Diet and Coronary Heart Disease* by the Department of Health and Social Security (H.M.S.O., London, 1974) and 'Prevention of Heart Disease' by the Joint Committee of the Royal College of Physicians and the Cardiac Society (*Journal of the Royal College of Physicians*, 10. 213, 1976). Both of these publications have an extensive bibliography. The modern management of heart attacks, and in particular the role of the coronary care unit, is discussed in A. Colling's book *Coronary Care in the Community* (Croom Helm, London, 1976), and in an editorial in the *Lancet* (1. 193, 1979).

15   *Those golden years – growing old*

Simone de Beauvoir's sensitive book *Old Age* (Penguin, London, 1977) should be read by everyone who wishes to understand the problems of ageing. Alex Comfort's *A Good Age* (Beasley, London, 1977) is written by a scientist whose interest has been in the ageing process. It is marvellously illustrated and sensitively written, complementing de Beauvoir's book. For the more technically minded the report by the Institute of Medicine *Aging and Medical Education* (National Academy of Sciences, Washington D.C., 1978) is well worth reading.

Although not specifically concerned with old people, E. Kubler-Ross *On Death and Dying* (Tavistock, London, 1976) should also be read.

In 1978, the Health Commission of New South Wales, Australia, published a handbook for older people called *Getting On*.

Our Elders, by Muir Gray and Gordon Wilcock (Oxford University Press, Oxford, 1981), provides a well-rounded account of all aspects of ageing.

INDEX

Acknowledgements

Illustrations by Illustra Design Limited.

Fig. 4 Reproduced with permission from J. Money, J. G. Hampson, and J. L. Hampson, 'Hermaphroditism: Recommendations Covering Assignment of Sex, Change of Sex, and Psychologic Management', *Bulletin of The Johns Hopkins Hospital* (97.284–300, 1955).

Figs. 5 and 6 Redrawn from J. M. Tanner *et al.*, *Arch. Dis. Childhood* (41.454, 1966).

Fig. 9 Source: C. Farrell, *My Mother Said* (Routledge & Kegan Paul, London, 1978).

Figs. 10 and 11 Redrawn from J. F. Kantner and M. Zelnik, *Family Planning Perspectives* (9.55, 1977).

Fig. 12 Modified from W. H. Masters and V. L. Johnson, *Human Sexual Response* (Little, Brown & Co., Boston, 1966).

Fig. 22 Based on information from A. C. Kinsey, W. B. Pomeroy, and C. E. Martin, *Sexual Behaviour in the Human Male* (Saunders, Philadelphia, 1948).

Figs. 26 and 31 Source: National Heart Foundation of Australia.

Fig. 30 Based on data from C. E. Hammond, L. Garfinkel, and H. Seidman, *Envir. Res.* (12.263, 1976).